BUSINESS PROCESS OUTSOURCING

A Supply Chain of Expertises

Second Edition

AF512266

VINOD V. SOPLE
Professor and Director
ITM-SIA Business School
Mumbai

PHI Learning Private Limited
Delhi-110092
2016

₹ 350.00

BUSINESS PROCESS OUTSOURCING: A Supply Chain of Expertises, Second Edition
Vinod V. Sople

© 2016 by PHI Learning Private Limited, Delhi. All rights reserved. No part of this book may be reproduced in any form, by mimeograph or any other means, without permission in writing from the publisher.

ISBN-978-81-203-5236-0

The export rights of this book are vested solely with the publisher.

Fourth Printing (Second Edition) . . . . . . **June 2016**

Published by Asoke K. Ghosh, PHI Learning Private Limited, Rimjhim House, 111, Patparganj Industrial Estate, Delhi-110092 and Printed by Mudrak, 30-A, Patparganj, Delhi-110091.

Contents

Preface

Today is an era of outsourcing. Indian industry is not exception to it. It is rather become a global hub for business process outsourcing. Availability of the large pool of talented workforce in IT domain at lower cost, compelled the foreign companies to outsource to Indian companies to keep them competitive in global markets. As companies increasingly rely on external BPO vendors to manage their business processes that are integral to their internal operations for customer support services, their relationships have evolved into close partnerships that are long-term in nature. Indian BPO companies need to ensure that they continue to deliver core benefits as well as enhance the overall value proposition to their clients. End-to-end domain knowledge in the industry verticals and geographical diversifications have been the key drivers to managing large customer relationships. The Indian BPO industry has continued to expand and evolve its service delivery capability over the past few years by investing in training and gaining end-to-end domain knowledge in key target industries and business verticals. It has also simultaneously upgraded its skill-sets from doing simple processes to complex processes involving both rule-based and judgmental services. The Indian BPO vendors have demonstrated continuing success in driving efficiency and productivity gains from innovation in sourcing inputs and running business processes, while ensuring quality and information security, by adopting superior technology, training methodologies as well as creating a deep-rooted culture for process excellence. BPOs are basically supply chains of expertise. This book attempts to discuss how these supply chains of expertise are managed, what their business models are, the regulatory and legal limitations, contractual, service level agreement responsibilities and obligations, BPO analytics and outsourcing in cloud environment. The book also discusses the upward journey of BPO outfits in the value chain, as well as their HR challenges and performance evaluation criteria.

The first edition of this book was well-accepted and received good response from the students. It gives me great pleasure to present to you **Second Edition** of this book. The following three new chapters have been added in this edition.

- BPO Analytics
- Outsourcing in Cloud Environment
- BPO Transformation Strategy

I invite all suggestions, comments and feedback regarding ways to improve the usefulness of this book. The readers may reach me at vinodsople@yahoo.com.

Vinod V. Sople

Acknowledgements

I wish to thank a number of people without whose contributions this text would not have come to fruition. I would like to thank all my colleagues, who contributed their time and talent, and in particular Prof. B.V.R. Murthy, Prof. Sajal Kabiraj and Mr. Amlesh Sharma, Research Scholar, for their review and suggestions for the improvement of this book, and also for helping me in reviewing and modifying the text to the present form. Several other persons have given me much reason to be thankful about, notably Mr. Thomas Paily and Mr. Sachin Chemburkar, who typeset the manuscript.

I gratefully acknowledge the efforts of senior PGDM students and research assistants at ITM Business School, Navi Mumbai, who helped me in developing the manuscript by way of data generation and information collection.

I cannot forget my spiritual guru, Shri Dada Maharaj Zurale, who inspired me to take up this project. Without his blessings, this book would not have seen the light of day.

I sincerely appreciate the efforts of the staff of PHI Learning, Delhi, towards the publishing of this book.

Finally, of course, there are no words for the gratitude I feel towards my family members. My wife Bharti, our daughter Aarti and son Abhishek constantly encouraged me to complete this book even at the cost of the time which I would have spent with them.

Vinod V. Sople

Chapter 1

Search for Competitiveness

Competitiveness, like charity, begins at home. An externally competitive economy thrives on stirring its internal competitiveness. An economy that suppresses its internal competitiveness is most unlikely to be globally competitive.[1]

In the past, the primary focus of initiatives to increase business competitiveness and success was on speed-to-market, cost optimization, and quality enhancement. For years, both economic conditions and the competitive environment enabled initiatives focused on these elements worked effectively. However, in today's dynamic markets, to face well-informed and demanding customers, aggressive competition, and innovative market paradigms, there is further quest for competitiveness. Core competency is one of the factors that is being addressed effectively by many companies and leveraged for outpacing the competition and delighting the customers. The core competencies are being further honed and non-core competencies outsourced to counter the threats that challenge organizations.

PARADIGM SHIFT

In the new millennium, marketers are experiencing competitive pressure and businesses are struggling not for growth alone but also for survival. This has forced the business organizations all over the world to re-look at their business processes as well as the ways in which they are organizing their back-end processes and delivering products and services to their customers. Business firms across the world have started looking beyond the organizational boundaries to improve on cost, quality, reliability, responsiveness and relationship to manage uncertainty. In order to survive and remain profitable, not only manufacturing organizations but also trading companies all over the world are concentrating on core competencies and outsourcing peripheral processes and intermediate products. Global buying and sourcing practices have undergone total changes over past few years. This has resulted into

1. G. Ramachandran, "Competitiveness begins at home", *Business Line*, 13 January 2005.

innovative management practices that are vastly superior in terms of inputs, processing and delivery to the customers. The products today are sourced from different parts of the world, assembled at different locations and shipped to various destinations to ensure greater customer satisfaction and squeezing out unproductive time and cost from supply chain cycle.

The pursuit of growth and the need to access new markets have been propelling business firms the world over to search for sustainable competitive advantage. This has led companies to greater customer consciousness and need for cost effectiveness. The global nature of business has forced business organizations to recognize the critical role of back-end operations in today's dynamic business environment. As the business firms are focusing on production, marketing and finance, greater attention is required in achieving customer satisfaction through effective and efficient operations of various processes in the business. Today outsourcing business operations has become a source for developing competitive advantage in the cost-conscious and customer-driven market-oriented economies. Hence the business firms today cannot afford to ignore the crucial role of Business Process Outsourcing (BPO) in their value chain, which if ignored will probably be suicidal for the business firm, not only for growth alone but also for survival.

The global business scenario has changed over the last few years. Today stress is no longer on size but on competitiveness. It is on capitalizing more on core competencies and leveraging them to have a multiplier effect. Management helps such organizations in retaining the local flavour amidst the global model of doing business. Hence the emphasis is more on building strategic alliances in the market place.

COMPETITIVENESS

Competitiveness is the need of the time, and for complete understanding it has to be considered at the following three different levels:

- ***Firm level:*** Ability to provide product and services more effectively and efficiently than the relevant competitors.
- ***Industry level:*** Ability of the nation's firms to achieve sustained success compared to foreign competitors without protection or subsidies.
- ***National level:*** Ability of the nation's citizens to achieve a high and rising standard of living.

At each level there are different indicators of competitiveness. They vary in what they imply about the present and future economic success or well-being of a firm, industry or nation. Some concepts of competitiveness are applicable at one level but not at all levels. According to B.R. Scott and G.C. Lodge, "A firm is competitive if it can produce products and services of superior quality and lower costs than its domestic and international competitors".[2]

Competitiveness at the firm level is measured through profitability, cost, quality, exports or foreign sales, and regional or global market share. Performance in the international marketplace provides a direct measure of the firm's competitiveness. R. Feurer and K. Chaharbaghi say, "Competitiveness is relative and not absolute. It depends on shareholder and customer values, financial strength which determines the ability to act and react within the competitive environment and the potential of people and technology in implementing the necessary strategic changes. Competitiveness can only be sustained if an appropriate balance is maintained between these factors which can be of conflicting nature".[3]

According to Buckley,[4] "Competitiveness includes both efficiency (reaching goals at the lowest possible cost) and effectiveness (having the right goals). It is this choice of industrial goals which is crucial. Competitiveness includes both the ends and the means towards those ends".

Industry level competitiveness covers the overall profitability of the nation's firms in the industrial sector, the industry's trade balance, the balance of outbound and inbound foreign direct investment, and direct measures of cost and quality at the industry level.

At the national level, competitiveness is exhibited by the standard of living of the citizens. In most countries, the standard of living is determined by productivity, which deploys national resources and the output of the economy per unit of labour and/or capital employed. A high and rising standard of living for all nationals can be sustained only by the continuous improvement of productivity, either through achieving higher productivity in existing businesses or through successful entry into higher productivity businesses. Thus, a nation's competitiveness is the degree to which a nation can, under free trade and fair market conditions, produce goods and services which meet the test of international markets, while simultaneously maintaining and expanding the real incomes of its people over the long term.

Competitiveness at Firm Level

At the firm level, an enterprise is called *uncompetitive* if it is not generating profits. Such firms do not have cost advantage, i.e., their product costs are higher than industry cost and market price. The value of the resources the firm is using (opportunity cost) exceeds the value of the goods and services it is producing. Resources are misallocated and not properly used. In a

2. Scott, B.R. and G.C. Lodge, "US Competitiveness in the World Economy", Report of the Select Committee of the House of Lords on Overseas Trade (1985), p. 3.
3 Feurer, R. and K. Chaharbaghi, K., "Defining Competitiveness: A Holistic Approach", Management Decision, Vol. 32, No. 2, 1994, pp. 49–58.
4 Buckley, P.J. et al., "Measures of International Competitiveness: A Critical Survey", *Journal of Marketing Management*, 1988.

homogeneous product industry, a firm may be unprofitable because its average cost is higher than the average costs of its competitors. The cost is higher than its competitors because its productivity is lower, it pays more for its inputs, or both. Its productivity may be lower because it is less efficiently managed, it operates at an inefficient scale, or both. However, in a differentiated-product industry, a firm may be unprofitable for the same reasons as given before for a firm in a homogeneous-product industry. The other reason is that its product offering may be less attractive than that of its competitors.

At the firm level, profitability, cost, productivity and market share are all indicators of competitiveness. Profitability is a major indicator of current competitiveness, although profitability is best measured over an extended period. Market share may also be a sufficient indicator of competitiveness if the firm is maximizing profits, i.e., not sacrificing profits in the pursuit of market share. Of course, a firm can be competitive in a market that is itself declining. In this case, competitiveness does not ensure future profitability. Average cost (relative to that of competitors) is a sufficient indicator of competitiveness in a homogeneous-product industry (unless low costs are achieved at the expense of future profitability). Unit labour cost may be an adequate representation of average cost if labour cost constitutes a large fraction of total cost, but this is becoming increasingly infrequent.

EXHIBIT 1.1
Insurance Company: Competitiveness through Back Office Support

Pan Insurance (PI) is in market for last 30 years and had continuously high growth in the past, to become one of the largest life insurance companies in the country. PI provides administration and contact center services for its own brand. PI's had been established as one of the well-known brands and has a presence in many markets including overseas.

PI engaged I-Connect Solutions Pvt. Ltd. (ICSPL) for its field center services across pan India. PI has over 700 contact center Insurance Advisers, as well as 150 back office employees providing operational support. PI's major objectives of the partnership with IS were to use WM Software (provided by the ICSPL) to support a blending strategy; identify spare capacity in the back office; implement consistent and automated management information tool and provide a centralized forecasting tool.

ICSPL with its software helped PI to encash the opportunity of improving the throughput of work and enhancing customer service capability. It also supported in the reduction of other demand drivers for an operation, such as reduced chaser calls to centers and even complaints. ICSPL identified that there were varying levels of call arrival rates throughout the day, across it's all the field centers. Hence, they concluded that the Field Centers Advisors had certain capacity at certain times of the day that was not being fully exploited. ICSPL believed that operational performance can be improved a lot by pooling the capacity of individuals to help deliver significant benefits. ICSPL management thought that feeding this back office work into the Field Centers would be an opportunity to achieve this. PI through its partnership with ICSPL arrived at a solution only to manage its back office and also field contact centers. ICSPL's real-time call management solution monitored call arrival rates, and identified when volumes are below and what is expected rates and which are collated into a smaller number of individuals making the capacity exploitable. Then, the notifications can be sent to Field Centers Advisors, asking them to switch to processing back office work. The Advisor then uses software to pull back office work to service it. The work is allocated to an Advisor based on the priorities of the outstanding work and the skills of the individual. This ensures that the right work is being done, by the right people, at the right time.

This solution also provided the opportunity for Field Center Advisors to access records of outstanding back office work, whilst on a call to a customer. This allowed them to provide accurate information on where their case is in the process, and when it is likely to be completed, or even complete it themselves. Thus, this helped them improving the customer experience by managing their expectations and reducing future demand.

Through the development of the enhanced blended environment, Field Center Advisors now could manage downtime judiciously and have good understanding of the businesses requirements and priorities. With the identification of extra capacity, ICSPL can now utilize the time for training modules to be delivered to the Advisor at their desk. The major benefits derived were; identification of spare capacity in the back office, significant increase in volumes on some key processes, turnaround times drastically reduced, work volume increases were absorbed and additional recruitment costs reduced resulting into firm level.

Total productivity of an enterprise measures the efficiency with which a firm converts the entire set of inputs required for production into output. If output is measured in physical units (such as million tonnes of cement, million metres of yarn, number of vehicles, etc.), nothing is said about the attractiveness of a firm's product offering. Thus, a firm's competitiveness should be measured by its profitability over a relatively long period rather than a limited period. The present discounted value of a firm's anticipated profit stream is the firm's market value. A firm is said to be uncompetitive if the market value of its debt and equity is less than the replacement cost of its assets. The ratio of the market value of a firm's debt and equity to the replacement cost of its assets is known as *Tobin's ratio*; if this is less than 1, the firm is uncompetitive.

The anticipated profits of a firm depend on its relative productivity and input costs, and the relative attractiveness of its product offering over time. The future profitability of a firm may be a function of its current spending on R&D, its patenting activity, or many other facets of the firm's strategy. It is generally assumed that the goal of a firm is to maximize the sum of its current and discounted future profits.

There are various ways in which a firm can exploit its stock of intangible assets. The objective is to exploit these assets to maximize the present value they generate. It is, however, not obvious when current and future profits are in fact being maximized. In some cases, a high market share is an indicator of success. In other cases, it is not. In some cases, low unit cost is an indicator of success, while in other cases it is not. It is extremely important not to confuse indicators with objectives. For the firm, the objective is to maximize the present value of profits. A high market share may indicate that this objective is being achieved. But a high market share is not necessarily desirable for its own sake. A high market share will have greater implications for profitability or wealth maximization when it is measured at the firm level, than when it is measured at the industry or national level.

A focus on firm-level competitiveness implies a limited role for government. A nation may be as competitive as its firms. Government's role in making firms competitive is carried out by providing an environment supportive to good managerial practice. The contributions from government are:

- Stabilizing the country's economy
- Creating a competitive environment
- Eliminating barriers to cooperation among firms
- Improving resources: human capital, finance and public services.

The quality of human capital available to firms depends on the quality of the educational system and the incentives to employees to improve their skills or acquire new ones. The terms on which finance is available depend on how the financial system is regulated. Governments can ensure that the policies evolved are implemented effectively.

EVALUATING COMPETITIVENESS

If a core competency results in a long-term advantage to the firm, it is called a *sustainable competitive advantage*.[5] The end-result of core competency is value creation for the customer (see Figure 1.1). A core competency is something that a firm can do well and that meets the following three conditions specified by Hamel and Prahalad (1990)[6]:

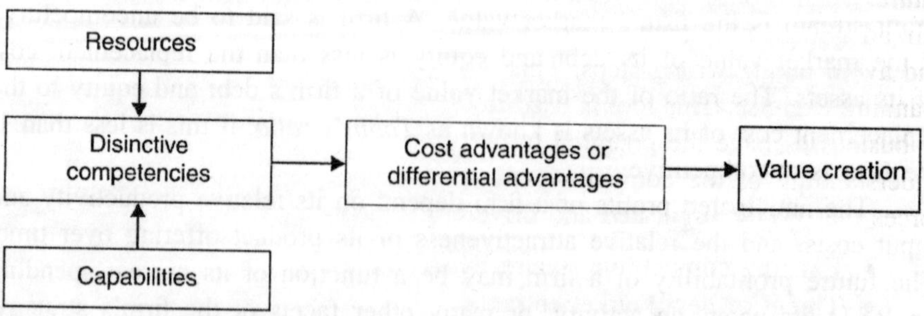

FIGURE 1.1 Porter's model of value creation.

5. Fred R. David, *Strategic Management: Concepts and Cases*, Prentice-Hall, 11th ed., 2007, pp. 156–157.
6. Gary Hamel and C.K. Prahlad, 'The core competency of the corporation', *Harvard Business Review*, May–June 1990, pp. 79–91.

- It provides benefits to customers
- It is hard for competitors to imitate
- It can be leveraged widely to many products and markets.

Core competency can be of various kinds, including technical or subject matter knowledge, a process having high reliability, and/or close relationships with suppliers and customers. It can also include product development or cultural matters such as employees' level of dedication. Today's business practices suggest that most activities that are not part of a company's core competency should be outsourced.

An example that can be quoted in this regard is Toyota's expertise in passenger vehicle manufacturing. Toyota focuses on its core competency of manufacturing and inventory management. The non-core activity of vehicle design was outsourced so as to expedite the new product development process. To take another example from the automotive industry, it has been claimed that Volvo's core competency is safety. This, however, is perhaps the end-result of their competency in terms of customer benefit. Their core competency might be more about their ability to source and design high-protection components, or to research and respond to market demands concerning safety.

When a firm sustains profit levels that exceed the average for its industry, the firm is said to possess a *competitive advantage* over its rivals. The goal of much of business strategy is to achieve a sustainable competitive advantage.

There are four basic tools developed by Michael Porter for evaluating competitiveness of a firm. These are:

Five competitive forces model

Porter's Five Forces tool (see Figure 1.2) is a powerful model for understanding where power lies in a business situation.[7] 'This is useful because it helps a company to understand both the strength of the current competitive position and the strength of a position that a company is looking to move into in future. With a clear understanding of where power lies, a company can take fair advantage of a situation of strength, improve a situation of weakness, and avoid taking wrong steps. This makes it an important part of company's planning exercise. This tool is used to identify whether new products, services or businesses have the potential to be profitable. This model gives us a good understanding of the competitive position of a firm in the market. The five forces that Porter suggested and drive competition are:

- Existing competitive rivalry between suppliers
- Threat of new market entrants
- Bargaining power of buyers
- Power of suppliers
- Threat of substitute products (including technology change).

7. Michael E. Porter, *Competitive Advantage: Creating and Sustaining Superior Performance,* New York, The Free Press, 1985, p. 5.

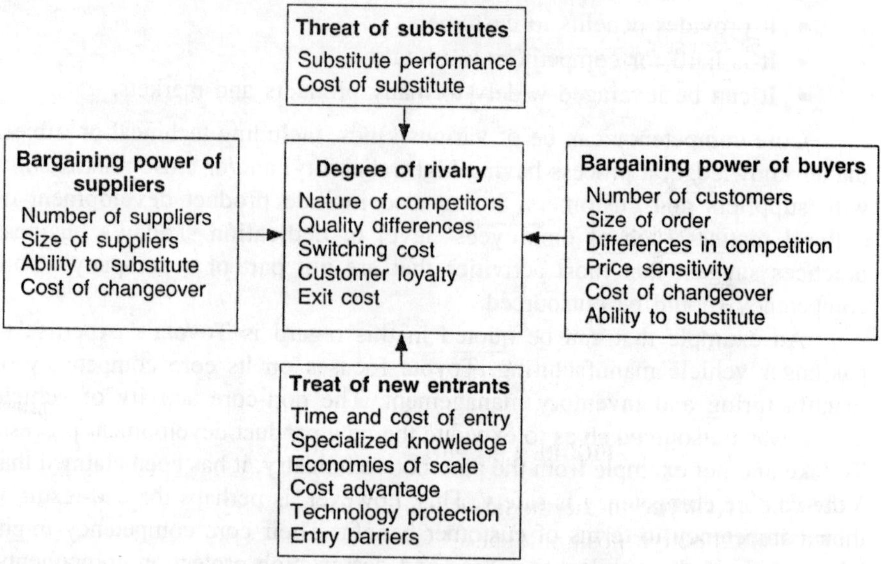

FIGURE 1.2 Porter's Five Forces model for competitiveness.

The five competitive forces determine industry profitability and attractiveness. These forces are important in shaping the prices that firms can charge, the costs they have to bear, and the required investments to compete in the industry.

The Five Forces model contains sub-points under each main heading, with the help of which a firm can carry out a broad-based sophisticated analysis of its competitive position to either develop strategy and plans or make investment decisions regarding a business or an organization.

Diamond model

Porter is also recognized for his competitive diamond model (see Figure 1.3), which is used for assessing the relative competitive strength of nations, and by implication, the industries therein.[8]

The diamond model, indicated in Figure 1.3, is used to analyze the business environment of the selected cluster. The determinants, taken individually and as a system, create a context in which a nation's firm is born and competes. Weakness in any one of those determinants constrains the industry's potential for upgrading and gaining competitive advantages.

In the diamond model, domestic rivalry for final goods stimulates the emergence of an industry that provides specialized intermediate goods. The diamond structure promotes clustering. Porter provides a detailed example to illustrate the system—the ceramic tile industry in Italy. Porter emphasizes

8. Michael E. Porter, *The Competitive Advantage of Nations,* Palgrave Macmillan, London, 1990, p. 72.

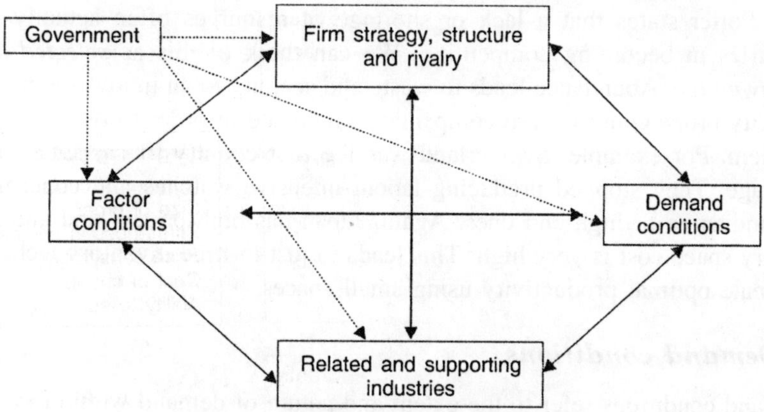

FIGURE 1.3 Porter's diamond model.

the role of chance in the model. Random events can either benefit or harm a firm's competitive position. These can be anything like major technological breakthroughs and inventions, acts of war and destruction, or dramatic shifts in exchange rates. When there is a large industry presence in an area, it will increase the supply of specific factors (such as workers with industry-specific training) since they will tend to get higher returns and lesser risk of losing employment. At the same time, upstream firms (that is, those who supply intermediate inputs) will invest in the area. They will also wish to save on transport costs, tariffs, inter-firm communication costs, inventories, etc. At the same time, downstream firms (those who use the industry's product as an input) will also invest in the area. Hence, attracted by the good set of specific factors, upstream and downstream firms (producers in related industries), those with similar inputs, or those whose goods are purchased by the same set of customers will also invest. This will trigger subsequent rounds of investment. In the diamond model, Porter has explained four determinants of national competitive advantage. These are:

1. *Factor conditions*

Factor conditions refer to production factors necessary for a given industry, e.g., skilled labour, logistics and infrastructure. Factor conditions also refer to inputs used as factors of production, such as labour, land, natural resources, capital and infrastructure. This sounds similar to standard economic theory, but Porter argues that the major factors of production (which can also be called *specialised factors*) are not inherited but created. Specialized factors of production are skilled labour, capital and infrastructure. General use factors such as unskilled labour and raw materials can be secure by any firm and hence do not create any sustained competitive advantage. However, specialized factors require heavy and sustained investment and are more difficult to duplicate. This creates a competitive advantage, because if other firms cannot readily duplicate these factors, they are of great value.

Porter states that a lack or shortage of resources often actually helps countries in becoming competitive. We can think of this as *selected factor disadvantage*. Abundance leads to waste and scarcity to an innovative mindset. Scarcity-prone countries are compelled to innovate in order to overcome their problem. For example, Switzerland was the first country to encounter labour shortage. They stopped producing labour-intensive watches and concentrated on innovative or high-end ones. Again, Japan has high-priced land and so its factory space cost is very high. This leads to just-in-time inventory techniques to create optimal productivity using small spaces.

2. *Demand conditions*

Demand conditions refer to the extent and nature of demand within the nation concerned for the product or service. Porter argues that a sophisticated and competitive domestic market is important for producing competitiveness. Firms that have a sophisticated domestic market are likely to sell superior products because the market seeks high quality, and a close interaction with such consumers allows the firm to understand their needs and desires better. One example of this is the French wine industry. The French are sophisticated wine consumers and therefore force and thus help French wineries to produce high-quality wines.

3. *Related and supporting industries*

A set of strong related and supporting industries is important to the competitiveness of firms. This includes suppliers and related industries. This usually occurs at a regional level as opposed to a national level. Examples include Silicon Valley and Detroit (for the auto industry) in the USA and Italy (for the leather industry). The phenomenon of competitors (and upstream and/ or downstream industries) locating in the same area is known as *clustering* or *agglomeration*. The advantages to locating in clusters are potential technology knowledge spillovers, market power, and availability of applicable labour force. However, disadvantages to locating close to one's rivals are potential poaching of firm's employees by rival companies and obvious increase in competition, thereby possibly decreasing margins.

4. *Strategy, structure and rivalry*

Thirdly, firm strategy, structure and rivalry create demand conditions. Domestic capital markets affect the strategy of firms. Some countries' capital markets have a long-run outlook, while others have a short-run one. Countries with short-run outlooks (like the USA) tend to be more competitive in industries with short-term investment (like the computer industry). Countries with a long-run outlook (like Switzerland) tend to be more competitive in industries with long-term investment (like the pharmaceutical industry). This is an important factor for individuals to base their career decisions on opportunities and prestige. A country will be competitive in an industry whose key personnel hold positions that are considered prestigious.

Porter further says that the best management styles vary between industries. Further, particular countries may be oriented towards particular styles of management. Therefore they will tend to be more competitive in industries to which their style of management is suited. For example, Germany has hierarchical management structures comprising managers with strong technical background. Italy has smaller, family-run business, while the USA has flat organizational structures.

Intense competition promotes innovation. Competition is rather fierce in Japan, as many companies compete vigorously in most industries. International competition is, in contrast, not as intense and motivating for Japanese firms. In international competition, there are often enough differences between companies and their environments to provide convenient excuses for firms who were outperformed by their competitors.

Implications for Governments. Government legislation and regulations involve market controls, resource conservation and healthy competition. The government plays an important role in Porter's diamond model. Like everybody else, Porter argues that there are some things that governments do that they should not, and other things that they do not do but should. As per Porter, the government's role is of a catalyst and challenger; it is to encourage—or even force—companies to raise their aspiration levels and move to superior levels of competitive performance.

Governments can have strong influence on all four of Porter's determinants through various actions such as subsidies for firms—either directly (money) or indirectly (infrastructure), tax codes relevant for corporation, business or property ownership, educational policies related to the skill level of workers, specialized factor creation and enforcement of tough product standards including environmental regulations.

Value chain analysis

Competitive advantage is created through the activities of the firm. The activities performed when competing in a particular industry can be grouped into categories, as these activities can be divided broadly into primary activities and support or secondary activities.[9] These activities are modelled into a value chain, as shown in Figure 1.4. Primary activities are those involved in the ongoing production, marketing, delivery and servicing of the product, whereas support activities are those that provide purchased inputs, technology, human resources or the overall infrastructure functions supporting the other activities. Every activity employs purchased inputs, human resources and some combination of technologies, and draws on firm infrastructure such

9. Michael E. Porter, *Competitive Advantage: Creating and Sustaining Superior Performance*, New York, The Free Press, 1985, p. 37.

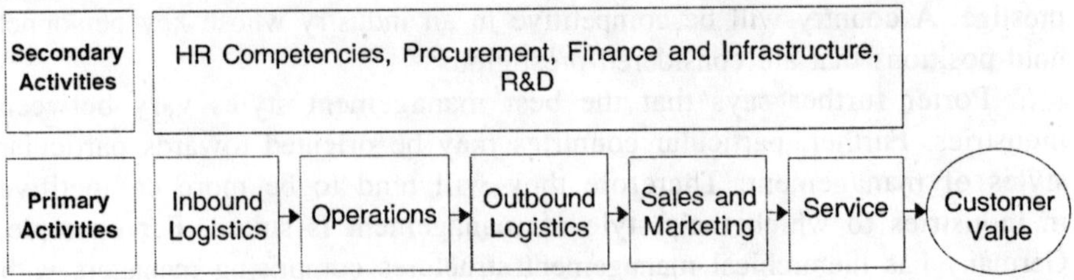

FIGURE 1.4 Porter's value chain model.

as general management and finance. Activities vary in their importance vis-à-vis competitive advantages from industry to industry.

All activities contribute to buyer (customer) value. Hence firms create value for their buyers through such activities. The ultimate value a firm creates is measured by the amount that the buyers are willing to pay for the product or service offered. A firm is profitable if this value exceeds the collective cost of performing the required activities. To gain competitive advantage over its rivals, a firm must do either of two things: provide comparable buyer value but perform activities more efficiently than its competitors (lower cost), or perform activities in a unique way that creates greater buyer value and commands a premium price (differentiation).

Firms gain competitive advantage by finding new ways to conduct activities, or by employing new procedures, new technologies, or different inputs. A firm is more than the sum of its activities. The value chain of a firm is an interdependent system or network of activities, connected by linkages. Linkages get created when the manner in which one activity is performed affects the cost or effectiveness of other activities. Linkages often create trade-offs in performing different activities that must be optimized. For example, a more costly product design, more expensive components, and more thorough inspection can lead to reduction in after-sale service costs. A firm must resolve such trade-offs, in accordance with its strategy, to achieve competitive advantage. Thus, strategy guides the way a firm performs individual activities and organizes its entire value chain.

Linkages also require that activities are coordinated. The coordination of linked activities leads to reduction in transaction costs, allows better information for control purposes, and substitutes costly operations in one action with less costly ones in others. The proper management of linkages can be decisive for securing competitive advantage.

Thus, creation of competitive advantage requires the management of the value chain as a system rather than as a collection of separate parts. Reconfiguring the value chain by relocating, reordering, regrouping, or even eliminating activities is often crucial for bringing about major improvement in competitive position.

In brief, the value chain provides a tool for understanding the sources of cost advantage. Securing cost advantage usually requires optimization of the linkages among activities, as well as close coordination with suppliers and distribution channels. This value chain also highlights various sources of differentiation.

Cluster map

Clusters are geographic concentrations of interrelated firms and institutions in a particular field. Clusters (see Figure 1.5) comprise an array of linked industries and other entities that are important for competition. They include, for example, suppliers of specialized inputs such as components, machinery, services and infrastructure.

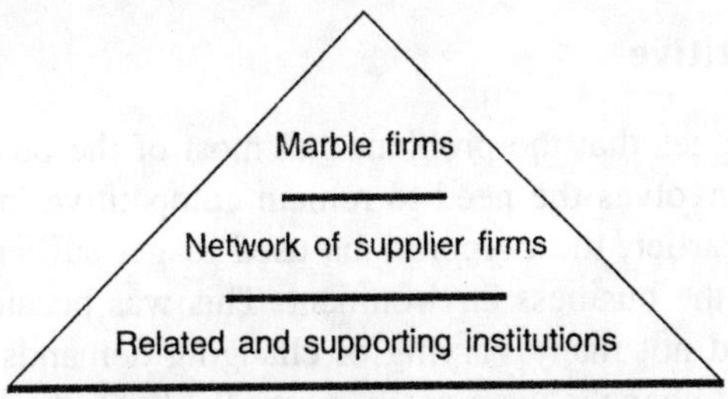

FIGURE 1.5 Cluster mapping.

Quite often, clusters also extend downstream to channels and customers and laterally to manufacturers of complementary products, and to firms in industries related by skills, technologies or common inputs. Finally, many clusters include governmental and other institutions such as universities, standards-setting agencies, thinktanks, vocational training providers, and trade associations, which provide specialized training, education, information, research, and technical support.

The cluster map clarifies all related and supporting elements of major industries. In addition, it illustrates linkages between such elements—strong or weak—and indicates absent industries. Cluster analysis provides a pattern for understanding how major industries carry out their business and the way they compete, whilst at the same time complementing and supporting one another.

Clusters affect competition in three broad ways:

- By increasing the productivity of firms or industries;
- By increasing their capacity for innovation and thus the growth of productivity; and
- By stimulating new business formation that supports innovation and expands the cluster.

Normally, clustering is revealed in the depth and breadth of clusters, which are most prominent in advanced economies. In developing economies, greater proportions of industries either are locally based or consist largely of foreign subsidiaries serving the local market. Exporting industries tend to be either resource-intensive or labour-intensive. Clusters in developing economies tend to rely primarily on foreign components, services, and technology. Often firms are forced to integrate vertically, create infrastructure and operate.

Developing good and supportive clusters is one of the essential steps in moving towards an advanced economy. Cluster formation in developing economies is limited by local education and skill levels, technological weaknesses, lack of access to capital, and underdeveloped institutions. In addition, government policy usually opposes cluster formation, and the monopolistic behaviour of firms protected from competition retards cluster development.

Staying Competitive

Michael Porter argues that the problem that most of the business corporations are facing today involves the need to remain competitive in various functions of the business. Earlier, the corporations used to get sufficient time to adjust to the changes in the business environment. This was because of lower levels of competition and not many varying or changing demands of the customers. The environmental changes were easily controllable by the corporations. They could do it through changes in organization structures or by adjusting the number of employees or some changes in administrative functions. However, to cope with the environmental challenges of today, business organizations have to be proactive in order to deal with highly competitive markets and the changing needs of the demanding customers. In addition, for remaining competitive, one has to do the job in the right way, at the first time, and in the shortest possible time-frame. To achieve this, the business organization has to ensure that all the business processes are cost-effective and efficient. But it is not possible for a single organization to have expertise in all of its business operations. They have to first identify their area of expertise, and for the process they do not possess expertise in, they have to take help of a third party, which has the competency to perform that function cost-effectively and efficiently. The way out to stay competitive is by outsourcing the non-core business functions.

In future the total competitiveness of an organization will be the sum total of the competitiveness in each of its functional areas. Hence, the main responsibility of the management will be to attain optimal process competitiveness in each functional area. There are always treats and opportunities in all functional areas in every business organization. Bad management of a function will throw the business out of competition. There are multiple examples of Indian business firms which had to close shop or are on the verge of dying out as they have not kept themselves sufficiently competitive to survive in the liberalized market-oriented Indian economy. The business process needs to be analyzed in light of the changing business environment. It is like adjusting continuously the acceleration process of the vehicle when it is required. In other words, it is a feedforward process that will keep the firm competitive today.

For staying competitive, organizations need to benchmark their business processes to attain the competitive edge. Innovation—process or product—is the keyword for competitiveness. Competitiveness normally emerges out of some mixture of the following:

- Quality of process delivery
- Continuous service improvement
- Speed of achieving required level of performance
- Reduction in cost.

To attain and retain an edge over their competitors, organizations have to keep abreast of industry changes, technological advances and new industry legislation. Training of employees is continually reviewed and updated as per industry norms, as training keeps the business up-to-date with the latest industry and global marketplace developments. Trained and motivated staff, who understand the specifics of particular business operations, can create a sustainable competitive advantage. They will give business the competitive edge by:

- Increasing productivity and quality standards in operations
- Being able to undertake a greater variety of work
- Allowing the firm to bid for more specialized, high-value contracts
- Assisting the firm to meet business objectives faster.

Training is vital to stay ahead and take advantage of new information technologies, which play a crucial role in many organizations. Trained staff will prevent business firms from suffering skill shortages in all areas relevant to the industry. Training should be flexible and can be customized for specific business operations.

ACHIEVING BUSINESS TRANSFORMATION

Outsourcing is nothing but simple re-engineering of the support system. Business firms are using outsourcing partners to achieve, sustainable improvement in enterprise-level performance. The primary objective of outsourcing is to cut cost and focus on the core activities. The earliest example of outsourcing, which shook the corporate world and is often quoted, is of Eastman Kodak that had outsourced its entire information technology function for a ten-year period at a cost of $250 million in 1990. However, today business firms are using outsourcing as a tool for business transformation. This is a more sophisticated approach as compared to the age-old cost approach. Today, firms are achieving an average 50% cost saving through outsourcing as compared to 20% saving reported in the early 1990s. In addition to the cost savings, the advantages the firms may have are:

- Enhancement in service levels
- Access to competitive skills
- Responsiveness to changing customer needs
- Re-engineering of business support process

Thus, business transformation is achieved through partnering with service providers or through the joint venture route.

BUSINESS MODEL FOR COMPETITIVENESS

For staying competitive, the organizations develop unique business models for product-market fit. For example, in the computer industry, Dell has a unique business model that sets them apart from competitors. As per Gary Hamel, business concept or model[10] (see Figure 1.6) consists of the following four major components.

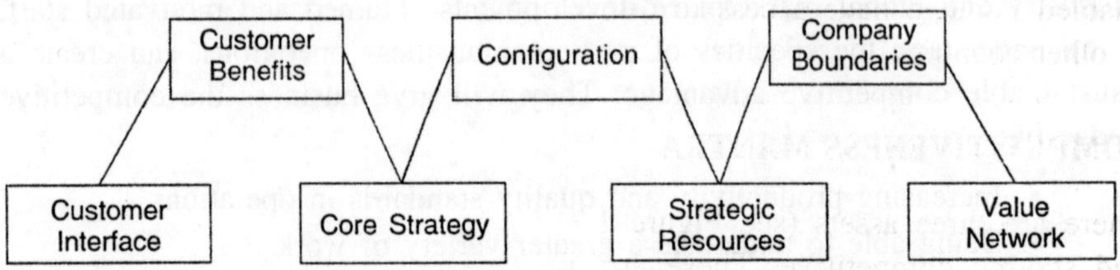

FIGURE 1.6 Components of business model.

1. *Customer interface*

The delivery of value or benefits to the customer requires both customer interface and the core strategy. Customer benefits link the core strategy directly to the needs of the customers. The customer interface covers order fulfilment through distribution channel and service support through service network. It also covers relations differentiation between transactional and valued customers. The differential pricing structure for bundling products and services to different customer segments is used to build customer interface.

2. *Core strategy*

The core strategy is the plan of the company about the way it is competing with its rivals. The elements involved in setting core strategy are the company's business mission, product-market scope and basis for differentiation.

3. *Strategic resources*

For having a competitive advantage a company should have resources such

10. Gary Hamel, *Leading the Revolution*, Harvard Business School Press, Boston, MA, USA, 2000, p. 96.

as core competencies (skills, systems and technologies) to create unique value for the customers. For example, Hindustan Unilever has branding and marketing distribution, and Dell Computer has direct-distribution competencies to market its products. The other strategic assets are brand, customer data, distribution coverage, intellectual property (patents, trademarks, copy rights and trade secrets). These are both rare and valuable, and are sources of competitiveness. The core processes are equally important as these processes transform competencies into customer value.

4. *Value network*

These are the ones through which a company acquires value. These include suppliers, partners and coalitions. For example, three automobile giants (Ford, Chrysler and GM) formed a single procurement organization (Convisint) to have cost advantage on the procurement front. Another example is P&G who are in vendor managed inventory (VMI) partnership with Wal-Mart. This enabled P&G to have access to difficult markets through Wal-Mart's entry in other countries.

COMPETITIVENESS MANTRA

There are three assets (see Figure 1.7) which are important for becoming and staying competitive. These are human assets, technology assets and relationship assets.

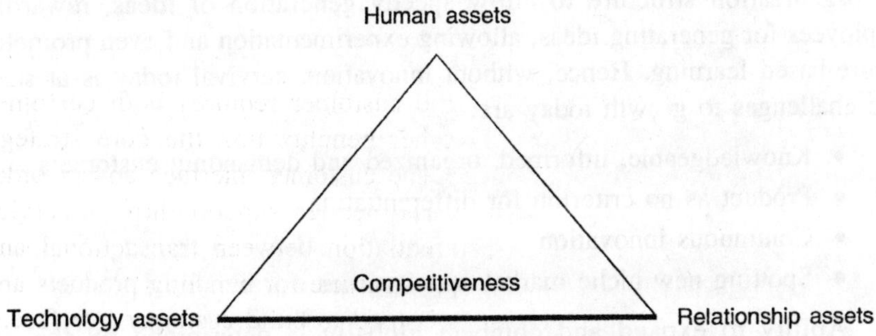

FIGURE 1.7 Components of competitiveness.

The human assets solve business problems and address business opportunities. They need to be up-to-date on technical skills; have an understanding of the business, which comes from client interaction; and have the ability to solve problems.

The technology asset is essential to integrating systems and making a process productive and cost-effective. Firms must also establish standards that limit the range of technologies that employees must support.

The relationship asset implies risk and responsibility for effectively applying technology in business. Top management must be involved in establishing priorities and forming steering committees that initiate a co-operative business relationship.

The rapid strides in recent years, such as economic progress linked to the explosion in information technology (IT), accompanied by globalization, has resulted in the demanding, aware, intelligent and involved customer. This has changed the total competitive dynamics of every industry. Today, physical borders no longer define markets. Companies can source products from the lowest-cost locations and sell to any profitable location. This is possible due to the communication revolution which has drastically reduced response times. The consumers demand value for money. This resulted in change in the nature of competition which is creating challenges for companies today. These challenges are about growth, cost, customer and quality.

The biggest challenge to companies today is in their ability to grow in the face of competition. The changing landscape has made it more and more difficult for organizations by limiting their competitive capabilities. The markets are getting saturated due to high penetration levels that challenge organizations to explore niche opportunities and expand their horizons into rural and international markets. These factors are driving corporation towards innovation in their offerings. The companies today recognize that ideas have a limited shelf life and are creating a culture where ideas flow continuously. Organizations are restructuring themselves around customers. They are now creating organization environments wherein they instil a deeper understanding of consumers and customers among their employees, flattening the organization structure to allow speedy generation of ideas, rewarding employees for generating ideas, allowing experimentation and even promoting failure-based learning. Hence, without innovation, survival today is at stake. The challenges to growth today are:

- Knowledgeable, informed, organized and demanding customers
- Product as no criterion for differentiation
- Continuous innovation
- Spotting new niche market opportunities.

Ability to expand and compete globally is determined by the cost competitiveness of the organization. This can be overcome with production at mega scale and by creating and tapping mega markets.

The challenge to Indian companies today is to overcome our "lack of a global mindset" in sourcing. Learning to function in the global sourcing arena, locating world-class sources and coping with multi-cultural negotiations is a must. To move towards world class is to benchmark every element of cost and take out or limit non-value-adding costs. The major challenges in cost reduction are:

- Ability to invest in scale and technology
- Deeper understanding of global sourcing

- Benchmarking out non-value added costs
- Reducing cycle time
- Driving supply chain efficiencies

One of the challenges is the mindset of selling on *price* and inability to sell *value*. The undue focus on price as against value is at the core of several businesses being unable to unlock their value potential adequately. The future will belong to companies that create robust cross-functional teams to provide enhanced customer value. Buyer–seller relationships are experiencing transformation around the world, with more and more instances of teamwork between the two.

The next challenge before the companies lies in eliminating errors in products and services as also improving the quality of input materials and processes to achieve global quality levels. The challenge calls for increasing investments in R&D as well as testing systems. Winning companies passionately create a Total Quality Management culture in the organization. Deep commitment of top management to quality and excellence is a major prerequisite for creating a quality culture in the organization. Hence, by facing the challenges mentioned with determination at the strategic, control, and operations levels, organizations can achieve competitiveness in the dynamic markets of today by resolving the issues in a systematic and planned manner.

SUMMARY

The pursuit of growth and the need to access new markets have been propelling companies the world over to search for sustainable competitive advantage. This has led companies to greater customer consciousness and need for cost-effectiveness. The global nature of business has compelled business organizations to recognize the critical role of back-end operations in today's dynamic business environment. As business firms are focusing on production, marketing and finance, a greater degree of attention is required in achieving customer satisfaction through effective and efficient operations of various processes in the business. Competitiveness is the need of the time. In order to understand competitiveness, it has to be considered at three different levels: firm level, industry level and national level. At each level there are different indicators of competitiveness. At firm level there are six qualitative indicators of competitiveness such as product quality and performance, customer satisfaction, product range, profits, costs, and production flexibility. For evaluating competitiveness, Porter evolved various models such as the five forces competition model, value chain model, cluster mapping and diamond model. Gary Hamel has suggested that businesses focus on critical components such as customer interface, core strategy, strategic resources, and value network. For any organization there are three assets, which are important for becoming and staying competitive. These are human assets, technology assets, and relationship assets.

Review Questions

1. Discuss competitiveness at different levels and the indicators of competitiveness therein.
2. Which are the four different tools for evaluating competitiveness developed by Michael Porter?
3. Explain Porter's Five Forces model of competition with regard to the BPO industry in India.
4. Analyze the competitiveness of the BPO industry in India using the diamond model.
5. Select any leading BPO service provider in India and analyze its components and competitiveness by using Gary Hamel's business model.
6. In today's context, staying competitive is a must for survival. Select a leading BPO firm and find out how it is creating value for the customer and achieving sustainable competitiveness.

Chapter 2

Need for Outsourcing

70% of GE's work would be outsourced. Of this, 70% would be done from offshore development centres. And of this, about 70% would be done in India. This ultimately boils down to about 30% of GE's work being outsourced to India.[1]

One of the benefits of outsourcing is that a business firm can save on every aspect of the business and increase profits. With outsourcing of non-core processes, the organization will be free to concentrate on its core business, and the firm's employees can be put to better use and it is possible to have a huge growth in firm's core business. Outsourcing can save the organization's time, effort, infrastructure and manpower. Since an outsourcing firm doesn't have to invest in infrastructure, it can also save on making unnecessary fixed investments. Outsourcing removes the need for changing or maintaining infrastructure and can also save on capital expenditure. Outsourcing can help the firm to save on training costs, because of no investment in manpower. As the job is assigned to a vendor who is an expert in his field, the result is high productivity, system efficiency and cost-effectiveness. The net effect is the creation of savings that will help bring about an increase in the firm's revenue and its speed to market. The other important advantage with outsourcing is the cross-pollination of latest technologies which the firm's vendor may be using for their operations.

INTRODUCTION

Outsourcing is the transfer to an external service provider the operation and day-to-day management of a business process, which can be done keeping in mind productivity, cost effectiveness and system efficiency. The customer receives a service that performs a distinct business function that fits into the customer's overall business operations.

Outsourcing can be defined as use of external agency to perform the business activity more cost-effectively and efficiently in the given time-

1. General Electric's CEO introduced the 70:70:70 rule. In an e-mail to GE employees across the world, Jack Welch stated this, as reported in *Business World*, 20 March 2000.

frame. The external agencies are called *vendors*. They are experts in their jobs and in addition they have domain knowledge of the customer's industry. They are either standalone outfits, i.e., experts in one particular activity or integrators having expertise in multiple functional areas. The integrators have the capabilities to integrate them as per the customer's needs.

The concept of outsourcing started with Ross Perot when he founded Electronic Data Systems in 1962. EDS would tell a prospective client, "You are familiar with designing, manufacturing and selling furniture, but we're familiar with managing information technology. We can sell you the information technology you need, and you pay us monthly for the service with a minimum commitment of two to ten years."

Outsourcing can be defined as a process in which an organization enters into a contract with another organization to operate and manage one or more of its business processes. *Outsourcer* refers to a company that contracts with another company to provide services that might otherwise be performed by its in-house employees. Many large companies now outsource jobs such as call centre services, e-mail services, and payroll. These jobs are handled by separate companies specializing in each service. There are many reasons why companies outsource various jobs, but the most prominent advantage seems that of saves money. Many of the companies that provide outsourcing services are able to do the same work for considerably less money, as they have the expertise to complete the job in the shortest possible time.

EXHIBIT 2.1
Back Office Process in Holiday Resort

KEM Resorts is into holiday rental business in India having more than 50 properties available for holiday rental. The holiday rental business is growing fast in India. This business is cost-driven and having stiff competition. The resort company has to give best of the offers and services to attract customers. It is possible only by reducing the overheads and the cost benefit should be passed on to the customers. The company is having its own team to promote and market the services. However, the management felt that looking into the marketing potential they have estimated, the volume of business they expected is not coming. Alternatively, they thought of outsourcing the services. After thorough market research they decided to associate with a BPO vendor—COVISION—in this industry space. BPO vendor proposed back office processing model. KEM initially had reservations in outsourcing their operation. However, COVISION developed a dedicated team to deliver back office outsourcing service for KEM's operation. The BPO operation is flexible and the KEM monitored the work directly through various reports and through daily interaction. Every individual in the team has been given target for providing customer service to the customers and their performance is monitored directly. The back office support included:

- Customer relationship and support.
- Marketing (offline and online).

- Coordination with property owners, travel agents and vendors.
- Reservations and online payment collection.
- Web management.
- Search engine optimization.

COVISION constantly analyzed the ways to improve the outsourcing operation using advanced quality techniques and organization methods, etc. The result was a grand success with gains; more than 45% process cost savings, customers were serviced faster and increased process turnover time, reduction in overheads created avenues to give the cost advantage to customers, increase in business volume, organized customer support created lot of reference and repeated customers and, finally, KEM has time to concentrate on new marketing campaigns.

Outsourcing also allows firms to focus on other business issues while having some processes handled by outside experts. This means that out of a large number of other resources, attention should be focused on productive resources within the firm. The vendor company that handles the outsourced work is usually streamlined and often has world-class capabilities and access to new technology that a firm can't afford to buy on its own. Also, if a firm is looking for expansion, outsourcing is a cost-effective way to start laying down foundations in other countries.

Outsourcing involves the delegation of tasks or jobs from internal production to an external entity (such as a subcontractor). This means buying goods or services instead of producing or providing them in-house. Outsourcing is not exactly a new innovation; it is a shift that has occurred recently due to industry trends. Thus outsourcing is done to save money, improve quality, or free company resources for other activities. Outsourcing was first done in the data-processing industry and has spread to other areas including telemarketing and call centres.

Today the business organization needs to remain competitive not only for the growth but also for survival. For this the management has to improve its performance on a continuous basis. The organizations are normally resorting to the following for improving the performance:

- Using latest management techniques
- Using improved or advanced technology
- Implementing suggestions of eminent consultants.

There are some disadvantages of outsourcing as well, particularly in marketing outsourcing. One is that outsourcing often eliminates direct communication between a firm and its clients. This prevents the firm from building strong relationships with their customers, and often leads to dissatisfaction on one or both sides. There is also the danger of not being able to control some aspects of the business process, as outsourcing may lead to delayed communications and project implementation. The sensitive information is more vulnerable, and the firm may become very dependent upon its service providers, which could lead to problems in the event of the outsourcing service provider backing out of the contract suddenly. Thus, while outsourcing may prove highly beneficial on many counts, it also has many drawbacks. It is important that each individual company accurately assesses its needs to determine if outsourcing is a viable option.

The modern techniques used by the organizations for improving the performance are TQM (Total Quality Management), BPR (Business Process Reengineering), CRM (Customer Relationship Management), Six Sigma, etc. These tools enable the executives to improve the business process and achieve competitive edge. However, it is not possible for the organization even after using these tools to improve its performance beyond certain levels, because of certain organizational limitations such as allocation of resources to non-core functional areas, where the focus is less. Also, the degree of success in using these techniques is different in different organizations because of the organization cultures and management priorities.

Today, outsourcing has become a new word in the IT vocabulary, although it is an old concept in the manufacturing industry, where most large manufacturers of mass-produced goods have traditionally used specialized vendors to supply sub-assemblies. However, in a business firm with IT enablement, information technology outsourcing may include a transfer of responsibility for management of data centres and networks (LAN, WAN, and telecommunications) to a third party.

WHY OUTSOURCING?

One of the major advantages of outsourcing is flexibility. It can be a lot easier to cut back on a vendor than an employee. Another advantage that the firms have is that they can attain expertise in every particular area. The most positive thing about outsourcing is its ability to save a firm's money. This will depend on the size of the company and what specific tasks are to be outsourced. For example, a company outsources the IT services (help desk, computer support and maintenance) and pays significantly less than they pay a full-time IT person to give the same level of support. Today, outsourcing continues to move into more strategic areas of the business. The firms are realizing that their best partner is the one that offers them the greatest value, not necessarily the lowest cost. Most business firms which go for outsourcing follow the following decision model (see Figure 2.1).

In the high-tech industry, original equipment manufacturers (OEMs) like Cisco, IBM, Nortel, Palm, and Compaq have outsourced manufacturing to specialists like Solectron and Celestica. These contract manufacturers have expanded their services to include shipping, repairs, and even product design. Thus by offering design services, the contract manufacturers help OEMs craft products in a more standardized way to cut costs and reduce the risk of component shortages, which can hurt a Cisco or a Compaq badly.

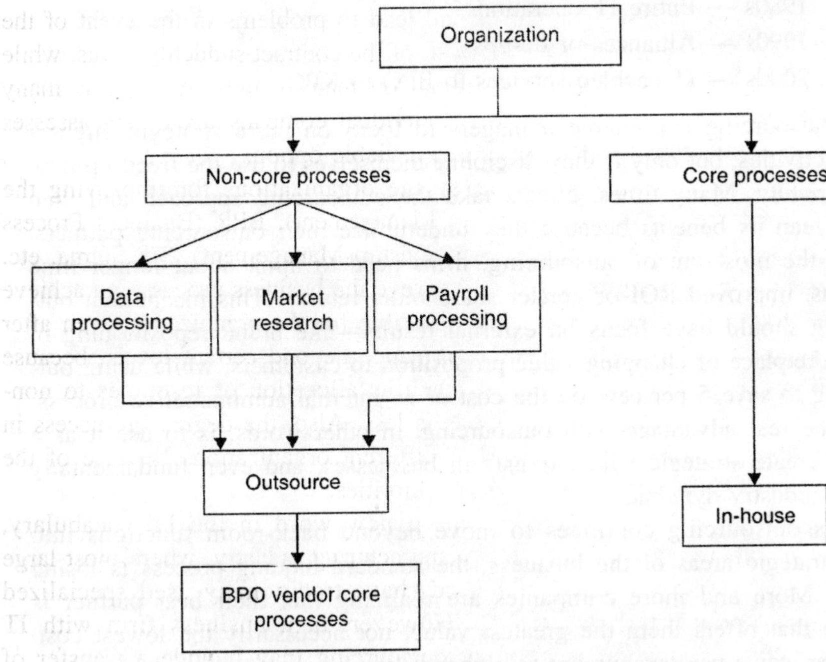

FIGURE 2.1 Business process outsourcing model.

There are some definite advantages to outsourcing. Contract work is often cheaper—especially if opted for off-shore development. Here, people are hired only for specific tasks. Outsourcing creates shareholder value by reducing costs and commitments to fixed and working capital. Outsourcing helps a firm focus on its core business, helping to create a competitive advantage within its industry. Other advantages include access to best-of-class capabilities and accelerating the benefits of reengineering. Another advantage outsourcing gives firms is a chance to get the best job possible from the vendors it hires. However, if the work is done in-house, there may be company ties which are hard to break.

SCOPE OF OUTSOURCING

Earlier, outsourcing used to be viewed as a tactic for reducing the costs of back-room functions such as payroll and IT. Before the 1990s outsourcing was not a breakthrough management idea. But things started to change in the early 1990s, as firms began outsourcing more strategically significant functions such as manufacturing and logistics, and even product design and other innovation-related activities. All of a sudden, outsourcing had turned into a critical management tool. Looking at the history, outsourcing undergone the following evolution:

- 1960s — Time-sharing
- 1970s — Parts of IT operations

- 1980s — Entire IT operations
- 1990s — Alliances or tie-ups
- 2000s — IT-enabled services to BPO to KPO.

Outsourcing can enable managers to focus on more strategic, higher-value activities, but only if they discipline themselves to use the freed-up time appropriately. Many times, clients take the outsourcing approach and then fail to reap its benefits because they underutilize their outsourcing partners. To get the most out of outsourcing, firms need to think about longer time horizons, improved ROI or greater shareholder returns. This means that outsourcing should have focus on external results—like brand repositioning in the marketplace or changing value proposition to customers, while using outsourcing to save 5 per cent on the cost of an internal administrative process.

The real advantage with outsourcing, in other words, is to use it as a tool to create strategic value, transform businesses, and even fundamentally change industry dynamics.

As outsourcing continues to move beyond back-room functions into more strategic areas of the business, the standard bidding process is losing favour. More and more companies are realizing that their best partner is the one that offers them the greatest value, not necessarily the lowest cost. However, some use outsourcing as a change-management tool to drive major, enterprise-level transformation. The following are the examples of outsourcing deals indicating its pervasiveness:

(i) NDTV ties up with Genpact for media outsourcing services.
(ii) Monument conservation outsourcing by Archaeological Survey of India.
(iii) Outsourcing of aircraft maintenance by cash-strapped airlines.
(iv) Legal service outsourcing by US legal firms to cheaper destinations.

OUTSOURCING: A CATALYST FOR CHANGE

In some companies, outsourcing is used as a change management tool to drive major enterprise-level transformation, such as a shift in competitive position or a major increase in market share or stock price.

Transformational outsourcing is often faster and more effective for organizations than other major change initiatives such as re-engineering or acquisitions. Companies have tended to use mergers and acquisitions to get themselves into new industries and change the limits of what they were doing. This is not the cup of tea for all the firms. However, with outsourcing a firm gets a firmer grip on its competitiveness.

Outsourcing has the potential to eliminate the cyclic nature of the business in many industries. For example, in times of strong or growing demand, OEMs like Cisco and IBM add cushions to the capacity forecasts they provide to their vendors. For the same reason, their manufacturers add cushions to their own forecasts for needed components, so that they don't get caught short. The result is speculative ordering on both ends of the value chain. This cushioning is completely independent of true demand; it wouldn't exist where manufacturing is done in-house, as changing a forecast in this case can be a very simple process.

Outsourcing creates an extra layer in the supply chain, and that typically means one more safety cushion. These cushions don't create industry recession in and of themselves, but they heighten its severity. Outsourcing allows the company to use external manufacturing capacity instead of having to build its own plants.

Thus outsourcing works where it gets at the some major sources of waste. That's why there's so much potential for outsourcing in the high-tech supply chain.

EXHIBIT 2.2
Air Lines Outsourcing: A Pressing Need

Airline industry is prime example of stiff competition as a result of deregulation. Almost all the airlines have used outsourcing as a method of cost control, increase profitability and improve efficiency. In their pursuit of high performance, airlines are outsourcing key business processes for a variety of reasons. For example, before the airlines were deregulated, the majority of air carriers conducted their maintenance in-house. After deregulation, with competitive pressures mounting and for airlines the outsourcing of maintenance became more prevalent. Not restricted to US airlines, outsourcing aircraft maintenance has become a global practice. Factors involved in the outsourcing decision range from a startup not having the capital to develop their own in-house maintenance program, to legacy carrier's cost cutting efforts, and all points in between. Today, it is more critical than ever to streamline operations without compromising service quality. Seeking new economies of scale is equally critical, as is capturing customer mind share to get his loyalty. Todays' competitive business environment has forced companies to identify methods to improve efficiencies. A solution is to outsource certain non-core business processes. Thus, the companies eliminate the distractions and focuses on the managerial attentions and resources on building their core competencies. With the increased air traffic volume of flight ticket booking has increased many folds. The in-house ticket billing process which was commonly done in-house has gone for a toss and resulted into backfiring of billing cycle. Air-Orion (AO) is the largest international airline carrying around 7.5 million passengers worldwide to over 250 destinations. As one of the world's longest established airlines, it has always been regarded as an industry-leader. Annually, Air-Orion handles 10 million tickets on the global scale. Around 10–12% of tickets are sold by other airlines. Billing recovery is huge task for in-house billing department. Air-Orion recognized the need of outsourcing billing process to outside vendor. They engaged 'Sigma Solutions' (SS) to take up the responsibility of ticket process and billing cycle management. SS took the job to provide an efficient and cost effective operation IT solution and AO decided to outsource its ticket processing to process 8 million tickets and has billing functions to create an archive capable of storing 20 million tickets. Considerable cost savings have been achieved through rationalization of the billing process and streamlining of the organization. AO can search the archive and retrieve ticket images in less than five seconds. The solution has enough capacity for growth without requiring additional investment. Considerable cost savings have been achieved through rationalization of the billing process and streamlining of the organization. This initiative builds upon the long-term customer relationship through the use of the very latest technology to get efficiencies in flight ticket processing. The AO is in the process of outsourcing many other management processes to get the benefits like: increased ancillary revenue generation, expanded distribution channels with reduced distribution costs, real-time business intelligence, decreased operating costs, better customer service, improved resource deployment and support for rapid growth.

OUTSOURCING: BEYOND COST ADVANTAGE

Outsourcing involves procurement of products or services from sources that are external to the organization. Firms should consider outsourcing when it is believed that certain support functions can be completed faster, cheaper, or better by an outside organization. Tasks that are not core competencies of the organization are candidates for being contracted out. Today, the outsourcing of selected organizational processes or activities is an integral part of corporate strategy. For corporations, benefits of outsourcing are substantial: reduced costs, expanded services and expertise. Outsourcing allows companies to refocus their resources on their core business. Corporations can buy technology from a vendor that would be too expensive for them to replicate internally. For outsourcing to be successful the decision needs to be an informed one. Effective management of the outsourcing relationships is an organizational imperative today. While cost-cutting may have been the original reason to outsource work, increasingly factors such as innovation and the need to increase focus are also being included in decisions on outsourcing. However, the final direction should not solely address the question of cost savings, but must also consider the benefits and the strategic position of the company in the marketplace to create the following benefits:

- Smooth peaks, troughs and staff shortages
- Access to specialist skills and knowledge
- Access to specialized content
- Reduction in content cost
- Reduction in research resource cost
- Reduction in overheads
- Undertaking of confidential research.

Information Technology is one of the primary outsourced job functions today. Everything from in-house servers being relocated to server firms around the globe to internal help support desk, programming, analysis and database management is outsourced to third parties. Human Resources is becoming another sought-after outsourceable function for all kinds of businesses. Other areas of outsourcing are Sales, Documentation, Utility, Financials, Insurance, Logistics, Secretarial Services. Consulting, Healthcare, Manufacturing, News and Media.

Outsourcing: IT and Business Processes

This term is used in IT industry to describe bundling of IT and BPO solutions provided by a vendor to its clients. In fact the very nature of these service streams is different. BPO covers a lot of real-time activities which need to be performed throughout the year. However, IT is more project-driven or initiative-based. The people and processes needed to undertake these activities would be very different. Problems will obviously arise to integrate these two vastly different service offerings. Most companies do not have a dual need for IT as well as BPO services at the same time. However, there are organizations looking for integrated IT and BPO services; but these are more an exception than the norm.

Another aspect that negates the total outsourcing of services is the decision-making chain for IT outsourcing and BPO. BPO/CRM offshoring decisions are typically taken at the board level with the operations or customer servicing heads driving the decision. The CIO, however, usually drives IT outsourcing, and most relationships currently exist here. Again, site visits are critical to BPO decisions, while reference checks may suffice in cases of IT outsourcing. Also, very important to BPO is experience. Delivery of IT services is very different from customer interactions and back-office processing in terms of the critical aspects of people and processes.

OUTSOURCING GUIDELINES

The goal of outsourcing is better quality at lower costs, but too often the outsourcing results are disappointing-to-dismal; the reason is that many buyers lack a clear outsourcing methodology. Using the outsourcing concepts, managers responsible for outsourcing should follow the following steps:

- Determine core competencies that should be kept in-house rather than outsourced
- Align outsourcing with overall corporate strategy
- Use outsourcing to support transformation strategies such as restructuring and TQM
- Evaluate, compare, and select vendors
- Negotiate win-win contracts, monitor how vendors perform, and evaluate financial savings
- Handle competition from vendors' as well as contractors' end.

The costs involved in managing the outsourcing process can be a cause for worry, but it need not be so. Firms need to make sure that there is clarity in planning out management strategies and adapting them to outsourcing. Irrespective of the size of business, for getting benefits out of outsourcing, a proper management framework to organize the process is integral. Better outsourcing management helps in optimizing resources for maximum performance.

There are certain areas of outsourcing business that need constant attention. Concentrating on these areas will greatly increase control over the direction of the outsourced project.

Cost

The main attraction of outsourcing is its cost reduction. To achieve this, firms must analyze the scope and price right at the beginning of the project and arrive at a reasonable consensus on cost.

Communication

It is essential to establish proper communication channels that facilitate open communication. The main advantage of maintaining good communication with the BPO partner is transparency in all activities. To ensure better communication the following should be in place:

- Establish good communication systems
- Regularly contact the outsourcing partner
- Give clear instructions and feedback
- Clarify all possible doubts that can arise.

Performance

It is necessary to strike a balance between the actual performance levels and the ideal performance standards of the outsourcing project. The core issue in performance management is the time factor. It is important to make sure that the project does not lag too much. To ensure this, targets have to be specified, and review and analysis has to be done on a regular basis.

Risk Management

Risk factors are the biggest sources of concern in outsourcing. A complete assessment of possible risks will give an upper hand in being aware of various risks and ensuring that they are managed well.

Crisis Management

Firms need to ensure that the management is financially and professionally equipped to deal with contingencies. With a good outsourcing partner, crisis management will not be a difficult issue as contingencies are supported with back-up plans.

Knowledge Transfer

Knowledge transfer has a direct influence on productivity. Hence, while transferring knowledge about the proposed project, there is need to make sure that complete information and knowledge is transferred to one's outsourcing partner.

Relationship

In the outsourcing business, both the parties enter into a long-term relationship for mutual benefit. As far as possible, business should be done with an ethical and credible partner. This will add to the profitability of business as the cost of maintaining the relationship will be reduced. In addition to evaluate the outsourcing partner, the outsourcing firm needs to know how to equip in-house capabilities to match with requirement. For this, they need to

- Evaluate in-house capability
- Distribute the workload between in-house and outsourcing processes
- Entrust a responsible person or team to monitor the outsourcing process
- Train employees on how to manage and organize an outsourcing business

Ultimately, the aim is to succeed in its outsourcing venture and that too with considerable profit margin. There is a need to establish the best possible management systems for going ahead with outsourcing of business processes.

OUTSOURCING ISSUES

In outsourcing business, choosing a service provider with integrity, honesty, efficiency and great communication skills will solve many issues. Before outsourcing a business process, one should ensure to ask the vendor for details such as number of years in business, number of employees, financial background to and get a thorough picture of the vendor's history. The following things need to be investigated in depth before awarding the outsourcing contracts:

- Capability of vendor to provide quality products or services
- Lifecycle cost of the products/services of the vendor
- Reliability in meeting delivery deadlines
- Security of firm's data in the hands of the vendor
- Risk analysis of the vendor

- Effects of the vendor's employee attrition on the contract
- Vendor's fairness and transparency in dealings
- Vendor's compliance with regulations
- Matching of vendor's organization culture with the firm's.

Finally, what a firm does not measure, it cannot monitor, and what it cannot monitor, will decay. Hence, it is extremely important to formulate a set of metrics before making the BPO outsourcing decision. It is crucial to apply those metrics in-house first to get a realistic estimate of how well the firm is executing its processes. Depending on the kind of process and its risk profile, appropriate techniques can be used to measure the quality of the process output. Once these measurements are made, a firm can go forth and negotiate a BPO contract which specifies the service level agreements and the means of tracking them unambiguously.

OUTSOURCING BEST PRACTICES

The focal point of outsourcing project is the Service Level Agreement (SLA). The aim of outsourcing is to gain value for the customer. However, there are several contrasting views regarding how to maximize value and minimize risk of outsourcing. The following guidelines can help when structuring SLA, and then implementing and maintaining a relationship with the chosen provider:

Relationships between personnel

To have real value out of the relationship between the key management personnel from both sides, there should be good understanding and strong working ties between them. In fact friendship between employees of the two organizations (client and vendor) is an important determinant in forming long-term relationships.

Setting achievable and quantifiable objectives

The performance criterion should be set in a way which clarifies the expectations to be fulfilled by the vendor. The comparable projects will serve as starting points for setting objectives which are negotiable. However these objectives should be understood by both the parties.

Incentives and penalties

Performance review of both the sides is a must. Performance should be linked to reward and penalty schemes to get results.

Periodic review

Review meetings to be organized periodically. During the meetings, both sides can discuss the performance of the teams and determine the future objectives or goals of the company accordingly. They can also discuss product reviews and deliverables during these meetings. Performance objectives should be continuously revised according to the changing business environment.

Communication for bridging cultural differences

Communication is the key to a healthy relationship. The parties involved in an outsourcing relationship usually belong to distinct cultures. The differences have to be accepted and bridged. Cultural understanding between the two organizations can be enhanced by organizing social events, educating about company background, participating in each others' quality programmes, etc.

It is challenging to manage an outsourcer relationship when the vendor is geographically thousands of miles away. Distance is a factor that must be taken into account when deciding on the outsourcing contract. In such events there are a few guidelines for creating and maintaining a successful relationship that can be used by both the parties:

- Manage the relationship as you would do with any outsourced activity, regardless of the geographical distance.
- Depute a manager on-site, particularly early in the relationship while the details are being worked out.
- Visit the site frequently till the relations are established and initial teething troubles are resolved.
- Have a local representative to oversee the relationship.
- Establish continuous communication linkage to avoid misunderstanding.
- Set up a formal daily review session, particularly early in the relationship, and encourage the development of informal channels.
- Monitor customer inquiries and evaluate the quality of the response.
- Conduct regularly a baseline survey (informal way) to determine customer satisfaction levels.

In addition, prior agreement on skill set of professionals to be deployed on the project is a must. Also, outsourcing project is to be defined in terms of CPM (critical path method) charts to easily evaluate the progress of the project. The norm of minimum use of internal resources during outsourcing project should be judiciously followed. Internal conflict needs to be avoided. Division of outsourcing project and project fees into clearly defined and measurable parts, so that in case the project as a whole fails to take off, its parts can be implemented, is highly desirable.

SUMMARY

Outsourcing is the delegation of tasks or jobs from internal production to an external entity (such as a subcontractor), where functions previously performed by an organization are supplied under contract from a third party. While outsourcing is not exactly a new innovation, the shifts that have occurred recently in this space are worth noting. The concept of taking out internal company functions and paying an outside firm to handle them is today most welcome. Outsourcing is done to save money, improve quality, or utilize company resources in other activities. Outsourcing was first done in the data-processing industry and has spread to areas, including tele-messaging and call centres. Outsourcing is the wave of the future. It implies a degree of managerial control and risk on the part of the provider. It is a long-term, result-oriented relationship with an external service provider for activities traditionally performed within the company. Outsourcing usually applies to a complete business process. One may ask: Why outsource? The answer is: because one doesn't have the time to do it by oneself; because one doesn't have the money to do it by oneself; because one would rather focus on mission-critical issues; and because one doesn't have the skills to do it by oneself.

Review Questions

1. "Outsourcing is a catalyst for change." Explain with illustrations.
2. What are the do's and dont's of outsourcing?
3. Explain the scope of outsourcing and its related advantages.
4. Differentiate between IT and BPO outsourcing.
5. What are the major issues in a Business Process Outsourcing contract?
6. What are guidelines for successful outsourcing contract?
7. Survey the BPO industries and find out the best prevailing practices in outsourcing.

Chapter 3

BPOs: Beyond Call Centres

Today's competitive marketplace demands operational productivity, administrative efficiency, business agility, shorter turnaround times and increased shareholder value. Business Process Outsourcing (BPO) is the survival key in transforming the business processes to achieve these end results.[1]

A call centre is a physical location, where calls are placed or received to handle the queries or the problems related to some particular product of a particular organization. In other words, by making a call to a call centre one can have a clear idea and solution to the problem about the product or service concerned. Call centres cater to the low end of business process needs of the customers. For high-end needs of the business processes, BPOs are the solution providers. BPO is a general term used to describe the outsourcing of critical, but non-core, business processes or functions of an organization to external vendors for long periods of time on a set of predefined performance metrics. BPO services have gained prominence during the past couple of years as more and more organizations have recognized the practical and enhanced value of externally delegating processes instead of doing them in-house. Thus the role of BPOs are much beyond the scope of call centres. The skills required in BPOs are technical-oriented rather than the communication-oriented ones which are required in call centres.

INTRODUCTION

Call centre is a term which covers a number of activities like reservation centres, helpdesks, information lines or customer service centres, irrespective of how they are organized or what types of transaction they handle. The term *call centre* is generally used for a refined voice operations centre that provides a full range of high-volume, inbound or outbound call-handling services. The most common services provided are customer support, operator services, directory assistance, multilingual customer support, credit services,

1. http://sourceamerica.net/HIM/WhatBPO.asp.

card services, inbound and outbound telemarketing, interactive voice response, and web-based services.

Call centres are becoming increasingly popular in today's business, where many companies have centralized customer service and support functions. Call centres are generally large offices with representatives who either make or receive phone calls. Depending on the type of work, call centres may have a single office employing a few people or large office with thousands of employees. The main activity in some call centres is answering inbound calls, such as in a bank that gives out a toll-free number for customers needing help. At the same time, there are some call centres that focus on outbound calls too.

With increase in outsourcing, call centres are also becoming popular. By way of outsourcing, companies contract out some functions to other companies located mostly in cost-effective destinations like India. In this field, India enjoys several advantages over a number of developed countries. The major one is a large pool of qualified people—English-speaking graduates and IT professionals. In addition to this, India has some other advantages like cheap labour, flexibility in working hours and time zone difference. This is the reason why a number of MNCs are outsourcing their business activities to India.

CALL CENTRES

A call centre is a service centre. It has telecom facilities, trained associates (employees), access to wide databases, Internet and other online information support infrastructure to provide information and support to a customer. It provides round the clock and year-round service.

A caller has access to a toll-free number that connects him or her to a customer support centre. When a typical call reaches the call centre, the caller is answered by a trained associate, who has access to a wide database of information (see Figure 3.1) and who is also been trained on the product or service being offered by the organization. The dedicated communication links connect a remote call centre to a parent organization through voice links and online computer database access. The database is central to effective customer

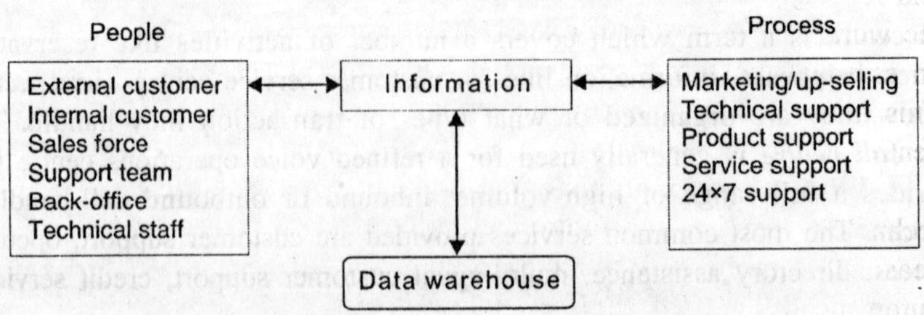

FIGURE 3.1 Call centre infrastructure.

support and maximum customer satisfaction. It allows the consultant to tap into customer history, customer-owned product attributes, etc. and exploits latest technological developments in global online information access and web-enabled database updation to respond to the caller.

In other words, the caller may be calling a local telephone number in the USA, but the call is being answered in India without any time delay. Call centres are operated by airlines and banks to provide services to customers or callers, investment banks, mutual funds, telecom services, and companies providing customized and high-value services. These services are very popular in countries such as the USA, Europe, Japan and Australia. The value-added services deployed as part of call centre design and operations are:

- State-of-the-art call centre environment
- Customized call handling applications
- 24 hours × 7 days × 52 weeks call response
- Online technical helpdesk services online
- Automatic call distribution
- Customer satisfaction, retention and relationship building
- Ongoing training programmes.

The service application areas that normally may be addressed by call centres include:

- Complaint handling
- Sales support
- Technical queries
- Relationship and account management
- Lead generation and follow-up
- Telemarketing
- Credit and billing problems
- Market research
- Database development.

In a call centre, due to increased volume of customer calls, coupled with growing complexity of staff scheduling (longer hours, weekend shifts, contract and regular workforce) a strong case for automation for the management of the workforce exists. Today, ACD (Automated Call Distributor) has become an essential tool for a professionally managed call centre across the globe. This is a solution with new generation technology adapted by leading call centres across the world.

With the help of historical and current call information, the new technology predicts the future call volume based on overall calling trends, seasonal factors and other predictable calling patterns. Forecasts are automatically updated with new information through a direct ACD interface. In the ACD system for staffing calculations, a telephone traffic engineering technique is used to determine the required number of staff based on the forecast workload. This technique called *Erlang C* takes into account the random arrival of calls into the centre as well as the "hold for the first agent" queuing that typically takes place. This software package is designed over the basic queuing theory. In this staff scheduling method, staff requirements along with nonproductive time estimates (for breaks, training, meetings, etc.) are used to determine a schedule requirement for each half-hour or quarter-hour period. Finally the optimal schedules are created on the basis of these requirements and a call centre's unique scheduling rules and constraints. The schedules thus prepared by the system are then assigned to staff based on shift bid rules and employee preferences.

The most critical component of a workforce management system is the intra-day comparison of actual performance against the plan. The automated workforce call centre management system compares the actual number of calls by half-hour to the call forecast, actual call handle time against estimated handle time, and actual number of staff on the phones to the schedule plan. This is needed to make necessary adjustments as quickly as possible. The automated system generally produces measurable improvements in the areas such as more efficient scheduling, automation of workforce management tasks, reduction in workforce shrinkage, reduction in network costs and of course increased revenues. In addition to these measurable benefits, there are many intangible benefits. The major one is addition of a sophisticated "what-if" planning capability that allows management to forecast and plan staff needs for the short term to respond to fluctuations to address long-term resource planning.

EXHIBIT 3.1
Outbound Call Centre Services

A renowned IT giant—Techofab—in the business of providing IT solutions to their customers, such as computer hardware, software and services. This was the first time this company opted to outsource outbound call centre services. Techofab had launched a new product in the market. The product was a software package that was highly technical in nature; it facilitated improved flow of communication in an organization. The role of call centre was to set up an outbound cold calling process with the main aim of generating sales leads. This required technically sound call centre agents, who were capable of communicating the features, advantages and benefits of the product to prospective customers of the Techofab in the country. The target customer segment for this new product was small and mid-sized companies. Call centre vendor set up an outbound cold calling process at their delivery centre with a dedicated team to promote the new software product. The call centre agents were recruited and trained by Techofab directly. These agents were provided with a database of prospective customers in the country and were given cold calling scripts, which were developed by Techofab. The calling process was unique and not routine, since every call that was made required a different set of technical queries to be answered by the call center agents.

Call centre vendor suggested certain reporting formats and templates as a value addition to the customer, which were well accepted. Reporting was done both on a daily and weekly basis. Daily reports were sent by the process owner to the Techofab, based on the performance of the outbound call centre agents.

A weekly check-in conference call was scheduled between the process owner, process manager and Techofab to brainstorm new ideas and address the challenges encountered by the outbound call centre agents. The call was useful to streamline the process of achieving enhanced conversion rates.

Stringent quality checks were set up at every stage of the process to ensure flawless execution in meeting the customer's requirements. Each voice call was recorded and subjected to quality checks to ensure that the outbound call centre agents performed well, in line with the customer's expectations. The performance levels of the call centre agents were constantly measured to ensure that vendor delivered high quality results, consistently.

The data gathered for the reports to be sent to the customer was checked and validated for spelling errors, grammatical mistakes and general correctness, before the reports were sent to the customer. The key differentiating factors of call centre vendor that led to high satisfaction at Techofab end were:

- Technically sound call centre agents working on the project.
- Clever handling of prospective customers' queries, leading to increased sales leads.
- Comprehensive reporting procedures.
- High accuracy levels of the delivered services maintained consistently.
- Excellent project management skills.

As a direct consequence of call centre vendor's services, the Techofab experienced a surge in new product inquiries and an increase in the sales figures of the new product.

Evolution of Call Centres

Call centres were started with the idea of basic phone services to attend to the customers and provide the immediate solution to their problems. However, over the years, call centres have evolved from phone services to full-fledged business enterprises. Business-oriented people have found that service is key to attracting and maintaining the customers, leading to revenue generation. The success of the call centre depends on customer satisfaction with regard to the responsiveness and the solution sought by the customers for their problems or queries. The key factors in customer satisfaction are minimum waiting period and shorter response time. To achieve this, the staff needs to be trained for continuous improvement on communication skills and accents.

The call centres cater to the low end of business process needs of the customers. The problems and their solutions sought at call centres are not so complex. For example, nursing call centres, which are coming up in large numbers in the western countries, are for health care delivery over the phones. A growing number of nurses are working out at call centres to dispense advice over the telephone to the patients. As this is a not-so-complex judgmental process, tele-nursing is getting widely accepted in medical circles as an efficient way to care of patients.

For a call centre job the basic requirement is good communication skills. Other than this, there is no higher educational qualification required to join the call centres. In most of the cases, graduates are preferred. These new recruits are trained for one to three months. The training focuses on pronunciation of British, American or Australian English, and oral communication skills in

- Conducting telephonic conversations
- Presenting the information
- Taking part in discussions
- Work on improving one's listening and speaking skills.

Medical transcription

In developed countries, as a doctor's time is at high premium, the current practice is for doctors to simply record their findings through a dictaphone or some such device. These sound tracks are then sent to datacom lines to overseas companies (where costs are much lower) that employ Medical transcriptionists who hear these recordings, transcribe them into reports and send them back electronically through datacom lines. Medical transcription has now become a specialized discipline. Here the main requirement is of employees with adequate training. Information and communication technologies are used to send the voice recordings on satellite lines to far-off low-cost locations, where these recordings are transcribed into reports, which are again sent back to hospitals or clinics digitally through the same lines and printed in the reports forms. Turnaround time has often as low as two hours. Today, to take advantage of lower costs, this work is sent to countries like India, Philippines, Mexico, and the West Indies, because of the availability of high-speed satellite links.

Data entry services

Industries such as banks and airlines require large-scale data entry and revenue accounting work to be done. For revenue accounting and other back-office accounting operations, paper documents or raw data are sent to remote locations, which are used for data entry and necessary reconciliation. Using high-speed datacom links for their back-office and data-processing operations, the banks, airlines and other organizations with extensive data turnover and customer interface are able to save costs and valuable resources. The prime concern of these companies is 100% availability of data and uptime of facilities. This can be ensured through high-speed datacom links from India to the parent country. In other words, such a centre should be realized simply as an off-shore extension of existing information and back-office operations promising constant availability. Over the last few years, there has been a steadily growing trend to outsource these services to major IT service providers with contract durations running into decades. The prime criteria of such projects are quality of organizational processes, availability of abundant manpower and ability to dedicate resources to client's needs.

Legal services

There is a constant need for lawyers who counsel clients to go through relevant laws and precedents in order to build up their case. This is usually done by very junior lawyers in legal firms. However, in the USA and other developed nations, even junior lawyers' services are highly priced. One of the ways to get around this hurdle is to have a readily accessible source of well-managed and intelligent information. One of the most promising and low-cost ways of having ready access to information is information technology. Therefore, many legal firms have started to outsource this work to organizations, which have large English-speaking, lower-priced workforces of trained lawyers. The job comprises working closely with the firms to create a database of their existing records, indexing on the basis of various useful and common understood criteria, keeping track of new documents being created and incorporating them into databases as per well-established parameters. Lawyers can then simply use their computers to draw up a history of like cases and draw a clear plan of action. Once again, the rules are clear and only average qualifications and ability are required.

Media content

New media content development is emerging as one of the fastest growing service segment in the global IT services industry. It caters to the needs of website management, production of content for new media such as compact disc, digital versatile disk and products of convergent technologies such as Internet-enabled TV. It offers a large potential as more and more offices, homes, institutions, students and professionals realize an ever-growing need to have easy access to information that can also suitably fused with other media. It consists of compilation and development of digital content for intra-organization dissemination, cross-institutional collaborative projects, public domain information, programmes for public/specialized education, web content development and management, and developing animated movies. It typically involves defining a set of rules and norms for collection of data, collating various unorganized sources of data, sorting, indexing and shifting compilation conversion into digital format and disseminating various users. In other types of digital content development, there is usually a contract between content provider and developers to review projects on an ongoing basis such as cartoon serials and movies. The opportunities are also available for acting as an offshore content developer for organizations such as Internet media companies and advertising companies. Today, web content development is becoming a multi-billion dollar segment. There are several other such areas where the potential is high. The acceptability of outsourcing such work to distant countries and the recognition of the cost savings is rapidly growing.

Customer support services

A caller uses a toll-free number that is generally connected to a customer support centre. When a typical call reaches the call centre, the caller is answered by a trained consultant with access to wide database of information and who is also been trained on the product or service being offered by the organization. The dedicated communication links connect a remote call centre to a parent organization through voice links and online computer database access. The web technology created to support the call centre ensures that the consultants have the most current information available, so that high standards or efficiency are met. For example, airlines overseas have toll-free numbers, where people call 24 hours a day, to make and change flight reservations, enquire about the status of booking, etc. What is required here is also a workforce of graduates who can read and write English. Since everybody is connected to the same central computing facilities, it does not matter if the call centre is located in the city of the caller or anywhere else in the world.

Captive Call Centres

Call centres for internal customers also represent a major opportunity for large companies and business groups. As an extension, most large companies would like to have call centres for their own customers, those for other group companies or even for responding to their large base of investors. From an investment perspective, outsourcing call centres to India represents a major opportunity for cost-cutting and boosting efficiency. By outsourcing call centres to India, the investments can be protected and further nurtured.

Call Centre Technology

Most of the recent trends in the call centre industry pertain to the technology behind the call routing and distribution function. Some of these trends will continue and include the following:

- Shift from proprietary to open architectural platforms is rapidly gaining acceptance, as vendors frequent introduction of PC-based routing and call management software.
- A shift toward 'turnkey' solutions is boosted by this trend to open platforms, which allows for easier integration with existing systems.
- In addition, open architecture is seen by those types of call centres operating in more non-traditional environments, e.g., SOHO, virtual call centres, telecommuting, etc.

- Price decline for products (due to level of technology and knowledge sharing).

Besides the preceding developments, call centre technologies are making a rapid shift to manageable solutions. For example, select companies in India have already developed extremely competitive and technologically advanced call centre solutions entirely based on PC technologies and platforms, as well as IP technologies. This helps to reduce the cost of the system and reduces change over time, as a major portion of technology is derived from software.

Success Factors in Call Centre

In a call centre the main task centres around serving an existing and potential customer base. This need is translated into providing satisfying and well-informed responses to a customer query and meeting the customer's expectations with regard to service quality. The difference in services can be made through a number of factors as follows:

- Integrating call centre service flow with the process of the customer for whom this service is being provided.
- Developing ability to satisfy the customer's query for the first time.
- Keeping minimum waiting period and response time for a query by benchmarking against some of the best call centre operations across the globe.
- Achieving quality certification such as ISO 9000 or other certification applicable to this industry. This includes full COPC-2000 (Customer Outsourcing Performance Centre) certification. This distinction means that the facility has met the requirements of all 32 areas described in the COPC-2000 standard. It thus helps to validate call centre's quality and continuous improvement initiatives.
- Quality of service rendered by an outsourced call centre should be equal to or exceed service levels already achieved by the clients' in-house call centre.
- Continuous training of call centre staff to help improve accent and diction capabilities, especially for the region being served.

BUSINESS PROCESS OUTSOURCING VENDORS

BPOs are way ahead of call centres. Business process outsourcing has become the latest business mantra around the world today.

BPO is the act of transferring some of an organization's repeated non-core business processes to an outside provider to achieve cost reductions while improving service quality. Because the processes are repeated and a long-term contract is used, outsourcing goes far beyond the use of associates. BPO results in increasing shareholder value. The main difference between

BPO and more traditional IT outsourcing is that BPO offers companies a way of achieving transformational outcomes much more quickly. In a typical BPO contract, a service provider takes over a specific corporate function. An effective BPO process covers much more than just changing the person who is responsible for performing the process. In BPO, the outside provider not only takes on the responsibility to manage the function or business process, but also re-engineers the way the process has been traditionally done. The next generation of business process outsourcing has emerged as a priority for businesses looking to better options in managing their application portfolios.

The first wave offered low-cost, off-shore development labour, but today firms are demanding new, less risky options for applications that are strategic, complex, or mission-critical, while still taking cost into consideration. Outsourcing has moved from a niche technology management tool to a mainstream strategic decision. Business process outsourcing leverages process-driven efficiencies in terms of organizational excellence, responsiveness and branding, financial efficiency and customer relationship. BPO is emerging as a powerful and flexible approach that business leaders can use to achieve a wide range of tactical and strategic aims. The most common business process that gets outsourced is the call centres. Call centres and helpdesks of many multinational and Fortune 500 companies are being outsourced to low-wage English-speaking countries such as Philippines and India.

EXHIBIT 3.2
Productivity through Business Process Outsourcing

Magnus Corp, a leading financial information provider invited the services of BPO Vendor—GLOBEOP—in finance sector to deliver round the clock services to its customers, supporting multiple languages across the globe. GLOBEOP developed an automated work-flow tool to enhance productivity and eliminate errors. Productivity increased by approximately 54% and savings to the extent of 35% of earlier expenses done annually.

Magnus is one of the world's leading real-time global economic and financial information providers of data, news, and analytic solutions. It uses large number of Financial Instruments running in millions through an array of sophisticated trading tools and services. Currently, it serves more than 1,70,000 clients worldwide with comprehensive and accurate financial information.

Magnus faced the several challenges across various streams of its business. They used to procure the earnings estimate data from an external vendor for the client. There were multiple quality issues in the data and the vendor was unable to rectify these errors. Magnus was catering to stock markets in various time zones and was providing its services in multiple languages. Control on operations at multiple locations was tedious and the efficiency was reducing. The seasonality in the flow of input files resulted in a peak in volumes every month end. With the increasing numbers and depth of customers serviced by the client, there was an increase in the backlog of pending files.

Magnus recognized the need for cost-effective and process-efficient operations. They wanted high quality of the extracted data and reduced process timelines, product enhancement by the core resources and zero errors in transcription. GLOBEOP provided a platform to the client to build the earnings estimate data. They built an advanced work flow tool built on the principles of queuing theory and assembly line production. This tool could manage the input, queuing, processing, review, and output of files. A quality control algorithm that minimizes review effort and maintains high quality levels, is an integral part of the work flow tool. With the error proof validations system and data transparency the quality review effort were possible. Data transparency achieved, enabled an internal auditor to double click on an extracted value and the tool navigates the auditor to the source document from where the questioned data element is captured. This navigation facilitated faster and efficient quality assurance.

GLOBEOP helped the Magnus to reduce their time to market by 55%, giving the client an edge over its competitors in publishing the most current information. The productivity enhancement was approximately 54%. This helped the client to increase the scope of work for each employee, while keeping the manpower same. This helped Magnus to save a lot annually. In addition, the enhanced productivity of the employees was utilized to introduce industry-specific financial measures with a comprehensive coverage of around 25,000 companies across the globe, covering 10 languages. With the extensive use of technology in data capture helped in improvement of quality from 70% to more than 95%.

Business process outsourcing occurs when an organization offers to perform a business function (i.e. accounts payable or purchasing) to a third party that conducts the activity based on a set of predetermined performance metric functions. Though some forms of BPO may include both IT management and business operations, the approach is primarily about outsourcing functions such as payroll, accounting, billing or even real estate management to a third party. Though these business processes may depend on IT, they are separate core IT operations such as data centre activities or network management.

Many Indian software companies take time to set up a BPO (vendor) facility in India. Actually, setting up a call centre is capital-intensive. An ordinary BPO centre that takes care of pure back-office operation (e.g. payroll, data entry) will not be as expensive as a call centre.

BPO saves precious management time and resources and allows focus while building upon core competencies. The list of functions being outsourced is getting longer everyday. For example, functions outsourced span purchasing and disbursement, order entry, billing and collection, human resources administration, cash and investment management, tax compliance, internal audit, payroll, etc. BPO is one way of increasing the firm's profit level. If done well, BPO results in increasing shareholder value.

For example, if a bank shifts work of 500 people from US to India, it can save about US$9 million a year due to lower costs in India. According to McKinsey, US pharmaceutical firms can reduce the cost of developing a new drug, currently estimated at between $ 600–900 million, by as much as $ 200 million if development work is outsourced to India. Thus the benefits derived from BPO can be summarized as follows:

- Productivity improvements
- Access to expertise
- Operational cost control
- Cost savings
- Improved accountability
- Improved HR
- Opportunity to focus on core business.

India, being one of the largest pools of low-cost English-speaking scientific and technical talent, has become one of the obvious choices to outsource to. Many companies like Dell, Sun Microsystems, LG, Ford, GE and Oracle have scaled up their outsourcing operations in India. Others like American Express, IBM and British Airways are leveraging the cost advantage by setting up call centres. Several foreign airline and banks have set up business process operations in India.

How does BPO Work?

BPO involves the complete transfer of a business process or function to an external service provider, who executes the transferred business process or function, with extensive usage of IT in the delivery process. Quality is the prime deciding factor and necessary performance metrics are pre-decided and built in SLA (service level agreement) signed between the outsourcer and the BPO vendor. The payment to the BPO vendor often depends on the quality delivered and nonpayment for delivering quality below the accepted limit is very common.

BPO is most easily applied across IT-intensive functions such as payroll processing, human resources, financial accounting, logistics, administration, customer interface applications (call centres, ATMs), etc. Internet and advances in communication technology have made it very easy for companies to outsource such functions.

However, BPO differs from traditional IT sourcing and the two terms cannot be used interchangeably. IT sourcing involves specific task management and/or task specific applications, which may be a part of a larger business process but most often do not involve an end-to-end process per se. For example, maintenance of servers or maintaining specific security applications are typical IT outsourcing tasks. There is no specific business process involved. On the other hand, a BPO would typically allow an organization to completely outsource a full process with all its sub-elements and focus on the core elements of an organization's strategy. As mentioned before, it is a complete transfer of process ownership from a company to a BPO vendor to avail of many benefits.

BPO Service Scope

Business process outsourcing today is seen as a strategic management option rather than just a way to cut costs. It helps the companies achieve their business objectives through operational excellence and an edge in the marketplace.

Every company today, has one or more of its services[2] (see Figure 3.2) outsourced so that it can focus more on its core competencies. The power of BPO as a business tool of unique versatility and flexibility is undoubted. Resources of the companies need to be focused on core business functions, and so the non-core functions need to be outsourced. Outsourcing gives a firm the right combination of people, processes and technology to operate effectively in the global market within the firm's budget and the stipulated time-frame. This is the reason why more and more companies are showing interest in outsourcing their activities to various off-shore locations. With the cost to bring a product from development to market having increased significantly, outsourcing is seen as a clear option. Quality and price are the two prime factors that come into play when searching for a reliable outsourcing service provider.

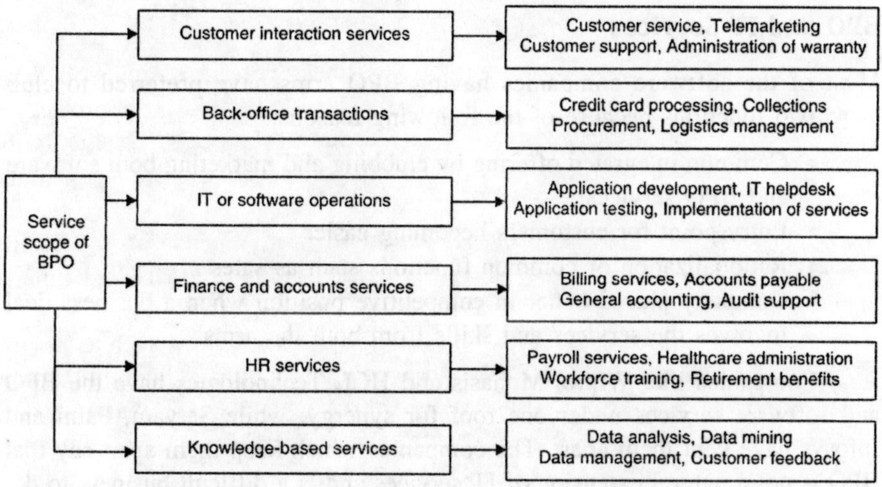

FIGURE 3.2 Service scope of BPO.

Benefits of BPO

Non-core business processes such as human resources, finance and accounting are critical, but also resource-intensive, time-consuming, and costly. Outsourcing improves operational efficiencies and drastically reduces costs without large, up-front capital investments. Business process outsourcing provides quantifiable benefits through improved efficiencies, lower overhead,

2. http://outsourcing.com/BPO/images/Elements-of-BPO.GIF.

reduced payroll and benefit expenses, and fewer capital investments. Companies seeking the business process outsourcing benefits generally engage themselves in a process led by the outsourcer, which is systematic and well-designed to ensure a positive and mutually beneficial experience for both client and provider.

BPO allows organizations to move non-core business processes to a services provider, so that they may focus on the more important strategic, revenue-generating programmes that create profitable growth and sustain business success. BPO provides access to proprietary workflow systems, process reengineering skills, and innovative staffing and delivery models, combined with world-class technology delivered by experts. Business process outsourcing provides the flexibility to respond to a rapidly changing marketplace and scale operations up or down as conditions dictate. Specifically, the benefits of BPO are as follows:

(a) Focus on core processes
(b) Cross-pollination of best practices
(c) Cost reduction
(d) Reduction in capital investment.

BPO and IT Services

Most of the software companies having BPO arms have preferred to club these two functions because of the following reasons:

- Common integrated offering by clubbing and marketing both software and BPO services
- Entry point for customers becoming easier
- Rationalization of common functions such as sales
- Company placed better in competitive position when a business deal involves the services and skills from both the arms.

Companies like Wipro, Mphasis and HCL Technologies have the BPO and software services under one roof for synergy, while Satyam, Patni and Infosys have kept them apart. The companies which keep them apart say that BPO is not a natural extension of IT services and is a difficult business to do, as there are some operational differences between them. According to some, BPO services are like factory operations while software services are obtained from creative vendors. The reasons for merging the two operations are:

- Client transitions from software to BPO
- Difference in the two operations
- Issues regarding customers and service delivery.

BPO usually refers to processes in organizations delivering services to customers, as opposed to those in organizations that "manufacture and deliver" products. Hence, BPO is generally discussed in the context of "services" organizations like banking, credit card, insurance, mortgage, and other financial services. However, today's organizations are very complex and even product manufacturers have 'service organizations' embedded within them. For example, customer service in a typical product company is a 'service organization'. Hence, BPO is relevant for such organizations as well. There are also certain kinds of organizational functions and processes that are amenable to outsourcing regardless of the precise activity that the organizations is engaged in, and such activities are common across all kinds of organizations, whether they are manufacturing or services. This also extends to organizations outside the commercial sector, including those in government, non-governmental organizations, multilateral agencies, etc. To conclude, in today's complex world there is hardly any organization for whom BPO is not relevant.

Manufacturing companies have been outsourcing the manufacture of components and sub-assemblies for a very long time. Such companies are very familiar with the basic economic concept of 'make or buy', wherein they can add machinery to 'make' a component in-house or alternatively to 'buy' a component from a supplier. This is possibly because manufactured products contain hundreds, sometimes thousands of parts, and it is not always possible to produce every single part in-house.

Improvements in technology in recent years have enabled companies to virtually control processes outsourced to distant locations of third-party vendors of outsourcing services. The rapid advances in Internet technology made this even simpler. This led to a trend of companies outsourcing more complex processes to outside vendors by keeping in touch with their vendors 24×7×365, thereby considerably reducing the risk associated with outsourcing work to a faraway location. Another big reason for the acceleration of this trend is the change in the mindset and thinking on part of the organizations as to what constitutes core and non-core activity. BPO and IT services can be differentiated on the following grounds:

Skills required

The skills required to manage technology are different from those needed to manage business processes. An IT outsourcer focuses on IT life-cycle management and PC uptime, whereas a BPO vendor manages people and processes. Hence transition management is more critical in BPO.

Quantifying savings from BPO deals can be difficult. According to past experience, more often the companies outsource to streamline processes, save time or leverage the strengths of third-party specialists and thus achieve savings in the 10% to 15% range.

Strategic outsourcing

A company's decision to outsource a business process typically supports a larger business strategy to add flexibility. Today's competitive marketplace demands operational productivity, administrative efficiency, business agility, shorter turnaround times and increased shareholder value. Hence, BPO is the survival key in transforming processes to achieve these end-results.

As the modern enterprise seeks to focus ever more narrowly on its core activities, BPO increasingly is being considered as a business strategy that provides access to 'best-in-class' processes. This growing trend for enterprises, to review their internal operations to more fully understand what their true core competencies are, and to focus only on these core competencies, is the primary driver behind the growth of the BPO market. However, BPO service providers face a number of challenges such as:

- Visibility of ongoing improvements in operational efficiency
- Reducing processing costs through continuous process improvements
- Maximizing BPO revenues within shortening BPO contract terms
- Increasing customer satisfaction by realizing business benefits sooner
- Improving service levels through process monitoring and reporting
- Achieve a faster ROI
- Defining and enforcing 'best practice' processes
- Implementing effective change management capabilities.

Project Management Approach in BPO

The success of a BPO project depends on its project management approach. Like a project an outsourcing transaction can be logically broken down into four basic phases: preparation, negotiation, implementation, and ongoing management.

- **Preparation:** In this phase, the management is responsible for identifying and helping to assess the legal and tax issues that are relevant to the particular transaction. The first task is preparation of the bid documents, including a proposed service agreement. In most major outsourcings, the customer—not the provider—prepares the proposed service agreement and defines the contract negotiation process.
- **Negotiation:** In this phase, the terms and conditions of the proposed relationship with the service provider are negotiated.
- **Implementation:** In this phase, there is orderly transfer of activities to the service provider. Such transfers may involve employees, technology, equipment, real estate and facilities, as well as intellectual property licences and other agreements. This phase involves ensuring that such third parties sign appropriate confidentiality, data protection, security and assignment of rights agreements. In multi-jurisdictional transactions, this phase typically involves arranging for the execution

of local companion agreements between the customer's and provider's affiliates, in order to effect local transfers and implement local invoicing arrangements.

- **Ongoing management:** This phase covers the interpretation of the agreement, and when necessary, to prepare, negotiate and assist with the implementation of amendments to the agreement.

Outsourcing as a strategy is not new. Some examples of outsourcing such as GM and EDS, Xerox and EDS, and Kodak and IBM, are more than a decade old. Over the years, the scale and scope of outsourcing has evolved considerably. It has also migrated from primarily Fortune 500 companies to large and mid-sized companies.

Since the 1970s, many western companies began manufacturing products in off-shore locations such as Japan, Korea, Thailand, and Taiwan. Despite the relatively high cost of transporting the goods by sea and air, it was cheaper to make them in the Far East (and in Mexico after the NAFTA treaty) than to keep manufacturing in the USA or Europe.

Most companies are now adjusted to manufacturing being done off-shore. What took place in manufacturing is now occurring in back-room processing and services. Manufacturing and service outsourcing have changed over the years. It is a macroeconomic trend to which every company needs to react. If a firm's competitor can make a product and provide associated services for less than the firm, then the firm needs to follow or to risk being put out of business.

Although initially low-skilled jobs such as manufacturing, call centre, and computer coding were shifted abroad, as more companies expand their offerings into outsourcing, new functions like human resources and knowledge skills like technology are outsourced. As the worldwide migration continues and the movement overseas matures, more high-skilled jobs such as accounting and engineering are sent abroad.

BPO and IT-enabled Services

IT-enabled services (ITES) or Business Process Outsourcing (BPO) as it is better known, holds tremendous potential for India. Though ITES in India has become almost synonymous with call centres in public perception, it covers much more. The term *ITES* can be defined as outsourcing of such processes that can be enabled with information technology, and it covers areas as diverse as finance, HR (human resource), administration, healthcare, telecommunication, manufacturing, etc.

ITES/BPO (see Figure 3.1) services include a scenario wherein one company hands over part of its work to another company, making it responsible for the design and implementation of the business process through the telecom and Internet media under strict guidelines regarding requirements and specifications from the outsourcing company.

Till 1994, the Indian telecom sector was under direct governmental control and the state-owned units enjoyed a monopoly in the market. In 1994, the government announced a policy under which the sector was liberalized and private participation was encouraged. The New Telecom Policy announced in 1999 and the introduction of IP telephony ended the state monopoly on international calling facilities. This resulted in drastic reduction in cost and brought a golden opportunity for the ITES/BPO industry to grow.

EXHIBIT 3.3
IT—Enabler to Reduce Multiple Vendors

Gallop Group with 1500 employees had ten independent SBUs and each had its own payroll system. The Gallop Group looking for a solution to reduce the financial and administrative burden by having one payroll system in place.

Gallop Group is in travel and tourism, marketing, entertainment, media, insurance, etc. With 1500 employees were located at multiple sites. They had 10 separate vendors to support the payroll at different locations. There was a substantial administrative and financial burden caused by outsourcing payroll. They were experiencing quality differential amongst the vendors and SBUs were spending much time in preparing the data so the vendors wouldn't get it wrong. Eventually, the decision was made that the best solution was to consolidate all of the separate vendors and bring them under one roof. They found one-ZYPE Solutions. Market feedback was excellent and being used in retail chain to with multiple outlets in multi-site environment. They found a cost effective solution to their problems. As they had lot of data being collated from multiple sources, which was often in different formats, they needed a flexible transition and ZYPE to adapt to these needs. One of the main benefits found through bringing their payroll under ZYPE is the amount of time it has saved. Day-to-day employee requests such as reproducing pay slips are now just a click away, rather than having to wait for multiple vendors to respond. ZYPE could provide detailed records to each division's individual finance function. With ZYPE they could reduce the day-to-day administration tasks of their payroll department by half. The speed of processing and range of reports Gallop got, has allowed Gallop to be more proactive with their MI (Management Information) data and provide useful information to HR team, such as hours worked and absences.

One of the first outsourced services was medical transcription, but outsourcing of business processes like data processing, billing, and customer support began towards the end of the 1990s, when MNCs established wholly owned subsidiaries which catered to the process off-shoring requirements of their parent companies.

Today, Indian companies are offering a variety of outsourced services (see Table 3.1) ranging from customer care, transcription, billing services and database marketing, to web sales/marketing, accounting, tax processing, transaction document management, telesales/telemarketing, HR hiring and biotech research.

TABLE 3.1 BPO and IT-enabled services

Customer interaction services	*IT-enabled services*
Marketing services	Medical transcription
Business intelligence	Document processing
Finance and accounting	Data entry and processing
Business transcription	Data warehousing
Hospitality management	IT helpdesk services
Transcription services	Application development
Transaction processing	Enterprise resource planning
Travel and transport services	Telecommunication services

Indian BPO Industry

With the other services industry growing at 10–11 per cent per annum, Indian BPOs are facing a manpower shortage, especially at the mid-management level. Presently, the Indian BPO industry is seen as follows:

- BPO industry was initially built around the model of cost-effectiveness. However, in the recent times, with wages continuing to rise at 15–20 per cent coupled with shortage of skilled manpower, this model no longer holds good.
- One of the most serious threats for BPO companies in India comes from the hidden cost of not-so-good infrastructure.
- As business processes are distributed across the globe through diverse complex and increasingly mobile networks and fast-growing industries, imperatives and challenges of creating a secure environment becomes paramount.
- India's true competitive advantage lies in the ability to apply technology to business processes. As of today, that potential is largely untapped.
- BPO industry is capital-intensive and requires huge additional capital infusion to fuel its growth.
- Most critical is the scarcity of the appropriate skills to be gained through the education system, which is low on quality and relevance.

Due to the current limitations, Indian BPOs need the following to be done:

- Brand-building exercises
- Creation of sound infrastructure
- Benchmarking for information security
- Focus on technology development

- Availability of risk capital and flexibility in taxation
- Raising the bar for the education system.

SUMMARY

A call centre is a service centre. The main activity in some call centres is answering inbound calls, such as a bank that gives out a toll-free number for customers needing help. At the same time, there are some call centres that focus on outbound calls too. The service application areas that normally may be addressed by a call centre includes complaint handling, sales support, technical queries, relationship and account management, lead generation and follow-up, telemarketing, credit and billing problems, market research and database development.

BPOs are way ahead of call centres. BPO is the act of transferring some of an organization's repeated non-core and core business processes to an outside provider to achieve cost reductions while improving service quality. BPO involves the complete transfer of a business process or function to an external service provider who executes the transferred business process or function—typically with extensive usage of IT in the delivery process. The BPO vendor completely takes over the execution of the process. In that sense it is the transfer of 'ownership' of the process. Quality is the prime deciding factor, and the necessary performance metrics are pre-decided and built in the service-level agreement signed between the outsourcer and the BPO vendor. The payment to the BPO vendor often depends on the quality delivered, and nonpayment for delivering quality below the accepted limit is very common. Thus BPOs are much beyond the call centres and higher in the value chain.

A success of a BPO project depends on its project management approach. Today's competitive marketplace demands operational productivity, administrative efficiency, business agility, shorter turnaround times and increased shareholder value. Business Process Outsourcing (BPO) is the survival key in transforming processes to achieve these end-results.

Review Questions

1. How does a BPO differs from a call centre?
2. Explain the benefits of BPO and its service scope.
3. "The success of a BPO project depends on its 'project management' approach". Explain.
4. Comment on the Indian BPO (service provider) industry in the present context and suggest what they need to do for competitiveness.

Chapter 4

Transition Management

***Transition management is a collective and cooperative efforts to work towards a transition in a flexible, stepwise manner, utilizing dynamics and vision.*[1]**

Transition management is a key aspect of the process of outsourcing. Transition management should form a part of the agreement between the outsourcer and the service provider and appear as a schedule to the agreement as new services. The outsourcing decision can have an adverse impact on the morale and productivity of in-house employees due to the worry of job loss and the possibility that the best people will start looking for other jobs. The purchaser's staff may be reluctant to work for the service provider and resign, taking valuable institutional knowledge with them. It will be critical for business continuity to be maintained during the period between the times when outsourcing is announced and implemented.

INTRODUCTION

For the organizations involved in outsourcing their business processes, managing the transition is critical to the success of the outsourcing project. Transition management is about managing the migration of the outsourced process from client to the third-party service provider.

In managing the transition, a variety of skills and competencies are required on the part of the transition coordinator. This role involves good communication ability, clarity in thinking and ability to convey ideas. The other requirements of this role are extensive interaction with the clients and strong project management skills. The outsourcing deals are complex projects by themselves and require expert management skills. The employees involved should be comfortable in working in a cross-cultural environment, as in offshore projects the project teams are based overseas. They need to have a very good understanding of the existing processes as the technology's role is pervasive and critical in the off-shore functions.

1. Matthias Weber and Jens Hemelskamp, *Towards Environmental Innovation System*, Springer, Berlin, Germany, 2005.

Apart from the day-to-day management of a migration, they have to manage the change management process for employees' attitude towards new work. To be successful, the manager needs to facilitate the changes that outsourcing brings about by ensuring that the migrations are done in an effective manner, and by demonstrating the transformational power of outsourcing.

The transition phase commences with the establishment of a Programme Management Office (PMO) that helps plan and execute transitions effectively. The PMO consists of representatives from the BPO vendor and the client, and is tasked with ensuring the efficient migration of the identified processes.

The transition planning phase is followed by transition execution, wherein domain, process and technology teams address each of the transition tracks that are deployed. This process of transition management[2] is explained (see Figure 4.1) as follows:

- Knowledge transfer, which includes the construction of operating procedures, preparation of training documents, and training executives to execute the process offshore
- Technology transfer that identifies the optimal network architecture, procurement of bandwidth and systems, and installation, testing and deployment of technical infrastructure
- Operating preparedness, which includes recruitment, induction and site preparation.

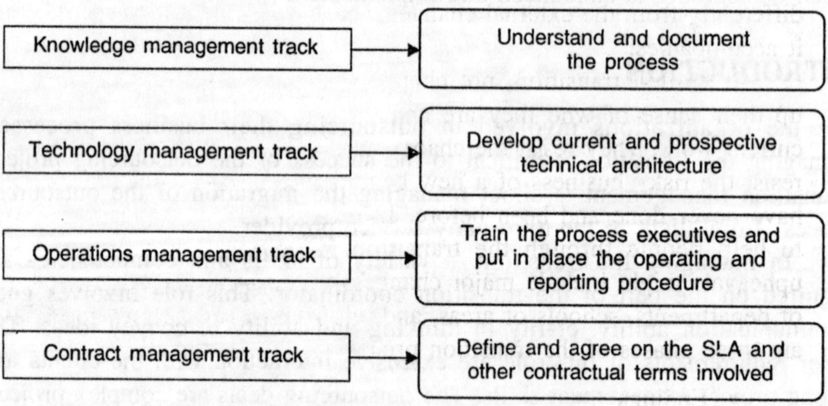

FIGURE 4.1 Transition management.

Transition is the process of migrating knowledge, systems and operating capabilities. It typically follows identification of appropriate processes and vendor selection. For the BPO vendor the process starts with the following:

2. www.progeon.com. Progeon, the business process outsourcing subsidiary of Infosys Technologies, has been renamed Infosys BPO recently.

- Preparing for a site to commence client operations
- Documenting the processes and training process executives to execute the processes
- Designing, procuring and deploying technology to access client systems as required
- Finalizing the SLA and contract parameters.

TRANSITION AND CHANGE

Transition is different from change, and it is very often the transition that people resist and not the change itself. The transition needs to be understood and managed, especially where the change is radical. Staff will be at different stages along the change curve, and the emotional response to change needs to be recognized. Leaders of change should also consider their own transition.

Change involves a shift in the external situation; it is about the events or circumstances which impact on and affect the organization, for example, a new leader, changes in government policy, technology, student expectations, and mergers. Thus, the change process is designed typically in terms of the outcomes or results required, in the sense that organizational change is usually a solution to someone's perception of a problem or an opportunity.

Transition is an internal, three-phase psychological re-orientation that people go through as they come to terms with change. It is a process—an inner experience not necessarily focused on outcome or results. It is timed differently from the external changes, and has less definition than the changes it accompanies.

It's often transition, not change that people resist. They resist giving up their sense of who they are and their identity as it is expressed in their current work. They resist the chaos and uncertainty of the neutral zone. They resist the risky business of a new beginning, i.e., doing and being what they have never done and been before. In order to effect change, it is important to help people through the transition. Transitions associated with major upheavals might include major changes to roles and responsibilities, mergers of departments, schools or areas, and, ultimately, loss of jobs. Basically there are three phases of the transition process:

- Endings
- Neutral zone
- New beginnings.

MANAGING TRANSITION

There are organizational, people-related and technical issues that have to be managed when an organization changes the way it works. The management task is to ensure that the transition is as smooth as possible between the old and the new ways of working. Research shows that preparing the organization for the change can consume more than 75 per cent of the resources for a project due to requirements for training, development of new processes, and so on.

The preparatory work should already have been carried out during the full proposal and draft contract stages, so that all staff know exactly what is to happen. A detailed transition plan will have to be included in the draft contract, drawn up after detailed discussions in which both customer and provider demonstrate their shared understanding of what is involved, the risks and the responsibilities of both parties. It is most frequently discussed by organization development (OD) specialists and commonly portrayed as occurring in three stages:

- Unfreezing
- Intervening
- Refreezing.

When organizations are unfrozen, either purposefully or by circumstances, they are characterized by uncertainty. In this atmosphere, roles and responsibilities are unclear, relationships that once seemed critical now seem questionable, and resources become more valuable than ever before. Philosophy, policy and practice are challenged and defended. People begin looking around trying to guess who will emerge at the top of the heap. Alliances and coalitions are quickly formed and just as quickly dissolved. In short, there's a great deal of confusion, and it reduces cooperation. As a consequence, the organization is less efficient and less effective than before.

If the organization is able to realize some new degree of stability, it will be more efficient and more effective than it was during the period of instability. However, assuming that the instability stems from the introduction of changes intended to improve matters, the organization will be more efficient and effective than it was before entering the period of instability. Whether the organization enters a period of instability as a result of sudden and unforeseen environmental pressures, or as part of a planned change effort, the primary objective once in an unstable situation is the same: maintain enough stability to operate on at least a survival level and afterwards at a higher level of performance.

Expanded Boundaries

One of the major effects of change is that managers suddenly find themselves with more "latitude" or "managerial discretion" than some of them know what to do with. Organizations must possess some degree of stability; they cannot afford to become static. So, the movement in question is not from one static state to another, but from one stable state to another and the stable states in question might well be quite dynamic. In stable times, the limits of a manager's accountability, authority and discretion are well-known and understood. Many managers, if not most, settle into well-defined roles and accompanying responsibilities, i.e., into a "comfort zone". The boundaries of these zones are defined by the organization through its rewards and sanctions and by the people themselves by way of norms, customs, and other unwritten rules that people have among themselves.

At the changing times, the roles and responsibilities are unclear and uncertain. As a result, the enforcement of the boundaries defining a manager's 'limitation zone' is less rigorous. This pervades all levels of management. Consequently, their problem is not really one of coping with change per se, but rather it is a problem of obtaining a new and clear understanding of their changed roles and responsibilities, especially as regards the limits of their accountability, authority and discretion.

Role Clarity

One way of easing the tension associated with the transition from one stable state to the next is to provide workshops on various role clarification methods and techniques, and asking all managers charged with implementing those methods and techniques to use them. These will be especially useful during the transition when roles and responsibilities might be in a continuous state of change. Clarity of roles and responsibilities is a tenuous attainment, especially in times of change. Job descriptions, organization charts and operation manuals are useless under such conditions. Hence, what is needed is a way of maintaining clarity in the phase-changing circumstances.

Responsibility Allocation

It is a simple, effective and flexible tool for clarifying organizational roles and responsibilities. It is a listing of people across the top and responsibilities down the side. It is easily maintained, even in times of turbulence, because it captures the essence of roles and responsibilities. The responsibility charting involves the preparation of a responsibility chart, but it is used more as the basis for intervention. It holds promise as an aid to managers caught up in a transitional period.

Experimentation

The main effect of the change is increased experimentation with new ways of getting the job done. People start deviating from past practice and are not clear about the results. In fact, they are engaged in establishing and testing the new limits of the managerial "operating zone". Moreover, they will establish them the "hard way". If the experimenters are unduly restrained, the task of restabilizing the organization will be hindered and delayed. This can be extremely costly to the organization. To mitigate this situation, it is necessary to communicate the fact that experimentation is both expected and necessary, that it is important to the restoration of stability. Another way is to reward the successful innovators. This encourages experimentation and, at the same time, makes it clear that rewards are related to success. However, for experimentation failure, there is no need to reward them, but great care should be taken to ensure that they are not punished. After all, they are doing exactly what is required.

Job Content Revision

In stable times, most of the content of manager's jobs consists of fairly stable routines, that is, set ways of doing business. In times of change, however, the majority of a manager's routines must be novel. They must be configured to meet the situation at hand.

Training

Organizations might find it beneficial to provide extensive training in problem-solving methods for its management force as well as selected members of the workforce. This enhances their ability to come up with right responses to new or different situations. It also provides them with a common platform for communicating among themselves about the organizational problems they are encountering and attempting to resolve.

Learning

In transition, many managers will be facing a new set of problems, resulting in suggestions to focus on learning as well as training. During the transition period and for some time thereafter, people will be in learning mode; they will be figuring out the solutions to the new problems as well as some new solutions to old problems. Managers can help by committing resources to sharing the learning that is taking place. This can be done by ensuring that the lessons learned by one group of people are communicated to other groups. Workshops and communications bulletins dealing with change issues are just some of the ways in which experiences can be shared. Another way of learning is through handbooks for various organizational functions. This can form the basis for training in the restabilized organization.

Employee Orientation

This addresses the new employee's need to learn about the new organization, but it is limited to some factual information (e.g., compensation, policies, history, security, etc.). More important, both to the individual and the organization, is the task of getting the new employee up to speed in his or her new job. The quicker is the better. In this regard, the employee's learning tasks involve learning about roles and responsibilities, organizational norms, and the styles and expectations of co-workers. This is a structured set of activities for the person to carry out that shortens the time it takes to get up to speed in the new job.

Efficient Communication

It is important to set up a change communication system early in the transition period. It is known that people can cope with good news and they can cope with bad news, but they can't cope with no news. In the absence of information, people resort to imagination and many people imagine the worst. Instead of clamping the lid down on information about impending changes and how changes underway are faring, managers are advised strongly to truthfully communicate it on a regular and, occasionally, situational basis. Otherwise, rumours will defeat the purpose of meaningful transition.

Organizational Loss

In times of stress, some people leave the organization; many of these are old-timers with knowledge and experience. When they go, they take their knowledge and experience with them. If enough of them leave, the "new" organization will be seriously hampered in its efforts to resolve some of the old problems. It will spend more time in relearning rather than in progressing further. Therefore, managers would do well to keep an eye on the number and the quality of the old timers that take their leave during the transition period and should be very careful in their identification of those who are to be eased out.

Retention

There are several things that the management can do to capture organizational knowledge and memory in the form of its old-timers. One is to place some of them on retainers as consultants to the organization. Others can be placed in formal mentoring roles for a period of time prior to their actual departure. Retaining knowledge and memory provides the organization with a much-needed historical perspective on future issues.

Extending Help

In transition, some people simply won't be able to adapt. Sooner or later, they will leave the organization. All that managers can do here is help these people make their way out of the organization with their dignity intact. Some people might be helped to find new jobs. Some executives might need help in making the transition to a retired status, and still others might require some assistance in the form of psychological counselling. This will help them to make their exit graceful and dignified.

FRAMEWORK FOR BPO EXECUTION

Business process outsourcing is getting very popular today and covering many other functional areas of business. With the benefits it is imparting and helping to have healthy ROI (return on investments), it is the most sought-after strategy of the businesses in the competitive markets today. However, it is necessary to implement BPO projects systematically to get desired results. If the BPO execution is not planned properly, it may not be beneficial in the long run.

There are six basic phases (see Figure 4.2) that the companies should go through in the execution process of outsourcing. These steps are: analysis, planning, partner selection, transition management, process control, and performance measurement and improvement.

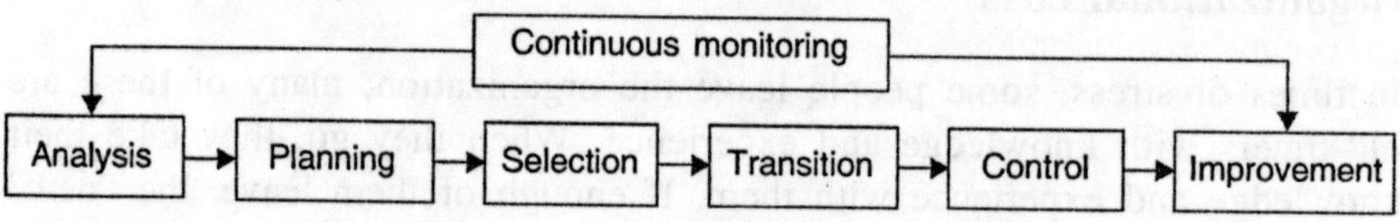

FIGURE 4.2 BPO execution framework.

Analysis

The analysis starts with the data or information collected. Detailed analysis is required on the process which is to be outsourced, competitors' activities, the best practices in the industry, anticipated performance risk, and total cost outgo.

Planning

BPO contracts are required to be completed in the stipulated time-frame, which may stretch from one year to three years or longer. Hence, activity and resource projections are essential for achieving time-bound project completion targets. Several factors such as the policy scenario, the quality of infrastructure and human capital, and the location of facilities can affect long-term outcomes. The steps to be followed are: reviewing existing processes, setting objectives, selecting the process to be outsourced, selecting the outsourcing partner, formulation of contract and the SLA with mutually agreed terms, and planning for resources.

Transition

The client who outsources the processes to BPO service providers stops its in-house activity and places its fate in the hands of another company. As outsourcing is a new area of operations for the employees, there may be many ifs and buts in the minds of employees of the client company during the transition stage. Hence, proper training and education of the employees is a must to infuse a sense of job security in the minds of the employees. This is a very critical phase and the success of the outsourcing initiative depends on how the things are handled during the transition phase. In many cases, this job is also outsourced to HR experts.

EXHIBIT 4.1
Improving Treasury Operations

ROCK Inc., a US-based $ 17 billion revenue company wanted to reduce its treasury operations cost of one of its world-wide media business and also to improve its regulatory compliance. A separate service department titled Internal Banking System (IBS) for forex hedging, funding, consultancy, remaking the invoices and financial reporting, etc. IBS has to face the challenge of delivering cost reduction in treasury service operations in growing in forty-nine countries keeping in view compliance to the applicable regulatory standards. Vendor had formed his team with technical experts in the field. This team provided services to IBS. They evolved centralized cash pooling system, automatic cash sweeping service and proxy payment system. The daily updates on accounts receivable and payables were carried on to effectively monitor and control the outcomes effectively. They used the back office information to help front office staff to execute the market contracts. The benefits ROCK got were; operational costs reduction by @ 40 per cent p.a., improved regulatory compliance and achieving zero non-conformities on successive transactions.

Control

Without appropriate checks and balances, companies run the risk of spoiling their customer relationships forever, resulting in termination of contracts. This may be because of delay in taking corrective actions when results are deviating from the agreed target. This requires periodic reviews of the performance and also a mechanism for correcting deviations in time. A dispute settlement mechanism in place is a must to avoid misunderstandings on both sides.

Improvement

For improving performance, both the parties are required to pay attention to the tasks of tracking performance through key predetermined parameters, identifying, developing and leveraging new capabilities, innovating on a continuous basis, and planning and designing process improvements.

A systematic planning and execution framework can help a firm get the right BPO partner for its business process outsourcing project. However, this involves a significant amount of change management planning for improvement.

SUMMARY

Transition management is one of the most important roles in any organization involved in outsourcing. The primary rationale to outsource any function is to benefit from the resultant cost reduction. The role of transition management begins as soon as any company begins to consider outsourcing. Transition management covers migration of the function or the process from the outsourcer's organization to the outsourcing organization. Because of the nature of the role, the manager responsible needs to have a variety of skills and competencies. He needs to be a good communicator, as the role requires extensive interaction with the clients; he needs to have strong project management skills, as most migrations are complex projects that require expert management skills; he needs to be comfortable in working in a cross-cultural environment, as most often the customer teams are based overseas; he needs to have a very good understanding of the existing processes and technologies, as these play a critical role in the offshorability of any function. Besides managing the day-to-day affairs of a migration, transition management is also about change management. To be successful, this role needs to facilitate the changes in a phased manner by ensuring that the migrations are done in an effective manner, and by demonstrating the transformational power of outsourcing. However, initially the manager responsible for transition is generally involved in creating the financial case for the project, and enabling the decision to outsource.

Review Questions

1. Differentiate between transition and change in the organizational context.
2. What is transition planning and how are different transition tracks addressed?
3. How are transitions managed during the outsourcing of a business process?
4. Discuss the execution framework for implementing business process outsourcing.
5. What are the factors that the client company needs to figure out when it selects its BPO vendor?

Chapter 5

BPO Business Models

Future success of the maturing BPO model will be based on improving the client's business capability, not simply providing commodity transactional services.[1]

With the rise in business complexity, high volumes and internal issues, customer behaviour has shifted towards the value-addition aspect. As the business volumes grow, organizations are forced to focus on their core activities, hence de-coupling all non-core, non-critical processes for outsourcing. While doing so, they aim to reap multiple benefits in end-to-end outsourcing, rather than just the economic ones. The critical success factor of the business model should address the business needs and challenges of the customer's business, namely, reduced or no capital cost, keep the operating cost variable rather than fixed, and ensure high degree of compliance and accelerated processing to stay ahead of competition.

INTRODUCTION

BPO services have gained importance during the past few years as more and more organizations have recognized the practical and enhanced value of externally delegating processes as opposed to doing them in-house. BPO usually refers to processes in organizations delivering services to customers, as opposed to organizations that "manufacture and deliver" products. Hence, BPO is generally discussed in the context of "services" organizations like banking, credit card, insurance, mortgage and other financial services. However, today's organizations are very complex and even product manufacturers have "service" organizations embedded within them, e.g., customer service in a typical product company is a "service organization". Hence BPO is relevant for such organizations as well. There are also certain kinds of organizational functions and processes that are amenable to outsourcing, regardless of the precise activity that the organization is engaged in. Such activities are common across all kinds of organizations, whether they are in manufacturing

1. "India BPO model is growing up to meet global demand for more complex services", 1 June 2004, http://www.xansa.com/shared/pressreleases/196149/.

or services. This also extends to organizations outside the commercial sector including those in government, non-governmental organizations, multilateral agencies, etc.

Manufacturing companies have been outsourcing the manufacture of components and sub-assemblies probably since the very beginning. Hence, BPO is not a new concept for them. Many larger organizations have been outsourcing non-core activities such as IT maintenance, housekeeping and security services for decades. These activities are relatively simple in nature and involve placement of low-skilled labour on-site (at the location itself). Critical activities were never on the agenda for outsourcing as companies were scared of losing control over such activities; moreover, it was assumed that it would be costlier to outsource them than to do them in-house.

All this has changed in the last 15–20 years. Improvements in technology in recent years have enabled companies to 'virtually' control processes outsourced to distant locations of third-party vendors of outsourcing services. The rapid advances in Internet technology led to a trend of companies outsourcing more complex processes to outside vendors by keeping in touch with their vendors 24×7×365, thus reducing the risk associated with outsourcing work to a faraway location. Another reason for the acceleration of this trend is the change in mindset and thinking on part of organizations as to what constitutes core and non-core activity.

BUSINESS MODEL

The business model (see Figure 5.1) itself is an important determinant of the profits to be made from an innovation. A mediocre innovation with a great business model may be more profitable than a great innovation with a mediocre business model.

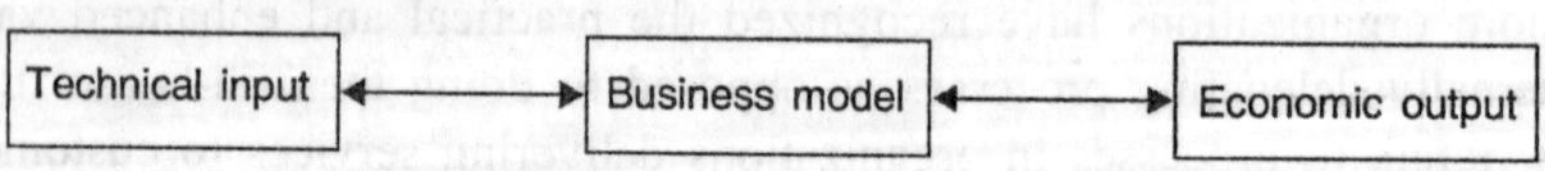

FIGURE 5.1 Business model.

Henry, Chesbrough (2002) searched literature from both the academic and the business press, identified some common themes and listed the following six components of the business model:

- **Value proposition.** The value of the product from the customer's perspective.
- **Market segment.** Segmentation and targeting of the different groups for unlocking the potential of an innovation.
- **Value chain structure.** The firm's position and activities in the value chain and how the firm will capture part of the value that it creates in the chain.

- **Revenue generation and margins.** How revenue is generated (sales, leasing, subscription, support, etc.), the cost structure, and target profit margins.
- **Position in value network.** Identification of competitors, complementers, and any network effects that can be utilized to deliver more value to the customer.
- **Competitive strategy.** How the company will attempt to develop a sustainable competitive advantage, for example, by means of a cost, differentiation, or niche strategy.

BPO CHALLENGES

BPO allows companies to concentrate or focus on core processes by outsourcing non-core activities. This makes companies lean and agile, thereby allowing the CEO and the top management to spend more time on the very purpose of their existence—the customer. They can spend time understanding the customer better and serve him better by understanding his tastes, preferences, changing trends etc., and in addition, react to them fast enough before they decide to change further.

Since BPO vendors specialize in specific processes, over time they acquire considerable expertise and domain knowledge in these activities. They are able to bring best practices to work and do a re-engineering of business processes, such that there is improvement in parameters like quality, response time, manpower requirement, etc. Very often, small and mid-sized organizations are unable to attract the best talent in functions like technology. Their technology knowledge and use is below the industry level. Outsourcing helps them to stay on the cutting edge, since the outsourcer is typically able to get the best talent.

Cost reduction is one of the biggest attractions of outsourcing. Some organizations have been able to achieve cost reduction of as high as 50% through outsourcing. BPO vendors are able to achieve this due to their economies of scale for each process as fixed costs is spread over large volumes of transactions spread across multiple customers. They also have the flexibility of going to the lowest-cost locations to perform the job. There are other reasons as well, e.g., for processes like those related to HR in a large multi-location company, there are low volumes at each specific location. But the volumes increase considerably once one combines the volumes across all locations. Also, since BPO vendors use the latest technology and best practices, they can streamline processes better and achieve optimum results in cost, quality and speed. It is this advantage that makes a BPO vendor more successful at such activities than the company that has outsourced them.

With outsourcing, organizations are able to save on both fixed and working capital required to perform business processes. They save a substantial amount of money as they need not spend to buy and maintain their systems, but their BPO vendors do the needful and bring in best practices from the world over.

When a process is being performed in-house, all the employees are paid fixed salary and benefits. There is also a fixed cost associated with investments in fixed assets. The costs are the same regardless of the level of work, productivity, etc. In contrast to this, if the process is outsourced, the customer pays only for the volume of output that the outsourcer gives. In the lean months, when the volumes are low. the cost reduces. The outsourcer will often ask for a minimum commitment, but by and large this system results in "pay as you go", wherein the costs are matched with the level of activity and the customer also gets part of the benefit of productivity improvement.

BPO faces many challenges. Firstly, BPO contracts (as against IT outsourcing contracts) are long term, which requires vendors to invest up-front in technology, people and infrastructure. Most BPO ramp-ups require customized solutions to back the re-engineered processes. Secondly, attrition, poaching of experienced people by competitors, leave of absence, stress, long training periods and the big investments associated with training are some of the serious HR-related challenges that BPO vendors face. Thirdly, a BPO vendor should be able to grow with the client. Large BPO contacts are usually bagged only by big BPO vendors, as the client has the confidence in their ability to deliver and manage the critical, yet non-core, process across different geographical areas, time zones, languages and situations. Fourthly, clients are usually extremely stringent about quality standards of the services provided by the BPO vendors and the time they take for the same. Fifthly, though the client outsources one of the several processes it performs, successful BPO vendors are expected to understand it in the light of the other processes. This is essential to help the BPO vendors understand the exact requirements in the larger scheme of things. This will have a positive impact on quality and delivery time. Sixthly, large capital investments generate returns over a long term. Initially, the vendor needs to create the infrastructure to manage complex processes, invest in technology, systems and people, and achieve critical mass to scale up and down with the client's requirements. Then, in the transition phase, the vendor has to over-hire since his productivity levels tend to be low as the outsourcing has just begun and his employees are not fully up to speed with the full process. The vendor ends up losing money in this time. Later, as the volume of business increases and additional investments in infrastructure are not required, the company enters a stage of profitability and improving margins. However, the initial period can be long and stretch up to two years in some cases. BPO vendors need to have patience and financial backing to carry on through such times.

TYPES OF BUSINESS PROCESSES

All the activities performed by various companies can be classified into certain broad categories as indicated in Table 5.1. Core activities are the basic reasons for a company's existence. Major examples are product design, manufacturing, branding, marketing, and sales management. Companies would like to and should keep these activities for themselves. Critical activities are ones that are time-sensitive: if they are not done within the specified time, there can be serious repercussions for the organization. For example, procurement is not a core activity, but is a critical one since if it is not done on time, material will not be available for manufacturing, and that could make the entire process go haywire. The world over, companies have started with the outsourcing of non-core and non-critical activities.

TABLE 5.1 Core and Critical Processes

Non-core and non-critical	*Non-core and critical*	*Core and critical*	*Core and non-critical*
Security	Customer care	Product design	Credit card marketing
Cafeteria	Payroll	Final manufacturing	Transaction processing
Housekeeping	Medical services	Branding	Account receivables management

Activities in Column 1 are non-core and non-critical. They require no Internet or IT support and very little communication technology support. They were easier to handle as the vendor sent his person to the company's premises to undertake the activity. Moreover, not much skill was required to perform such activities. Hence, they were completely in the company's control and this gave a strong sense of comfort.

Activities in Column 2 (non-core and critical) are the current favourites for companies as far as outsourcing is concerned. Logistics outsourcing is already very popular with several logistics providers offering various options to companies. Even in HR, administrative activities such as parts of the recruitment process, maintaining records for employee benefits, payroll, travel and expense reconciliation are also being outsourced.

Activities in Column 3 are core and critical activities; they are the reason for the company's existence. A company is known and recognized for such activities and will hence never outsource them. However, in manufacturing, companies still outsource parts such as manufactured assemblies that are used in the final assembly. There are cases where the entire manufacturing process is outsourced; however the company keeps branding, quality control, etc. under its own control. This means that the companies identify their core activities and do them on their own, preferring to concentrate on them. The rest is left to their outsourcing partners.

Activities in Column 4 (core and non-critical) have become very easy to outsource after the advances in telecommunication technology and the Internet. The best example is of various kinds of transaction processing such as credit card payments, reconciliation statements, mortgage payment processing, basic accounts-related functions such as general ledger and vouchers. Such processes require extensive linkages to core IT functions across various parts of the distributed organization and require close control over the outsourcer. As mentioned before, technological advances have made this feasible.

Thus, organizations tend to outsource their "back-office" areas, including HR, finance and accounting, and administration. Generally, the more successful BPO areas involve transaction-intensive processes that are highly standardized, relatively centralized and involve large volumes.

STRATEGY FOR BUSINESS PROCESS OUTSOURCING

With the advent of technology, lateral thinking and the ever-growing competition in market space, the focus of the organizations and businesses has simultaneously been on reducing costs and increasing the revenues. Here is where the concept of business process outsourcing comes in.

When business executives come under pressure to improve corporate performance, they look less at growing revenues and more at cutting costs. To cut costs, management increasingly goes for outsourcing certain business functions and processes to BPO services organizations. The philosophy behind BPO is simple: stick to your core competencies and leave everything else to low-cost third-party providers called BPO vendors.

BPO as strategy is not new. Some examples of BPO, such as GM and EDS, Xerox and EDS, Kodak and IBM, are more than a decade old. Over the years, the scale and scope of BPO has evolved considerably. It has also migrated from primarily Fortune 500 companies to large and mid-sized companies.

However, for many managers and decision-makers, the BPO opportunity is accompanied by rising fear because of lack of confidence. For journey through the unknown territory of BPO, management will need to answer three principal questions:

- What is the right business model for the firm's BPO strategy?
- How can the organization create the right relationships?
- What steps must the firm take to ensure meeting of business objectives?

The importance of business process outsourcing (BPO) on every organization's bottomline cannot be ignored; however, it is imperative to base outsourcing decisions on more than just cost savings. Business strategy should also be included in the decision process.

PROCESS OF OUTSOURCING

Each outsourcing decision involves several steps, and it is important to go through them. Experience shows that most 'failed' outsourcing transactions occur because they didn't follow these steps.

- **Step 1:** Listing out available in-house resources.
- **Step 2:** Assessment of in-house resources compared to services available in the marketplace to perform the same function more effectively.
- **Step 3:** Identification and evaluation of prospective bidders through market intelligence and finding out experiences of other companies with outsourcing.
- **Step 4:** Competitive bidding procedure, including request for proposals, evaluation of bids according to selected criteria, and clarification and comparison of bids through visit to vendors' premises and assessing their capabilities.
- **Step 5:** Negotiations, including a letter of intent and usually a contract with terms and conditions.
- **Step 6:** Signing the contract.
- **Step 7:** Transition phase, where the functions from the client's facilities are transferred to those of the vendor. The involvement of top management is mandatory if it means job losses.
- **Step 8:** 'Steady state' period, which marks the end of the transitioning phase and the beginning of the cost-cutting phase for the company.
- **Step 9:** Renegotiation or termination. Renegotiation happens after the contract period is over and company wants to continue with the outsourcing project with the same vendor. Termination occurs in case the relationship turns sour with the vendor over quality of service issues and/or if the company has found better vendor to do the same task.

ITO vs. BPO

Understanding the similarities and differences of an ITO (Information Technology Outsourcing) and BPO becomes important at the very outset of an outsourcing project. A key difference between the two is the relative importance of regulatory compliance. A typical ITO involves activities that are not heavily regulated (e.g., desktop management). The opposite is usually true in most BPOs (e.g., an accounting function). Although compliance issues cannot be ignored in an ITO, they normally have greater significance in a BPO.

An ITO and BPO share many common features, but they are fundamentally different exercises and it is important to understand how they are dissimilar. In an ITO (e.g., desktop management, network management, server management, application development), the customer's primary goal tends to be cost savings. The provider generally tends to offer a solution where it has or can achieve excellence of standardized processes, labour arbitrage and economies of scale across a large set of customers with the same or similar needs. A reverse auction or bidding process is commonly utilized to identify the provider that will perform the particular functions subject to specified service level commitments and at the lowest cost. In a BPO (e.g., call centre, HR administration, finance and accounting), the customer may seek cost savings, but typically it also targets other "value-added" objectives. The provider seeks to achieve excellence of process and even labour arbitrage, but the solution offered to the customer tends to be far more tailored to the customer's particular needs. In certain instances, a BPO may change the customer's value proposition in the marketplace—for example, it enables the customer to provide its clients with "real-time" access to account information, or significantly faster credit application procedures. Because BPOs often target these broader and deeper objectives, the "reverse auction" process generally proves to be inappropriate for these transactions. The ITO–BPO differences are:

- BPO may involve the transfer of personal data to the service provider, and then to its sub-contractors. Such transfers are now heavily regulated outside the USA under data protection laws, and they are subject to regulation in the USA under laws such as Gramm–Leach–Bliley (GLB) Act and Health Insurance Portability and Accountability Act (HIPAA). An ITO may raise cross-border data protection issues, but normally not to the same extent as a BPO, given that the provider's access to and use of personal data in the customer's possession will be more limited.
- BPO may involve services that squarely implicate the internal control environment of a company. An ITO may also implicate the customer's control environment, but satisfying the resulting regulatory requirements is normally less burdensome for the provider.

CLASSIFICATION OF BPO OUTFITS

Any organization has a variety of core, critical, non-critical and non-core activities that they can choose to outsource. Depending on the type of activities handled, there are essentially three kinds of BPO. These are as follows:

1. Transactional
2. Niche
3. Comprehensive.

Transactional

Transactional BPO handles one aspect of a process only. The customer has to carry out a significant part of the process in-house and hence the customer owns the risk of the process. In transactional outsourcing, many aspects of the process in a transactional mode leads to complex fragmentation, which can pose a threat to productive delivery. Using transaction providers has many benefits, but the more processes you outsource, the more fragmented your processes become. In essence, you still have an in-house department to manage. In transaction outsourcing, most of the operational risk stays with the client.

Transactional providers typically handle only one process and not the entire activity. In that sense, they are at the low end of the value chain. For example, in payroll, BPO vendors will not take over the entire department but will be responsible only for one activity, like issuing cheques. Such contracts are short (generally annual or less than two years), have less contract value, and herein performance metrics are decided per transaction. Companies have total control over the whole process and have to maintain an in-house department to organize and monitor it.

EXHIBIT 5.1
Transactional Model—Lead Generation Services

A leading logistics company having a fleet of 5000 trucks and serving 350 clients to transition from traditional transportation company to online model, the management has opened up e-Logistics wing, which they found is growing fast. This company has strong presence in Indian market. The prime goal for the customer was massive lead generation in order to cater to the expanding sales team. The client used velocity.com to manage the sales process. The tasks accomplished by the market research team was collecting information related to business from specific websites and generating leads. The challenge here was a timely updating of these lead data on the volocity.com website, getting lead lists filled with a number of potential customers with the data in variable formats, unstructured data, inaccurate information and ineffective leads. The major concern of e-Logistics was to let the sales team concentrate on the sales process rather than updating the lead-data on the velocity.com. They needed the sales team to improve the conversion ratios (prospects to customer) considerably.

The velocity.com designed a process for lead generation according to the e-Logistics business requirements. Initially, they designed a lead generation process based on a number of pre-defined parameters. Some of them included the type of industry, geographical location of the company, annual turnover and the core-products of the company. These leads were updated periodically in velocity.com. The primary lead lists were customized to have a common structured format, which could be directly imported to velocity.com. This process ensured that all the regional sales teams had enough leads in the buffer to reach the conversion ratio targets. The benefits accrued were; higher conversions in the sales process, upgraded management capabilities in the sales efforts, considerable cost-savings due to cutback in the operational costs.

Niche

A niche BPO carries out three or four aspects of a process. A niche BPO, which also makes certain investments in the customer's process, aims at improving the efficiency of the process. The vendor in a niche BPO works in close coordination with the buyer, sometimes seeking the services of the customer's employees. Both the vendor and the buyer share the risk of the process.

Niche providers focus on two to four processes. Niche providers will hire client's employees. They will invest modest amounts of capital to release some of the client's asset value. Niche providers are generally domestic, and their deals range from three to five years in length. Niche providers aim to make selected processes more efficient, by lowering costs and raising service levels. They are paid on the basis of outcomes, such as lowering employee turnover or reducing hiring time from 120 days to 90 days. In niche outsourcing, the risk is typically shared evenly between client and provider. Although the providers will hire the firm's people and be responsible for outcomes, they make only limited investments in capital and only impact a few processes. Thus, clients continue to shoulder the other processes in a function.

Niche providers handle a wider range or sequence of transactions than transactional BPO vendors—typically three to four processes. But they still don't handle the entire activity. They invest some amount of capital, which helps the outsourcing company to release its working capital. These deals tend to be longer in duration—typically three years and more; and the contract value is also more than those of transactional providers. They have good domain knowledge, and are also able to effect productivity and quality improvements over a period of time. Niche providers aim to make selected processes more efficient by lowering costs for companies and raising service levels. Many times, payment for such vendors have a fixed element and also a variable element based on outcomes.

EXHIBIT 5.2
Niche Model—Credit Analytics Financial Research

An asset management wing of leading bank faced with two major challenges; one, the lack of structured and standardized operations environment that made timely delivery of research products, unfeasible; and the second, inability of onshore analysts to focus on front-end activities and procure additional business. This was due to major focus of the wing on back-end work only. Additionally, the wing also needed enhancement of its operations window availability. The bank decided to outsource project to a BPO vendor. After a rigorous selection process, they selected the vendor to cover the following; provide financial assessment of the tenant, generate market data for fact sheets based on its latest financials, presentations and client query resolution, carry out calculations and analysis of the fund's liquidity position to ensure whether enough cash is available to meet obligation over the next year and update existing models that project financial statements for individual companies on publication of company results.

BPO vendor transformed the approach for calculating key financial numbers by building a dedicated team of skilled analysts, improving the client's approach for calculating key financial numbers and creating a sustainable business model. This enabled the client to focus on key engagements. The benefits delivered were; increased scope and product coverage, built a client-dedicated team staffed with highly educated, skilled, and committed analysts, reduced turn-around time from seven days to three days for appraisal, maintained a library of more than 300 research reports on a weekly basis.

BPO vendor team supported 18 processes on a day-to-day basis, which includes high-end research like preparing financial models, writing credit reports and performance reporting for funds. They have created customized products/templates to suit the client's diverse requirements, created a process manual to get consistent results for all processes covered, standardized the approach for calculating key financial numbers, such as Enterprise Value (EV), Earnings before Interest, Taxes, Depreciation and Amortization (EBITDA) and Free Cash Flow (FCF) among others. They have also created a sustainable offshore business model enabling the client to focus on key engagements.

Comprehensive

Comprehensive providers handle almost all the transactional and administrative processes in a function, or even several functions, such as HR and financial accounting. For instance, there are 22 processes in HR and 33 processes in finance and accounting. Comprehensive BPO prefers global deals, which are typically seven to ten years in length and higher in costs. These providers will buy client assets and will take on hundreds and sometimes thousands of client staff. Comprehensive providers strive to make interrelated processes more effective; so they aim to reduce the total cost of a function by introducing best practices. They are accountable for cost savings as well as outcomes for an entire function, so that clients pay for outcomes, not inputs. Comprehensive providers shoulder 70 per cent of the operational risk of the in-scope processes, because they are responsible for the information technology, transactions, and administrative elements of those processes. Furthermore, they invest significant amounts of capital in the relationship, and they absorb most client personnel.

This comprehensive model is new and has been in existence for the past three to four years. Interestingly, transactional BPOs act as sub-contractors to niche outsourcers, and both act as sub-contractors to comprehensive outsourcers. They together effectively act as Tier III, Tier II and Tier I outsourcers.

BPO MODELS

Overall, the choice of the business model for clients' need should to be very satisfactory for both the parties concerned. The major factors that contribute to this success are the partner selection process on both sides and the rules of engagement. Both need to be clearly defined and are transparent. The BPO vendors have adopted certain business models based on clients' need and their capability to make profits on the core competencies. The business models commonly used in BPO industry are:

Revenue distance model

Companies in the quest for competitiveness have discovered that outsourcing some tasks to cheaper locations is one way to deliver efficiencies and cut costs. But the simple act of outsourcing to a lower-cost base has evolved into a complex process that can cause considerable damage if not dealt with in a scientific manner. The damage can range from not achieving the expected cost savings to losing control to a third party, particularly when a company's more essential processes are outsourced.

Before outsourcing a business process, the management should ask, "How much does this process, compared to other processes, contribute to our product being better than the competition's product?". Evaluating and ranking each business process for its contribution to creating value for customers and to capturing that value for the company is a central part of the Revenue Distance Model.

In other words, the Revenue Distance Model captures the importance of a business process for the company. Those that are ranked high are critical for revenue generation and thus are best held close to home, and those that have low rankings could be, and perhaps should be, outsourced.

The Revenue Distance Model also recognizes that the relative importance of value creation and value capture will be different for different industries. For instance, a company in a nascent industry would rank processes that help in value creation as very high. For mature industries such as retail, banking and hospitality, however, value capture will be more important than value creation.

Global delivery model

Global delivery model[2] (see Table 5.2) is the most successful outsourcing model. It is a combination of onsite model and offshore model but unlike the onsite and offshore models wherein the offshore development centre of the service provider is located at only one place, in the Global Delivery Model the service provider has its offshore development centres spread out across the entire globe.

2. www.prithvisolutions.com/engagementModels.html.

TABLE 5.2 Global Delivery Model

At client site	*At global development centre*
Project	**Project**
Analysis and planning	Project management
High-level design	Detailed design
User interface design	Coding
Project co-ordination	Testing
Onsite testing implementation	Documentation
Post-implementation support	**Post-implementation support**
Rapid reaction	Bug fixes
Support	Warranty support
	Maintenance

In this model the service provider need not have their own offshore development centres across the globe, but they can use the resources of their partners located around the globe. This provides the client with a large working team with varied qualities and expertise in different fields.

Tasks accomplished by the onsite team:

- Understanding the client's requirements
- Directly interaction with the client to understand their needs
- Acting as a mediator between the client and the offshore centres
- Planning and designing the initial steps of the project
- Allocation of tasks amongst the available resources
- Testing the outcome of the project in tandem with the client's team
- Executing the project successfully at the client's place
- Provide the required support for maintenance.

Tasks accomplished at the offshore development centre:

- Detailed design that will be continuation of site team designs
- Deciding any specific technological requirements for the project
- Development
- Testing before handing over to onsite team
- Continuous technical support.

The Global Delivery Model is preferred where the client requires that the job be done quickly and successfully. Also, where the project is very big, requiring sufficient skilled manpower to complete the task, this is the only model, which proves functional. In this model the level of risk involved is also minimum, since even if any of the offshore development centres face any disaster the project work will not be stopped, as the work can be transferred immediately and continued by the remaining offshore development centres. The advantages of the Global Delivery Model are:

- **Lower risks:** In case of any disaster or emergency at one of the offshore centres, the work continues at or is transferred to other offshore development centres.
- **Round-the-clock productivity:** $24 \times 7 \times 365$ work cycle becomes possible because of the time-zone difference.
- **Best results:** Accomplishment of high-quality work is possible, as the client will get the benefit of skilled manpower spread out across the globe.
- **Shorter lead-time:** Shorter project completion time is achieved, as the work is completed by a number of offshore development centres working together with the same target.
- **Cost benefits:** The cost saving benefits for the client resulting from offshore outsourcing is also appreciable.
- **No employee additions:** The service provider can provide the client with a large working team with varied skill sets, which the client may not be able to employ for just the task at hand.
- **No communication gap:** The onsite team, which will be in direct contact with the client, is able to understand the client's needs in a better way.
- **Responsiveness:** Because of the onsite team's presence, response to changes in client's requirements is fast.

Some of the challenges in putting into practice the global delivery model in any organization are as follows:

- Having perfect co-ordination between all the offshore development centres and that too in accordance with the client's satisfaction is a big task.
- Project teams are culturally and geographically much diversified. Managing and executing an IT project with such a team is very difficult and requires a lot of training and experience.
- Managing projects gets more nebulous when it involves organizing the efforts and schedules of individuals, teams and resources from across the globe.

Global Delivery Model (GDM), pioneered by Infosys in the early 1980s, emerged as a disruptive force in the industry and led to the rise of offshore global outsourcing. Today, offshore global outsourcing has gained widespread acceptance as a crucial aspect of business strategy.

Enabled by the availability of highly-educated, technically-skilled and low-cost talent in India and other emerging economies, GDM has achieved broad acceptance through its ability to deliver lower costs, higher quality, and productivity. Offshore outsourcing is at the core of the global delivery model, which refers to the philosophy of:

- Breaking pieces of work into logical components, and
- Distributing components geographically throughout locations to perform them where it creates maximum value.

GDM was developed by Infosys to help enterprises at any maturity level realize the full benefits of global sourcing, it provides both a conceptual foundation and a set of actionable frameworks for business and IT leaders to:

- Think about outsourcing services at an enterprise-wide level to create alignment between business, operations and IT
- Structure business and IT assets and their execution phases in a well-defined modular fashion to achieve flexibility, and
- Act on a global level, using strategic global delivery, to ensure predictability of cost, quality, risk, and meeting of shared business objectives.

It is a model for enterprises to be in step with continuously changing business realities. As such, it represents a conceptual shift in thinking about IT and business process services outsourcing on a global scale. It defines a set of actionable frameworks and steps that business and IT decision-makers can undertake to put the concepts into practice to realize operational efficiencies and enable business innovation, regardless of their current level of sourcing maturity.

The savings from the Global Delivery Model (GDM) allows the firm to invest in pilot projects, which the client couldn't have made because of resource constraints. This adds to the firm's competitive advantage as well. GDM assures the following:

- Best product quality, which cuts down costs of fixing defects, maintenance and hence, the TCO (Total Cost of Ownership)
- Advantages coming out of continuous improvements, which keep improving all the key parameters
- Gives access to the best global talent
- Increases chance of process innovation.

Build-operate-transfer (BOT) model

As a simple and layman definition, the Build-Operate-Transfer Model (see Figure 5.2) refers to the case when a firm contracts with an offshore partner to build a shared services or offshore development centre, operates it for a fixed interim period and transfers it at the end. Organizations try this with the expectation that the offshore partner can initiate operations and reach operating stability much faster than it can with an in-house effort.

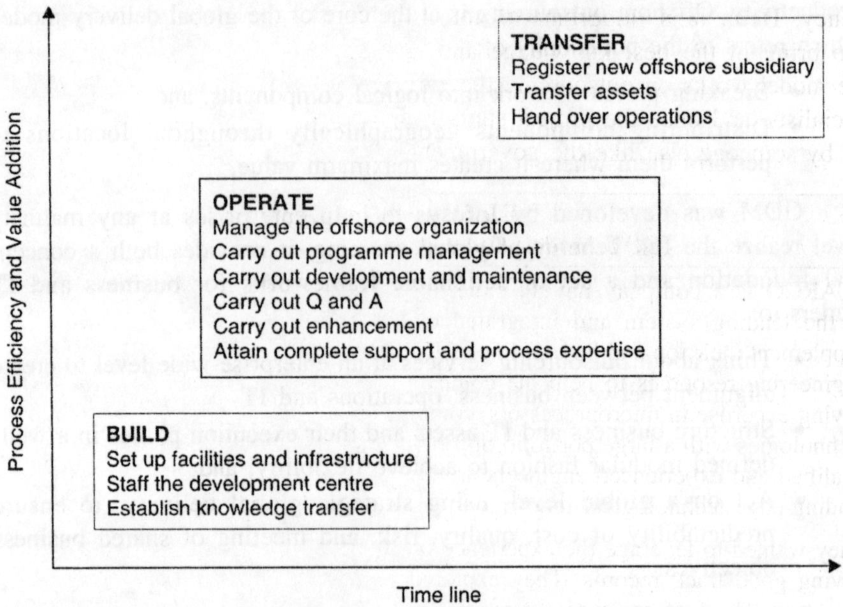

FIGURE 5.2 BOT model.

In order to enter the market rapidly, many companies need a flexible combination of application development and outsourced system. BOT delivery option is designed for such clients who focus on important strategic areas of their businesses while wanting to bring new service offerings to the marketplace.

Under this model, dedicated infrastructural facilities, team, and other resources are assigned to the clients. This facility is like an extension of the client's own facility. The captive facility is staffed on either a dedicated or a hybrid basis, that is, either by using the existing outsourcer's resources, or by using the client's resources, or by resources hired specifically for engagement, or a mix of them all. BPO organizations offer well-defined mechanisms for the smooth transition of the facility to the client. Clients see the following benefits by working with this model:

- Faster time to market
- Lower establishment costs
- Risk reduction
- Flexibility
- Process expertise
- Option of owning the facility.

The BOT model has been very successful in the infrastructure and construction industry. The vendor, for example, builds a highway or bridge, will operate it for a period of time and later hand it over to a government agency. Here, it is important to note that this model rests on specialists, who bring in the best knowledge and skill-sets for setting up this project. The model works on outsourcing the early stages of project execution to the specialists, and once the project starts running smoothly it is taken over and run by someone else like the government in this case.

EXHIBIT 5.3
BOT Model: Outsourcing Engineering

STARCO is a company having expertise in embedded processor technology to the leading system and integrated circuit suppliers across the globe. To supplement their top and bottom lines they decided to explore low-cost, offshore engineering resources to help the company in their base country. STARCO is having expertise in microprocessors, compilers and electronic design automation technologies with a large portfolio of Technology Intellectual Property. Team of qualified and experienced engineers are their real asset continuously developing leading-edge technological innovations.

They wanted to leverage the experience of other technology companies in India having good track records. They explored four different options to meet their objective. The first one was outsourcing in India, wherein outsourcing a set of tasks to a service company outside the country and these service companies would provide expertise and complete the task. Here, STARCO felt that their investment would be too high. They also felt that they may lose the value they created in the training process and IPs provided. Hence, turned down this option.

The second choice was to set up a subsidiary which will addresses the concerns of IP protection as well as the training investment. However, it comes with an initial investment in infrastructure and organization overhead, which STARCO felt to be too high for the scale of operation they will have.

The third choice was acquisition with an advantage of bringing in a team that already exists. However, building up a well-qualified engineering team in India is a difficult and long drawn task. They explored this option, but eventually abandoned the idea as no prospect was found that met their needs in terms of engineering expertise, location and cost.

The last option was to go for Build-Operate-Transfer (BOT) model. They decided to hire and build a team dedicated to STARCO projects in partnership with a company having domain knowledge, infrastructure and expertise. They chose TYCO to be their Indian partner. They worked with them to build a team and operate it under their guidance for about a year and a half. The project will be transferred to STARCO when there is a "critical mass of engineers to justify the cost of infrastructure and service overheads. In the deal, STARCO agreed to pay TYCO a fixed per-month per-engineer fee. The project transfer to STARCO's will occur after 2 years at a negotiated transfer fee. A team of engineers whom they have hired and trained are aware that within a period of time, they'll become STARCO employees. Towards motivation the Indian engineers were given STARCO stock options and receive other incentives.

Even though BOT is a good model to start with low initial investment, low risk and quick infrastructure and legal setup, but the BOT partner need to be trustworthy and open about communication and has the bandwidth to service needed. Here, for success, it's absolutely essential that the US managers associated with offshore project be fully committed to the effort. Without this commitment, the burden of the work and the inevitable hiccups will defeat the purpose of the BOT project.

BOT means that the client has a right to own the facility, while the third-party vendor builds it, hires the employees, gets the operation running for a certain period of time (usually a period of three to five years) and hands over the operations to the client after the said period. During the contract period, the vendor and the client work closely with a senior client representative monitoring the operations. At the time of the transition, the vendor is suitably compensated.

Thus the BOT model gives an opportunity and liberty to customers (offshore) to get the Offshore Centre (OC) built and operated as per their specific needs and also to set up the processes in various stages to suit their business needs. The staged process helps the client to evaluate the risks involved and also helps them to check the feasibility before investing in a full-fledged manner. This model offers the right to the customer to acquire the operations of such a centre at the end of the contract period, if they desire so.

This model is beneficial to an organization which plans to commence business in a country where it does not have its base. The organization would look at getting a local company to reduce the risk of its new venture in the country. Such an organization doesn't have the expertise in that process, and wants to pool in specialized and dedicated resources to execute it. Here the organization will tie up with a mature player who already has expertise and knowledge for it. The important factors to be addressed in a BOT model are:

- Who has the controlling stake when the project starts, and what would be the composition of the board
- Which of the partners will have what kind of powers on the board appointments
- Which milestones need to be tracked to ensure that the project is in line.

Thus, the BOT model helps large corporations to jump-start their operations in crunched-cycle time. They enjoy all the benefits of an established company, including the brand equity of the service provider, and also leverage all the best practices and learned lessons of the successful company during the formative years of the company and build upon it thereafter.

Blended offshore outsourcing model (BOOM)

The Blended Offshore Outsourcing Model (BOOM) (see Figure 5.3) methodology provides a blended approach towards IT outsourcing for small- and medium-sized project management enterprises (SMEs). BOOM provides dual advantage to the client by shifting the non-critical stages of the project life-cycle to the local Offshore Development Centre (in India), while still retaining project coordination and control at the client site, supported and coordinated by an onsite project manager and account manager. However, the project is closely monitored and controlled by the offshore project manager (located offshore) through regular coordination with the onsite project manager who interacts regularly with the project manager of the customer.

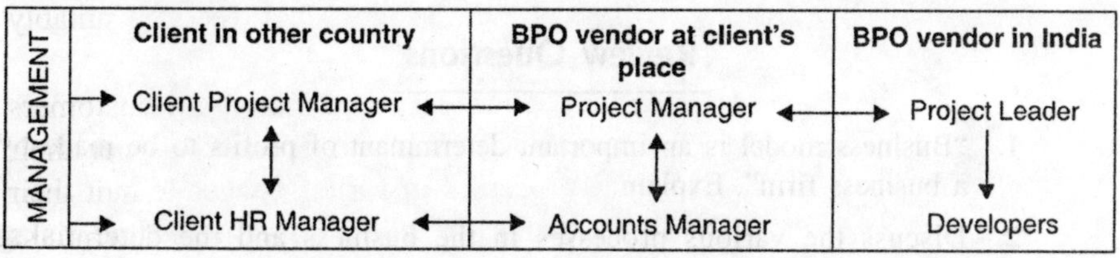

FIGURE 5.3 BOOM model.

This model is designed for the small and medium-sized project management enterprises (SMEs) in the other countries. The methodology also provides a good price to performance ratio by reducing the major share of the workload from onsite to offshore.

From the preceding discussion it is evident that BOOM recommends only the non-critical parts of the project to be done offshore. The following are the phases of the BOOM methodology:

Project Initiation — Onsite
Project Planning — Onsite
Project Execution — Offshore
Project Controlling — Onsite
Project Closing — Onsite

BOOM is a domain-independent but process- and methodology-driven outfit, giving organizations flexibility and complete understanding of their requirements. It enables the client to have complete control over the project at any point and provides a comprehensive solution completely woven for onsite clients with predictable yields.

SUMMARY

BPO involves a mix of decisions, from deciding about the partner and redefining processes to manage the relationship and multi-sourcing. However, the fundamental aspect is the mutual growth-oriented relationship between the client and the outsourcing partner based on constant innovation. The key to any BPO venture is the relationship that it manages to create with the carriers from whom they provide the service. Therefore the BPO model must choose the breadth and depth of the relationship very carefully. There are three key motives for BPO: cost, focus and flexibility. These issues should be built into the BPO model. There are three types of BPO: transactional, niche and comprehensive. Each has its advantages and disadvantages. The Global Delivery Models are onshore, offshore and inshore, based on the client's need and convenience. BOT is the most preferred model in the BPO industry. BOOM is a domain-independent but process and methodology-driven outfit, giving organizations flexibility and complete understanding of their requirements.

Review Questions

1. "Business model is an important determinant of profits to be made by a business firm". Explain.
2. Discuss the various processes in the business and the determining factors for being outsourcers.
3. Differentiate between IT and BP outsourcing.
4. Classify the BPO vendors and discuss their features.
5. What are different models for Business Process Outsourcing? Discuss their relative advantages and disadvantages.

Chapter 6

BPO Governance

BPO governance is not just compliance with current process, but a way to maximize a BPO relationship business value for both parties. It is a key to successful outsourcing strategy. Governance should address both 'hard' concerns like cost and technology issues as well as 'soft' i.e. people and business knowledge.[1]

In the past few years, there's been a great deal written about governance; yet it's still a misunderstood subject. In most cases, it's an afterthought, only considered once the "transaction" is complete and the service provider is selected. Unfortunately, this practice relegates governance to no more than a box to be checked off on the path to programme implementation. In order for governance to have a chance to realize the business case for which it was created, it must be more than this.

INTRODUCTION

In the competitive markets, corporations are always exploring the ways to remain cost-competitive. The majority of the business firms adopt outsourcing as a business strategy to remain competitive. In a BPO process the savings are there; but labour arbitrage alone does not make a successful venture. It requires control through discipline, which is called *governance*. The importance of having a good governance structure should never be underestimated. For success in BPO contract, firms must ask the following questions before its implementation:

- Is the organization in a position to make the transition?
- Are the processes properly documented?
- Does the organization have the right people to make the transition?
- Are there commitment and controls?

Outsourcing is a long journey and one must realize that one has to pick up a 'strategic partner' and not a 'vendor'. The customer wants a fair

1. http://www.go4outsourcing.com/articles/managing_bpo_governance.asp

price, but in the end the customer shall get what he pays for. Driving for rock-bottom prices will get you a service provider that looks for every excuse not to improve the process, thereby giving you sub-standard results. Hence, one has to define the financial targets that must be achieved to meet the business plan. Then, when reached, one has to back off and focus on the relationship.

CORPORATE GOVERNANCE

Corporate governance involves commitment to values and ethical business conduct. It is about how an organization is managed. This includes its corporate and other structures, its culture, policies and the manner in which it deals with various stakeholders. Accordingly, timely and accurate disclosure of information regarding the financial situation, performance and ownership of the company is an important part of corporate governance. This improves public understanding of the structure, activities and policies of the organization. Consequently, the organization is able to attract investors, and enhance the trust and confidence of the existing stakeholders.

Corporate governance guidelines and best practices have evolved over a period of time. The Cadbury Report on the financial aspects of corporate governance, published in the UK in 1992, was a landmark. It led to the publication of the Viénot Report in France in 1995. This report boldly advocated the removal of cross-shareholdings that had formed the bedrock of French capitalism for decades. Further, The General Motors Board of Directors Guidelines in the USA and the Dey Report in Canada proved to be influential in the evolution of other guidelines and codes across the world. Over the past decade, various countries have issued recommendations for corporate governance. Compliance with these is generally not mandated by law, although codes that are linked to stock exchanges sometimes have a mandatory content.

The Sarbanes–Oxley Act, which was signed by US President George W. Bush into law in July 2002, has brought about sweeping changes in financial reporting. This is perceived to be the most significant change to the federal securities law since the 1930s. Besides directors and auditors, the Act has also laid down new accountability standards for security analysts and legal counsels.

In November 2003, the SEC approved changes to the NYSE (New York Stock Exchange) and NASDAQ listing requirements. The changes focused mainly on Board independence, independent committees of the Board, audit committee composition, code of business conduct and ethics, and related party transactions.

The Higgs Report on non-executive directors and the Smith Report on audit committees, both published in January 2003, form part of the systematic review of corporate governance being undertaken in the UK and Europe.

This is in light of recent corporate failures. The recommendations of these two reports are aimed at strengthening the existing framework for corporate governance in the UK enhancing the effectiveness of the non-executive directors and switching the key audit relationship from executive directors to an independent audit committee are part of this. These recommendations are intended as revisions to the Combined Code on Corporate Governance.

In April 2004, the governments of the 30 countries belonging to the Organization for Economic Co-operation and Development (OECD) approved a revised version of the OECD's Principles of Corporate Governance, adding new recommendations for good practice in corporate behaviour with a view to rebuilding and maintaining public trust in companies and stock markets. The revised principles call on governments to ensure effective regulatory frameworks and on companies to be more accountable. The principles include increased awareness among institutional investors, enhanced role for shareholders in executive compensation, greater transparency and effective disclosures to counter conflicts of interest.

In India, the Confederation of Indian Industry (CII) took the lead in framing a desirable code of corporate governance in April 1998. This was followed by the recommendations of the Kumarmangalam Birla Committee on Corporate Governance. This committee was appointed by the Securities and Exchange Board of India (SEBI). The recommendations were accepted by SEBI in December 1999, and are now enshrined in Clause 49 of the Listing Agreement of every Indian stock exchange. SEBI also instituted a committee under the chairmanship of N.R. Narayana Murthy, which recommended enhancements in corporate governance. SEBI has incorporated the recommendations made by the Narayana Murthy Committee on Corporate Governance in Clause 49 of the listing agreement. The revised Clause 49 has been made effective from January 1, 2006. Thus, sound corporate governance is critical to enhance and retain investor trust. Hence, corporate governance philosophy is based on the following principles:

- Satisfy the spirit of the law.
- Corporate governance standards should go beyond the law.
- Be transparent.
- Personal conveniences and corporate resources should be separated.
- Communicate to stakeholders about how the company is run internally.
- Comply with the laws of the land.
- Have a simple and transparent corporate structure to serve business needs.
- Management is the trustee of the shareholders' capital and not the owner.

At the core of the corporate governance practice is the Board, which oversees how the management serves and protects the long-term interests of all the stakeholders of the company. Hence, an active, well-informed and independent Board is necessary to ensure the highest standards of corporate governance.

INDIAN PERSPECTIVE

Indian BPOs first have to comply with Indian law. Then, they must comply with the relevant laws of the land that offshores business processes, such as COBIT for IT management, Six Sigma, ISO, COPC for quality management and Sarbanes–Oxley Act, 2002 for auditing. BPOs themselves should design their own process standards or to comply with some well-known international standards such as SOX for going for overseas contracts. Compliance to regulatory frameworks such as the Sarbanes–Oxley Act by the BPO industry can act as a signal to global stakeholders that a firm is following best practices for corporate governance. This has become an important enabler, as India's BPOs are proposing to list in international vendors' lists.

ETHICS IN DECISION-MAKING

Many times, business organizations encounter the dilemma of ethical decision-making. However, ethical compliance leads to a strong public image and upholds the integrity and character of an organization. Whether personal or professional, not many of us want to associate with unethical individuals. It makes a lot more sense to do business with ethical organizations, as it has a direct influence on the overall functioning of a business. Ethics creates a space for itself and ensures the smooth running of businesses. When there is mutual trust and responsibility towards each other, a crisis management mechanism will automatically evolve. The best indicator of whether a firm's action is ethical or unethical can be best judged by the way firm's outsourcing partner reacts during a crisis.

The core concern of outsourcing ethics is confidential information security. If the firm's outsourcing partners do not have adequate information security measures, it might be wise to stay clear of them. Legal perceptions may differ from one nation to the other and ambiguity could arise when a dispute occurs, leaving both parties in a fix. The association becomes easier when the parties have a legal, moral and ethical obligation to comply with the agreement, with due respect to international law.

There are many companies that offer services at very low cost. An ethical concern might seem to be a costlier choice. However, the price difference could be deceptive as the variation will only be in the initial cost. In the long run, the overall cost will prove to be much lower when you are working with an ethical partner.

Vendor reliability is the basis of trust, that makes someone wants to outsource. The outsourcer has to weigh the dependability and reliability of the organizations to which you want to outsource. A clear definition and practice of the ethical rules and privacy policies of the organization, like non-disclosure of trade secrets, secrecy and non-disclosure contracts with staff, third-party service providers and visitors is a prerequisite. This will reassure the outsourcer that it is safe to do business with a partner who is thousands of miles away.

Information security will largely depend on the people who handle the information. Organizations that implement tough employee credibility measures have a direct implication on their outsourcing ethics. The other sign of ethical company is clear and open communication channels. When a project does not go the right way, an ethical partner will always keep the firm informed of the problem, possible solutions and the time needed. However, the following list is an indicative of ethical practices met by the outsourcing partner:

- Proper information security systems
- Trade secret protection measures
- Infrastructure
- Training and upgrading the security skills
- Electronic data storage safety
- Presence of a whistleblower
- Proper arrangement with third-party service providers.

Invariably in the long run, in an unethical partnership the cost of maintaining the project and the relationship will be high. On the other hand, in ethical partnership there is common focus in problem resolution, knowing the risks and managing them together. The result is reduction in cost and risk.

Before making an outsourcing decision, the outsourcer should also be clear about the responsibilities that can be shared. This will help in building a healthy relationship base such as:

- Willingness to discuss
- Manage expectations
- Last agreed document should be the basis
- Build flexibility to contracts
- Openness to wider scope and price reviews.

PRACTICES IN PLACE

The quality standards that Indian BPOs have adopted represent a mix of issues that the BPOs must address. Some are the important standards that directly affect the quality of service offered by the service providers, including COPC, ISO and Six Sigma. In addition, Indian BPOs have adopted standards that create quality final service for the overseas clients. Under this category are the ones such as COBIT, ITSM and BS7799. In addition, many organizations are adopting procedures such as *whitehat hacking*, in which ethical hackers hack and test security. Third-party BPOs have been using these audit reports to highlight their security compliance to their customers.

COBIT is an IT management standard. It identifies certain control parameters, the dependencies on IT resources and puts certain practices in place. Any organization becoming progressively more complex from the IT point of view needs to have some kind of COBIT compliance. However, one may not replicate the exact COBIT standard in the organization. Many IT vendors are now creating information structure management software compliant to these standards. For example, HP OpenView is based on the ITSM COBIT standards. The Indian IT Act, 2000 is still somewhat opaque on the data protection front. There is a need for increased recognition for these standards of the BPO environment, and to create laws to prevent loopholes.

CHALLENGES IN BPO INDUSTRY

Security in BPO industry is a great challenge. There are three dimensions to this challenge which are HR Management, Techno-Legal Compliance and Technology Solutions.

1. *HR perspective*

Computer or a technology device is a technology risk point. However, the human risk point is complicated with BPO employees as they are less predictable, self-intelligent and prone to factors such as greed, jealousy, and mischief. Managing risk in such a situation is not as easy as managing adoption and implementation of technology.

2. *Techno-legal perspective*

The techno-legal aspects refers to providing a technical cover for prevention of intrusions, prevention of loss or compromise of information, disaster recovery and business continuity. The legal compliance ensures that any breach of technical security aspect does not result in a liability to the Information Asset owner. This will prompt him to proceed legally for recovery of damages or to cover himself with an adequate insurance facility.

3. *Technology solutions*

In BPO, human-related risks and legal risks can not be entirely reduced as the number of transaction handlers is huge. However, a substantial part of the risk can be reduced by handling it through technology solutions, which are being used by the IT industry.

Security Management

Security management may not be core competency of BPO outfits. Hence, considering the criticality of the problem as well as the survival of the BPO firm, there is a need for a third-party organization to deal with security aspects relevant to the industry. Some of the activities that this organization will manage are:

- Maintenance of employee data
- Conducting of background checks under BS 7858 standards
- Practising "Professional code of conduct"
- Impart ethical training to BPO employees
- Implement technical security solutions for disaster recovery
- Encryption for information protection, digital signatures, secured archival, etc.
- Conduct IT security compliance audits
- Conduct techno-legal compliance audits
- Conduct HR-related risk management programmes
- Training and education for techno-legal compliance
- Introduce a conflict resolution mechanism.

ETHICAL HACKERS

Similar to business corporations employ auditors to routinely examine financial records, BPO service providers should audit security policy. Just as accountants perform book-keeping audits, ethical hackers perform security audits. Without security regular audits and compliance controls, no real security exists. There are many individuals waiting to test and probe the organization's security stance. These individuals range from government and corporate spies to hackers, crackers and script kiddies, or those who write and release malicious code.

An ethical hacker is most similar to a penetration tester. The ethical hacker is an individual who is employed or contracted to undertake an attempted penetration test. These individuals use the same methods as those employed by hackers. Ethical hackers have written authorization to probe a network. Only then is this attempted hack legal, as there is a contract between the ethical hacker and the organization.

Primarily, ethical hackers are employed in groups to carry out penetration tests. These groups are commonly referred to as 'red teams'.[2] These individuals are being paid by the organization to poke, prod, and determine the overall level of security. Again, what is important here is that they have been given written permission to perform this test and have detailed boundaries to work within.

2. www.washingtonpost.com/wp_srv/politics/govt/fedguide/stories/ap021699.htm

The certified ethical hacker will be responsible for the following security testing:

1. Ethics and legal issues
2. Footprinting
3. Scanning
4. Enumeration
5. System hacking
6. Trojans and backdoors
7. Sniffers
8. Denial of service
9. Social engineering
10. Session hijaking
11. Hacking web servers
12. Web application vulnerabilities
13. Web-based password cracking techniques
14. SQL injection
15. Hacking wireless networks
16. Virus and worms
17. Hacking Novell
18. Hacking Linux
19. IDS, firewalls, and honeypots
20. Buffer overflows
21. Cryptography.

These domains comprise a full body of ethical hacking knowledge. In India, ITES Grads is offering Mile2 Certification Training through Axiom Technologies, Hyderabad.

CODE OF ETHICS

The provisions of the code of ethics are designed to promote honest and ethical conduct, including the ethical handling of actual or apparent conflicts of interest between personal and professional relationships. All employees, officers and directors of the company must comply with the provisions of the code.

In the course of performing the various roles in the company, each of the employees will encounter ethical questions in different forms and under a variety of circumstances. To provide answers to these questions, the ethical code with rules and procedures help the employees, officers and directors recognize and respond to situations that present ethical issues.

The reputation of the company relies on the character of its employees. In order to protect this, the company should not tolerate unethical behaviour by employees, officers or directors. Those who violate the standards in this code need to be subjected to disciplinary action.

Compliance

An Indian company with international operations is subject to laws and regulations both in India and abroad. Company policy requires that all employees, officers and directors of the company comply fully with company's rules and laws of the land. In the conflict situation the employees should seek clarification from the ethical officer.

Conflicts of interest

A conflict of interest arises when an employee takes actions or enters into relationships that could possibly oppose the interests of the company, or could possibly interfere with the employee's performance or independent judgment when carrying out his or her duties. The company should strictly prohibit its employees from taking any action or entering into any relationship that creates, or even appears to create, a conflict of interest without the prior approval of the management. Furthermore, employees may not use company property, information, influence or their position in the company for personal gain.

Fair dealing

Although the prosperity of the company depends on the ability to outperform the competitors, the company should be committed to achieving success by fair and ethical means. Company should prohibit employees from engaging in any dishonest, unethical or illegal business practices.

Controls and disclosures of accounts

The company requires that all its books and records be maintained accurately and with honesty. This requires that no fund, asset, liability, revenue or expense be concealed, or improperly or incompletely recorded for any purpose. All entries must be supported by documentation adequate to permit the books and records to be verified by auditors.

The Audit Committee of the Board has the responsibility of reviewing the company's policies and practices with respect to financial reporting. Auditors should have unrestricted access to all company documents and records. All employees are required to cooperate fully with internal and external audits.

Reporting Procedures

All employees have a duty to report any violations of the code of conduct, as well as violations of any laws, rules, or regulations. Employees also have a duty to report any transaction or relationship that could reasonably be expected to give rise to a conflict of interest. The company should have procedures in place to make reports, which may be made in person, by e-mail, by telephone or in writing by sending a description of the violation and the names of the parties involved.

Disciplinary action

The company should implement the disciplinary policies to ensure that prompt and consistent actions are taken in response to violations of ethical code such as:

Range of penalties. This includes (i) an oral or written warning, (ii) a reprimand, (iii) suspension, (iv) termination, and/or (v) restitution. Violations will also be reported to the appropriate regulatory agencies or other authorities.

Disciplinary process. The penalty for a particular violation should be decided on a case-by-case basis and shall depend on the nature and severity of the violation.

Consistent enforcement. To give consistent, equal treatment to all employees, officers and directors with impartiality.

MODEL FOR BPO GOVERNANCE

When BPO arrangements with partners fail, companies and their outsourcing providers pay the price in lost time and money. Moreover, customer satisfaction and competitiveness can suffer as companies fail to achieve the efficiencies and cost savings promised by BPO vendors.

These scenarios can be avoided if companies carefully analyze the nature of the processes they are outsourcing and establish the right contractual relationship with their vendors. The correct fit between processes and BPO relationship governance can improve the odds that the arrangement will generate the competitive advantages that outsourcing promises. There are three relevant process dimensions which need to be addressed.

1. *Complexity*

The extent to which the people performing the process must adopt different methods or procedures to do their work and the degree to which these individuals fail in establishing solutions to process problems.

2. *Independence*

The degree to which a process can be analyzed and changed without affecting other processes in the organization.

3. *Strategic importance*

The extent to which the process manages to provide the organization a competitive advantage.

Any process can have relevance to BPO. But to improve the odds of a successful outsourcing arrangement, the approach to relationship governance should reflect the nature of the process in question. That means that the BPO governance structure should match the nature of the outsourced process.

In outsourcing relationships, the two configurations are particularly aligned. In the first, the outsourced process is characterized by low complexity, high independence and low strategic importance. To outsource this kind of process, it is suggested that a company should establish contract with a best-of-breed specialty provider, in which the user firm has little operational involvement in the management of the outsourced process. These contracts have low levels of information exchange and the emphasis is on control of assigned tasks.

In some BPO configurations, the outsourced process is characterized by high complexity, low independence and high strategic importance. In such cases the BPO governance model would include a partnership arrangement with the vendor. This would include joint ownership of the outsourced process, high levels of information exchange, and an emphasis on coordination tasks.

SELF-GOVERNANCE

In the past the BPO industry entered into no-poaching pact. Poaching is prevalent in the industry wherein there is no trainer talent available to support the growing businesses and the need of trained manpower is immediate. In head haunting, usually firms land up picking up professionals from rivals to meet the time-bound project completion deadlines. However, the pact existed on the paper itself. But today, many large Indian BPOs are using self-governance as a tool for employee retention. In self-governance, the BPOs specifically avoid recruiting people from organizations which provide support to them as an alternate vendor.

Indian companies have already put in place or are currently honing their privacy and security measures even before the government finishes with the legislation. It is common to see employees swipe identity cards through readers, have their bags and pockets searched, deposit devices like cell phones, PDAs, pens and notebooks in lockers, and shred notes of client conversations after the shift ends. Visitors are not even allowed into the working area, and if they are, they must fill out a form promising not to communicate any knowledge of what they see inside. Call centre operators such as MphasiS BPO, Wipro Spectramind, and 24/7 Customer, as well as back-office subsidiaries of companies such as General Electric, have added state-of-the-art systems to monitor phone conversations, guard data, and watch workers' every move. E-mail, CD-ROM drives, hard drives, and other means of storing, copying, or forwarding information are removed from computer terminals. Indian employees can view information from overseas servers only for specific tasks. Video cameras are installed all over the area. Phone conversations are recorded and monitored. Disgruntled former employees attempting to commit data theft can be locked out and their access to PCs and phones cut three minutes after a resignation. The companies like Infosys use biometric security, including retina scans and palm reading, to identify employees against their records. Employee background checks, magnetic access cards, monitoring access electronically, physically searching bags on entry and exit, and video security are staple security features at all these companies.

APPROACH TO GOVERNANCE

In successful outsourcing, partners work together to share ownership, accountability, and responsibility of product and service delivery, which lead to accomplishments in the marketplace. The success of an outsourcing relationship is the consequence of an intimate working relationship that defines rules, disciplines, success factors, roles, and accountability. Governance supervises outsourcing by building a formal corporate structure to ensure consistent success. The goal of governance is to have:

- Aligned cultural foundation
- Focus on business results
- Consistent and disciplined methodologies, processes and communication protocols
- Agreed-upon decision-making authority and processes to resolve disputes
- Shared accountability for all parties.

The criteria for evolving good governance should be based on the following:

Organization culture

Culture generally refers to the unwritten rules of how things get done, what is acceptable behaviour and what is not. A framework for culture must include the following:

- Values accepted throughout both organizations
- Rewards and recognitions aligned to the values
- Activities that reinforce values.
- Deterrents or taboos that are enacted when culture is violated.

Outsourcing relationships succeed in direct proportion to cultural alignment and focused governance formalizes the unwritten rules and sets the tone for the business relationship.

Discipline

Effective outsourcing cannot be based on the good relationships of a few key individuals. To scale a outsourcing relationship, commonly agreed-upon methodologies and processes need to be in place. Consistent and repeatable delivery processes are common in any mature industry. However, less common are non-technical processes like communications, relationship management, and conflict resolution. Governance enables the building, documentation, and adherence of these processes on an enterprise-wide scale for both organizations.

Defining roles

Governance establishes a decision-making structure in the outsourcing process. It clarifies strategic and tactical ownership roles by fixing responsibility at one of the three tiers. One of the best practices that governance builds is the approach of "equal accountability and individual responsibility". This is achieved by putting in place shared critical success factors for both vendor and customer. Team objectives must be structured to align with incentive compensation. The goal is to award bonuses to both the vendor and customer associates only in case the team objectives are met. Failure to meet team objectives results in investigating the causes and not penalizing the individuals. The shared accountability encourages each team to work together to reach defined goals of the relationship.

Measuring success

An effective governance model must monitor and measure the outsourcing relationship. Monthly reports should measure the project deliverable parameters. Customer and vendor feedback surveys should be conducted by an independent team for measuring the criticality of the issues involved in the relationship. The measurable metrics include:

- Offshore or onsite leverage ratios
- Blended rates
- Quality
- Head count
- Revenues and cost
- Cost and revenue per deliverable
- SLA parameters
- Time and materials utilization.

Real-time monitoring of these metrics through online tools is necessary to prevent time and cost deviations. Measuring, monitoring, and ensuring action on the results is one of the most crucial functions of governance. Early identification of action items enables quick problem resolution, which is a critical success factor for intimate relationships.

KEYS TO SUCCESSFUL TRANSITION

No BPO transition is simple, even if ultimately successful. However, if done for the right reasons, and with the right expectations, any transition can deliver returns far exceeding the time and energy invested.

The trick is to recognize not only obvious organizational barriers to progress, and managerial tactics that can aid it, but also to address the blind spots. For success following six keys are prescribed in Table 6.1.

TABLE 6.1 Keys to Successful Transition

Keys	*Actions*
Manage change	Secure the commitment of senior leaders and by recognizing subtle cultural differences that can undermine initial transition efforts
Assess organizational readiness	Assess for a BPO transition from a mental as well as technical standpoint keeping realistic expectations to manage them actively.
Anticipate risks	Anticipate risks and their gravity in terms of loss of business and image, to formulate a plan for mitigating them.
Establish project-management infrastructure	Manage process of transition carefully.
Create a governance mechanism	Collect feedback from the TPM and other key stakeholders and provide formal executive oversight and guidance.
Evolve measurement metrics	Measure outcome qualitatively and quantitatively.

In transition process organization should invest sufficient time on knowledge transfer. This will eliminate the chances of hiccups in the starting as information is vital to process performance in post-transition phase. An effective governance model (including considerations for decision-making, dispute resolution and innovation) is important at the day-to-day, process-management level. This will help immensely in retaining the knowledge and in establishing the practical and psychological foundations needed to stabilize process performance.

BEST PRACTICES

Some key outsourcing best practices emerge from successful governance are:

- Set plan of action
- Define roles and responsibilities
- Outline the business goals

- Let goals be understood by all players
- Monitor and measure issues
- Evaluate progress against benchmarks or targets
- Share cultural do's and don'ts, so that all parties understand what is acceptable.

A comprehensive governance system which addresses culture, accountability, decision making, discipline and goals, is imperative to guarantee continuous improvement and predictable outsourcing service success.

SUMMARY

While cost-effectiveness is still a key consideration, BPO buyers are increasingly giving more importance to factors other than cost while deciding on BPO vendors. Corporate governance, for example, is high on the list of such non-cost deciding factors. The correct fit between processes and BPO relationship governance can improve the odds that the arrangement will generate the competitive advantages that outsourcing promises. There are three particularly relevant process dimensions, which are: complexity, independence and strategic importance. Any process can have relevance to BPO. But to improve the odds of a successful outsourcing arrangement, the approach to relationship governance should reflect the nature of the process in question. For success the BPO governance structure should be matched to the nature of the outsourced process. Today many large Indian BPOs are using self-governance as a tool for employee retentions. They go for self-regulated hiring process as against official agreements with the competitors. In self-governance, the BPOs specifically avoid recruiting people from organizations which provide support to them as alternate vendor.

Review Questions

1. Explain what is corporate governance in the context of BPO.
2. What is the ethical decision-making process in an organization?
3. Discuss the various challenges in BPO industry with regard to governance.
4. What is 'code of ethics' in the BPO? Explain the role of ethical hackers in a BPO.
5. Discuss the best practices which can be adopted for BPO governance.

Chapter 7

Legal Issues in BPO Contracts

It's always better to invest in a fence when you are on the edge of a cliff than to invest in an ambulance.[1]

It's always better to spend extra time in drawing up a good BPO contract than trying to plug holes later. It's advisable to spend time with a vendor and find out about particular local laws that have to be complied with. Also, time should be spent in drawing clear non-solicitation laws where a customer wanting to set up a captive centre cannot poach employees from a vendor. Key issues while negotiating a BPO deal are setting up of a negotiating team. This team should be represented by people from several departments of the organizations—from finance, and legal to operations. The top management can step into the negotiations later. The other important factor for the vendor is the closing time of the deal. The longer the negotiation, the lesser the bargaining power of the vendor.

INTRODUCTION

Outsourcing is the delegation of in-house operations by companies to independent contractors. The recent Information Technology boom in India has been a direct result of outsourcing of IT-enabled services by foreign multinationals to Indian IT companies. Large multinational companies consider India an outsourcing destination because of the low cost of skilled workforce, the high quality of work, and the availability of English-speaking and computer-literate people. The work is undertaken on specific projects by way of an outsourcing contract. However, while entering into an outsourcing contract, the parties must keep certain factors in mind, such as protection of Intellectual Property Rights and taxation issues under the Transfer Pricing regulations of the Income Tax Act. Any outsourcing transaction raises following legal issues:

1. Nishit Desai, "Master the art of BPO negotiations: Getting the basics right is paramount while drawing up BPO contracts", NASSCOM ITeS BPO Strategy Summit, 13 June 2003.

- Intellectual property
- Income tax
- Transaction tax
- Insurance claims
- Bankruptcy or insolvency issues
- Employment governmental controls
- Regulatory compliance on foreign investment
- Industry sector regulations
- Foreign exchange controls
- Public company regulations
- Transfer of technology
- Activity-specific regulations and mandatory "public policy" laws
- Competition dispute resolution.

In addition to these legal considerations, any outsourcing transaction today that involves an "offshoring" component should take account of the emerging body of so-called "global sourcing" legislation. In the USA, for example, both the federal and state levels, legislatures presently are considering a variety of bills that essentially seek to inhibit the transfer of jobs overseas. Many of these bills only affect government contracts and where the work can be performed. Other bills, however, impose obligations on call centre activities (i.e., location identity requirements) or additional restrictions on transfers of personally identifiable information (e.g., financial information). Most of these bills may never enter into law and, to the extent they are, may be challenged as violating the regulations.

INTELLECTUAL PROPERTY RIGHTS

Protection of intellectual property rights owned by IT companies, such as the software, copyright, trade secrets, inventions, ideas, formulas, source and object codes, knowhow, improvements, etc. must be taken into account in the outsourcing contract. Under Indian copyright law, there is an automatic assignment of copyright from a software developer to his/her employer, so long as there is no contract to the contrary. However, this is not the case with an independent contractor. Furthermore, with reference to Indian patent law, there are no automatic assignment provisions, and inventions have to be assigned by both employees and consultants. It is, therefore, imperative that there is an assignment of any new invention by the independent contractor and its employees to the client during the course of the contract as well as an assignment of the final work product.

Consider the following situation. Company A outsources certain services to Company B, an independent contractor. Company A provides Company B deliverables, which contain confidential or proprietary information of third parties, to generate the work product. In the course of developing the work product. the employees and independent contractors of Company B make certain inventions. In this case, confidential and proprietary information must be protected by Company A at three levels, i.e.:

- Company A's deliverables;
- Work product and related inventions developed by Company B; and
- Future work product developed by Company B.

Client's deliverables

In most cases of outsourcing, the client provides the contractor with third-party confidential information to enable it to carry out the contracted services. The client must ensure that the contractor maintains the confidentiality of such information and uses the information only for the specified purposes. Moreover, the contractor must be made to enter into contracts with its employees stating that they will not infringe the proprietary and intellectual property rights of the client or third parties.

Work product and related inventions

The contractor must be under an obligation to keep confidential the work product that is developed during the course of the contract. There must be an exclusive, royalty-free, irrevocable, perpetual and worldwide assignment, to the client, of any new invention that the contractor or its employees develop during the continuance of the contract. The contractor must not be permitted to retain any right to use the work product or challenge the validity of the client's exclusive rights to the work product.

Future work product

The client must ensure the assignment of the work products not only during the subsistence of the contract, but also those developed in the future out of the client's deliverables.

For outsourcing in India, IPR laws in India are always undergoing amendments, according to the needs of the changing times and in unison with International Laws and Practices. India has accepted the World Trade Organization (WTO) Agreement, which came into force on January 1, 1995, and has also become a party to the Agreement on Trade Related Intellectual Property Rights. In the last few years, India has effected several legislative changes in copyrights, trademarks, designs, patents, and other issues besides enacting new legislations on bio-diversity and geographical indications. These measures have drastically reformed Indian laws on intellectual property.

TRANSFER PRICING (TP) GUIDELINES

While entering into an outsourcing arrangement, one must keep in mind the

TP regulations that are used to compute income from international transactions between associated enterprises. The TP regulations become applicable only if the enterprises are regarded as or are deemed to be associated enterprises. In an outsourcing arrangement, enterprises are deemed to be associated when:

- The manufacture or processing of goods by the contractor is wholly dependent upon the use of the intellectual property of the client;
- One enterprise, or any person specified by it, supplies and influences the prices and other conditions relating to ninety per cent (90%) or more of the raw materials and consumables required for the manufacture or processing of goods or articles carried out by the contractor; or
- When the goods or articles manufactured or processed by the contractor are sold to the client at prices and conditions that are influenced by the client.

The income arising from an international transaction is required to be computed having regard to the *arm's length price*. Arm's length price means a price which is applied or proposed to be applied in a transaction between persons other than associated enterprises, in uncontrolled conditions.

Further, an international transaction means a transaction, whether an oral or written arrangement, between two or more associated enterprises, either or both of whom are non-residents, in the nature of:

- Purchase, sale or lease of tangible or intangible property;
- Provision of services;
- Lending or borrowing money;
- Any other transaction having a bearing on profits, income, losses or assets of such enterprises.

These provisions, however, do not apply in a case where the aggregate value, as recorded in the books of account, of the international transactions does not exceed ₹ 10,000,000 (Rupees One Crore) (US$208,350) in a financial year.

DATA SECURITY

Data privacy and security are not new concepts in outsourcing. When there is transfer of sensitive and confidential information, concerns about a leakage or abuse do arise. For anti-outsourcing parties, data privacy and security are one of the main reasons to curb outsourcing. Some consider the security risks to be the same if the data were handled offshore or onshore, while others are unsure about the data privacy and security laws in countries like India and view it as a serious deterrent to their decision to outsource.

BPO vendors in the USA and the UK are under increasing pressure from legislation that insists on them guaranteeing the privacy of their customers' financial and medical data. Indian companies realize that they need to scale up their security in order to cater to these concerns before they actually turn out to be a problem. From individual companies to associations like NASSCOM, proactive measures are being taken to ensure that India's unique value proposition is "trustworthy outsourcing".

India does not have laws which are as stringent as those in the USA, but the government and associations such as NASSCOM are working towards ensuring that laws are at par with international legislation.

Other than legislation, measures set up between companies which outsource to India and Indian vendors ensure that there is little left to chance. Confidential data is stored on the servers of the companies that are outsourcing and their Indian vendors have tightly controlled access. Therefore, if there is a security breach, the US or European company outsourcing the work is legally responsible.

However, these are technicalities which cannot be used to skirt the issue and Indian companies realize this. In the instance of a single security breach the publicity created will not only destroy the reputation of the concerned company, but of India's well-established name as the foremost outsourcing destination.

It is indeed extremely important for India to have in place a distinctive legal regime promoting data protection. This is necessary to create confidence among investors and foreign companies that data sent to India for back-office operations is indeed safe and that there appropriate statutory mechanisms in place should any breach of data take place.

One of the main arguments raised against outsourcing to India is related to lack of data protection laws and how that renders data insecure. The Government of India has been sensitized about the issue and is presently working to put in place a legislative mechanism to legally enable data protection and data security.

OTHER ISSUES

The provisions in the agreement will vary depending on whether the proposed deal is early or late-stage, but commonly include the following:

- The parties' respective performance and compliance obligations;
- Payment structures, e.g. milestones, etc.;
- Collaboration and co-operation between the partners;
- Exclusivity and non-competition;
- Warranties, indemnities and liability issues;
- Term, termination and obligations on termination;
- Dispute resolution.

Irrespective of the type of company outsourcing and buying-in services in relation to R&D, clinical research, manufacturing, logistics, sales or support functions, in the transactions the key terms will relate to the precise service to be provided and at what price. In addition the other issues covered are:

- Joint investment or contribution;
- Dealing with intellectual property and knowhow;
- Continuous improvement;
- Compatibility of the technical and commercial agreements.

LAWS IN INTERNATIONAL CONTRACTS

In a cross-border contract, the national legal regime of any single country becomes inadequate to tackle the situation. When the parties to the contract are located in different countries, at least two systems of law comes into picture to deal with transactions. The best way to ensure the application of a particular legal system to international contracts is to choose a particular law to govern this contract. This law is called the "Proper Law of the Contract". The courts have held that "Proper Law" is the law which is acceptable to both the parties.

Indian Courts—Choice of Law

When the parties in the contract make choice of law, the Indian courts have always recognized such choice of proper law. In the US, though courts generally honour the law chosen by the parties, the same was limited due to the holding that there should be some "reasonable relationship" between the transaction and the chosen law. This created some uncertainty. This legal quandary was fully removed by the New York General Obligations Law, (NYGOL), which became effective on 19th July, 1984. However, Indian courts have upheld laws chosen by the parties.

Under Indian law, parties are free to stipulate their terms of contract and lay down the law by which the contract is to be governed. Courts in India have held that the intention of parties would decide as to the law of which country would govern the Contract and which court would have jurisdiction. Sections 13, 15 and 44A of the Indian Civil Procedure Code and Section 41 of the Indian Evidence Act, govern the conclusiveness and enforcement of foreign judgments in India. If there is a reciprocal arrangement between India and the foreign country whose judgment is sought to be enforced, then under Section 44A of the Indian Civil Procedure Code the said foreign Decree could be executed as if it were a Decree passed by the Indian court without the need to file a suit. If there is no reciprocal arrangement between the foreign country concerned and India, then the said Judgment/Decree can be enforced in India by filing a suit on the foreign judgment.

Guidelines for International Contracts

Companies enter into international contracts, as they are always profitable. The following aspects should be considered while entering into international contracts, which would safeguard the interests of all the parties to the contract:

- There should be an express choice of law governing the contracts.
- Court recognizes the law chosen as the proper law for enforcement.
- In cases where contracts are signed in a country which is different from the country whose law is chosen, it should be ensured that the formal requirements of that place of contract are fulfilled in all respects.
- Where the chosen law is Indian law and if Indian judgment is to be enforced on any foreign soil, ensure that the said foreign soil has a similar law on the lines of Section 44A of the Indian Civil Procedure Code.
- Where arbitration is chosen as the method of dispute resolution, the place of arbitration and other aspects have to be properly determined.

BUSINESS GOALS

In best-of-breed outsourcing contracts, these business goals will be reflected in carefully structured and negotiated terms involving pricing, quality, risk management, process design, termination and privacy rights.

Pricing structure

It will shift from FTE-based compensation to transaction-based compensation. This shift will depend on increasingly automated or structured service delivery models.

Quality assurance

It shows up in many clauses. These cover process transformation, service transition, training requirements for externally-facing service agents, process integration and improvement (leading to complex issues relating to intellectual property streams), and sole source liability of vendors for process integration. Enforceability of QA clauses requires careful vendor selection and drafting.

Risks

Every outsourcing agreement will contain provisions to allocate risks. Ordinary commercial risks include certain legal compliance, performance measurement, exchange rate fluctuations and human resources life-cycles. Extraordinary risks include force majeure, disaster-recovery services, third-party litigation and major shifts in market dynamics for both the service provider and the enterprise customer. Outsourcing contracts need to map out and allocate emerging risks in both ordinary and extraordinary categories.

Process design needs management

Intellectual property conflicts increasingly pitch the enterprise customer's desire to own and exclusively control the proprietary processes (and improvements made during the outsourcing relationship) that it has historically used against the service provider's desire to build a library of re-usable business processes that support the enterprise customer's entire industry. As seen in the ERP software suites, long-term efficiency might be best serviced by permitting some form of standardization on processes, particularly those that are mandated by law or accounting rules.

Terminations

The contracts need to set up a plan for post-termination transitions. This will require greater attention to portability of services for future consumption. The termination plan needs to be ready for implementation midstream; so phase analysis (with appropriate financial charges) should be built into the contract.

Individuals need protections of privacy rights

Privacy and data protection continue to be the fulcrum for political activism and compliance risk. Protectionism for labour may persist, but protectionism for personal data and privacy will get more traction. It may no longer be enough to simply exclude any third-party beneficiary rights.

Regulatory issues

A review of legislative, regulatory and political issues in the past suggests that there will be more regulation of both outsourcing and offshoring. However, the following key issues will be covered:

- Whether offshoring violates privacy rights under local law where the data is subjected to processing;
- Whether, for enforcement, clear privacy rights, laws and criminal sanctions will be applicable;
- Whether offshoring to a foreign country that has anti-terrorist laws will violate the domestic law on personal privacy;
- Whether importation of services is subject to special taxes;
- Whether enterprise customers or their service providers will own derivative works and how collaboration can be structured so that both protect their vital business interests;
- Whether employment rights, including pension rights, are honoured by the employers; and

- Whether the degree to which service providers are to be regulated as such, to protect regulated industries; insurance of risks in outsourcing, particularly in regulated industries.

SERVICE-LEVEL MANAGEMENT IN OUTSOURCING

Service-level management consists of defining, measuring and managing service levels to conform to the contractual requirements. Service Level Agreements (SLAs) establish the guidelines that govern the delivery of the managed services. In case of a call centre, the time for response is a typical SLA. In information technology, server uptime is a key SLA. When designing SLAs, enterprise customers should consider the impact of having the outsourcing service provider drive its quality of service solely in terms of the contractual SLAs. The terms and conditions of the agreement should therefore integrate with the SLAs to fill in gaps and adopt policies.

INDIAN LABOUR LAWS APPLICABLE TO BPOs

The following are the employment related labour laws applicable to commercial establishments, located within the limits notified by Government of Maharashtra and functioning as BPOs, Software Companies and IT Companies under its jurisdiction.

The Bombay Shops and Establishments Act, 1948

The Software, IT Companies and BPOs are covered under 'Commercial Establishments' defined under this Act. Chapter VI of the Bombay Shops and Establishments Act, 1948 covers work timings for young persons and women in a commercial establishment. The Section 33(3) states that no woman shall be required or allowed to work in an establishment after 9:30 pm. The Schedule II of this Act under Exemption No. 476 (for Software and IT establishments) including Customer Service Care Center operating through Computer in the state of Maharashtra states that Section 33(3) shall be subject to the following:

- As per this Act the employer must make special arrangement for protection of female employees working before 6:00 am and after 8:30 pm including transport.
- Female employees should be provided jobs jointly or in groups.
- Arrangement for rest rooms and lockers should be made for woman employees.

Section 34 A of this Act states that no young person or woman working in any establishment, whether as an employee or otherwise, shall be required or allowed to perform such work as may be declared by the State Government by notification in the Official Gazette, to be work involving danger to life, health or morals.

The Minimum Wages Act, 1948

The Minimum Wages Act applies to Commercial Establishments as the employees of a Commercial Establishment fall within Entry 17 of the Schedule to the Act. This Act applies to any person employed in a commercial establishment as defined in the Bombay Shops and Establishments Act, 1948. However, as the salary of employees in Commercial Establishment is normally quite high, compliance with the Act is usually not a problem.

The Employment Exchanges (Compulsory Notification of Vacancies) Act, 1959

This Act applies to establishments, which operate in the private sector, hence Commercial Establishments are covered. However, the Act will only apply in a Commercial Establishment where ordinarily 25 or more persons are employed to work for remuneration. The Act mandates that, in the event of a notification to that effect by the appropriate Government (Government of Maharashtra in Maharashtra), a private sector establishment before filling up any vacancy in any employment in that establishment shall notify that vacancy to such employment exchanges as may be prescribed.

The Employees' Provident Fund and Miscellaneous Provisions Act, 1952

This covers the statutory rules for 'Provident Fund' applicable to commercial establishments. The Act applies to any establishment employing twenty or more persons and it is the employer's responsibility to ensure compliance of the provisions under Provident Fund Act.

The Maternity Benefit Act, 1961

The Maternity Benefit Act applies to any establishment in which 10 or more persons are employed, or were employed, on any day of the preceding 12 months. In this Act the portion describing applicability of the Act uses the word 'persons' and not 'women', meaning that it is not necessary that there must be a minimum of 10 women in an establishment for the Act to apply, only 10 persons, including at least one woman. This Act is for the benefit of working women who are pregnant, or have given birth or suffered a miscarriage. The employment of women in such establishments for certain periods before and after child birth regulates under this Act. The women will be entitled to maternity benefits as per the provisions of the Act.

The Payment of Gratuity Act, 1972

The Payment of Gratuity Act applies to any establishment in which ten or more persons are employed, or were employed, on any day of the preceding twelve months. It provides for the payment of gratuity to an employee, after he has rendered continuous service for not less than five years, on his superannuation, retirement or resignation, or on his death or disablement due to accident or disease. The five year continuous work requirement is not necessary if service is terminated due to death or disease, and upon death, the gratuity is paid to the nominee of the deceased employee.

The Payment of Bonus Act, 1965

In Maharashtra, the Payment of Bonus Act applies to commercial establishments with 10 or more employees on any day during that accounting year. The Act lays down a scheme for the calculation of bonus for the employees, as well as payment of maximum and minimum bonus, deductions from bonus, etc. The Act provides for filing of various returns.

The Employees Compensation Act, 1923

Under Bombay Shops and Establishments Act of 1948, Section 38A states that the provisions of the Employee's Compensation Act, 1923 (VIII of 1923), and the rules made from time to time thereunder, shall, *mutatis mutandis* apply to employees of an establishment to which the Act applies, as if they were workmen within the meaning of the Employee's Compensation Act, 1923.

The Employees' State Insurance Act, 1948

The ESI Act applies to industries and establishments within a geographical area which has been notified by the appropriate Government as an area covered by the Act. In case a Commercial Establishment has been brought under the purview of this Act by the appropriate Government, the Act will cover employees whose compensation is up to Rupees Fifteen Thousand.

Now, if an employee is covered under the ESI Act on account of his salary being under the Rupees Fifteen Thousand cap, he is not eligible to receive benefits under The Employees Compensation Act. In a Commercial Establishment, therefore, employees who are below the Rupees Fifteen Thousand cap shall be eligible to benefits under the ESI Act and those above, shall be covered by the Employees Compensation Act.

The Industrial Employment (Standing Orders) Act, 1946

The Industrial Employment (Standing Orders) Act, 1946 covers establishment wherein 50 or more workmen are employed on any working day. The Act provides for model service rules which are applicable to Employees falling within a definition of 'Workman' under Industrial Disputes Act, 1947.

The Contract Labour (Regulation and Abolition) Act, 1970

The Act applies to an establishment of a principal employer in which twenty or more workmen are employed as contract labour. To constitute the number of 20 contract labour, not only the workers employed by one contractor is to be counted, but the total number of contract labour engaged by different contractors have to be counted. Under Section 7 of the Act, a principal employer has to obtain registration, even when the establishment engages less than 20 contract labour through one contractor, but engages 20 or more contract labour through different contractors. This Act is also applicable in case if the commercial establishment employees through a service provider for carrying out various jobs such as security, cleaning, loading and unloading services, etc. The registration of establishment under this Indian employment law is mandatory. The principle employer is responsible for payment of wages and all statuary compliances. This Act shall apply to housekeepers hired by the establishment for upkeep of the premises and other menial duties.

The Equal Remuneration Act, 1976

The Act is applicable to commercial establishments. It provides that employers cannot discriminate against men and women in matters of recruitment. According to this Act it is the duty of employer to pay equal remuneration to men and women workers for same work or work of a similar nature.

SUMMARY

With the economic slowdown around the world, several foreign multinationals are eyeing India as an outsourcing destination for their IT needs. Outsourcing contracts between the client and the contractor must be meticulously drawn to protect the intellectual property rights of the client. Moreover, the TP regulations must be borne in mind to determine their applicability to the contract. To avoid the filing of multiple suits, Indian law should govern the contract, which will make it quicker for the client to obtain injunctive relief in India in the event of a breach of the contract.

Legal issues mirror the business, social and political issues of international sourcing and delivery of niche business process services. The biggest legal issues stem from the biggest business issues. Hence, business executives engaged in cross-border outsourcing contracts in the global environment need to look into legal issues first to pursue multiple goals for a distributed globalizing enterprise. In this environment, modern supply chain management dictates the biggest business requirements: cost management, pricing predictability, scalability and reliability.

Review Questions

1. Which are the various legal issues in an outsourcing contract?
2. What is data security in a BPO contract and how is it addressed in India?
3. What are the guidelines for entering the international BPO contract with regard to legal issues?
4. What is 'transfer pricing' in a BPO contract and how is this issue addressed in the latest amendment issued by the Indian government?
5. Discuss various issues in protection of IPR in BPO contracts and how Indian IPR laws are helping to resolve these issues.
6. Discuss the various Indian labour laws applicable in BPO sector.

Chapter 8

BPO: Regulatory Issues

Regulatory compliance mandates are becoming increasingly pervasive and onerous in western countries. They have become the driving force in influencing affected organizations' investment areas of attention and activities; and in extreme cases, strategic direction. BPO regulations has become a new and uglier "BPR".[1]

BPO clients insist that regulations are adhered to, as this can result in business being attracted or lost. If a BPO vendor fails to comply with the required regulatory compliance provided by the client, the vendor loses out on business. As a BPO business depends on outsourcing from customers in international markets, then it is essential that Indian BPOs should focus on the issue of compliance to quality standards and also the prevailing government regulations in both the countries. First, they have to comply with Indian law, and then they must comply with the relevant regulation of the country and industry of the land that offshores business processes, such as COBIT for IT management, Six Sigma, ISO, COPC for quality management and Sarbanes–Oxley Act, 2002, for auditing.

INTRODUCTION

The importance of Information Technology and its potential has been realized by policymakers, and it has been noted that IT has the potential to influence extensive economic development in the country. IT is now one of the top priorities of the Indian government, and favourable policies are being formulated to extract maximum benefits from the industry. The government has initiated favourable policies for making India a BPO or IT hub. The reforms have reduced licensing requirements and made foreign technology and investment accessible to help the Indian IT and BPO industries.

In pursuance of liberalization and globalization, the Indian government has been formulating and implementing more transparent and investment-friendly policies. This is now reflecting in many areas. Till 1994, Department

1. Stan Lepeak, "The impact of regulatory compliance mandates on Business Process and IT Outsourcing", http://www.thefreelibrary.com (September 5, 2005).

of Telecom (DoT) was the sole provider of basic telecom services in India, but the new telecom policy opened the field to the private operators as well. It has made India one of the fastest-growing countries in the field of telecom. Another significant example of the liberal policy of the Indian government is the IT Act. The IT Bill passed in 2000 provides a legal framework for the recognition of electronic contracts, prevention of computer crimes, electronic filing of documents, etc.

Recognizing the importance of venture capital funding, the Ministry of Information Technology has set up a National Venture Fund for the Software and IT Industry with a corpus of ₹100 crores. The main aim of the venture capital fund is to provide venture capital to start up software firms and small IT units.

NASSCOM has been playing a crucial role in helping the IT industry achieve the IT and ITES Vision and make India far ahead of other players in the field of IT and BPO. NASSCOM has helped the government implement almost all the original recommendations of the last NASSCOM–McKinsey Report, 1999, concerning the capital markets, venture capitalists, SEBI and the Companies Act.

BPO AND COMPLIANCE

India's success in the BPO industry is largely because India is a low-cost destination with an adequate supply of qualified manpower. The BPO scenario consists of businesses that depend entirely on repeat business for growth. Clients invariably start small and strike bigger business deals over time as they develop confidence in the delivery capability of the service provider. Given this, the key differentiators are quality and the adoption of standards that are relevant in the outsourcing business.

As the BPO business depends on outsourcing from customers in international markets, it is essential that Indian BPOs should focus on the issue of compliance to quality standards and also the prevailing government regulations in both the countries. First, they have to comply with Indian law. Then, they must comply with the relevant laws of the land that offshores business processes, such as COBIT for IT management, Six Sigma, ISO, COPC for quality management and Sarbanes–Oxley Act, 2002 for auditing. Sometimes the customers may have their own unique practices that Indian BPOs must adopt. Sometimes, BPOs themselves may have designed their own process standards or may like to comply with some well-known international standards such as SOX on their own.

Compliance with government regulations and following of the industry standards may not by itself help in business growth. However, not having quality certifications can certainly come in the way of business growth. The vendor selection criteria these days for large deals specifies minimum adherence to quality standards and regulation. Compliance to regulatory frameworks such as the Sarbanes–Oxley Act by the BPO industry can act as a signal to global customers that a firm is following best industry practices for governance.

In a country like the USA, in addition to these, the BPO vendors need to comply with other regulations such as Health Insurance Probability and Accountability Act, Gramm–Leach–Bliley Act, Computer Fraud and Abuse Act, and Electronic Communication Policy Act. Similarly in the UK, the BPOs need to comply with Data Protection Act, Regulation of Investigatory Power Act, etc.

BPO REGULATIONS: INDIAN vs. GLOBAL SCENARIO

In business process outsourcing, service providers have to abide by the regulations that their clients follow. The BPO industry is driven by technology. The technology component of BPO will only increase as the industry moves from low-end services such as customer support and medical transcription to premium, high-end services—research and analytics, IT helpdesks, medical insurance processing, and media services. It is only natural that technology plays an important role in helping the average BPO vendor comply with the prevailing regulations that each outsourcing deal involves. Technology has to be put in place along with policies and procedures to ensure that there is compliance in all areas. Although most BPOs are clear about compliance as far as certifications are concerned, awareness with regard to the following spread from 2004 onwards:

- The Sarbanes–Oxley Act
- The Gramm–Leach–Bliley Act
- The EU Data Protection Act

The Indian outsourcing industry can be broadly categorized into two segments such as in-house (captive) centres and third-party providers. In case of in-house centres, outsourcing is done by of the parent organization and business processes are located at low-cost and high-skill offshore locations (like India). In this case, the central unit itself will take care of enforcing all the regulatory issues that the offshore centre is subject to. This is because captive BPO is just an extension of the business that happens to be located outside the country.

In the case of third-party outsourcing centres, the scenario is different. These organizations must have compliance with the latest quality and technological regulations in order to stay competitive in the global marketplace. Data privacy and integrity that relate to outsourcing are the biggest concerns for an offshore BPO's customers. This is especially true in the case of businesses that have IPRs (Intellectual Property Rights) to protect, or banks and others that must maintain the confidentiality of their customer records. If BPOs fail to implement the required level of information security, they lose out on business. Implementing ethical practices for client confidentiality are almost mandatory. In banking operations, outsourcing data about account holders is passed on to the BPO vendor. In this case, data is processed outside the country and hence the BPO vendor company has to follow the relevant privacy laws.

Fraud is an ever-present problem. Strong security policies have to be there in an ITES–BPO organization. The issue of client confidentiality—addresses, phone numbers, credit card information, etc.—must be addressed. This trend is assuming increased prominence as higher service quality levels become the norm. In such an environment, certification and regulatory compliance can help a BPO company to be a differentiator.

Most Indian BPO companies are BS 7799 and ISO 17799 certified. According to Ernst & Young (E&Y) and the Indo-American Chamber of Commerce (IACC) Offshore Outsourcing Survey, BS 7799 and ISO 17799 security certifications are in place at 43 per cent of surveyed BPO companies in India. E&Y confirmed that in terms of global certifications and standards, Indian BPOs are at par with the rest of the world.

On the service management front, ITIL (IT Infrastructure Library) is used as a foundation by most BPO companies. Here, Indian BPO outfits have an advantage over other industry segments that haven't caught up on this front. The effective use of ITIL means that BPOs have a comparatively easier time in catching up with upcoming standards such as BS 15000 and the COBIT (Control Objectives for Information and related Technology) framework. On the quality accreditation front, an E&Y–IACC survey found that ISO 9000 is the most popular quality standard followed by COPC and Six Sigma.

Even after certification, Indian BPO companies have to catch up on the regulations front. The principal regulations that affect Indian BPOs are:

- COBIT
- British Standard 7799
- ISO/IEC 17799 (Data privacy policy)
- The Sarbanes–Oxley Act
- The Healthcare Insurance Portability and Accountability Act (HIPAA)
- The Gramm–Leach–Bliley Act, 1999 (GLBA)
- The UK Data Protection Act (DPA)
- The Fair Debt Collection Practices Act (FDCPA)
- The US–EU Safe Harbour Agreement.

COBIT

It is an IT governance framework and supporting tool set that allows managers to bridge the gap between control requirements, technical issues and business risks. COBIT enables clear policy development and good practice for IT control throughout organizations. COBIT emphasizes regulatory compliance, helps organizations to increase the value attained from IT, enables alignment and simplifies implementation of the COBIT framework.

British Standard 7799

The British Standard 7799, is the most widely recognized security standard in the world. May 1999, edition included many enhancements and improvements on previous versions. In December 2000, it was republished again, and evolved into ISO17799. It is comprehensive in its coverage of security issues. It contains a significant number of control requirements, some extremely complex. Compliance with BS7799 is consequently far from trivial task, even for the most security conscious of organizations. Full certification can be even more daunting.

ISO/IEC 17799 (Data privacy policy)

It establishes guidelines and general principles for initiating, implementing, maintaining, and improving information security management in an organization. The objectives outlined provide general guidance on the commonly accepted goals of information security management. ISO/IEC 17799:2005 contains best practices of control objectives and controls in the areas of information security management, security policy, organization of information security, asset management, human resources security, physical and environmental security, communications and operations management, access control, information systems acquisition, development and maintenance, information security incident management, business continuity management and compliance. The control objectives and controls in ISO 17799:2005 are intended as a common basis and practical guideline for developing organizational security standards and effective security management practices, and to help build confidence in inter-organizational activities.

The Sarbanes-Oxley Act

An act passed by the US Congress in 2002 to protect investors from the possibility of fraudulent accounting activities by corporations. The Sarbanes-Oxley Act (SOX) mandated strict reforms to improve financial disclosures from corporations and prevent accounting fraud. SOX was enacted in response to the accounting scandals in the early 2000s. Scandals such as Enron, Tyco, and WorldCom shook investor confidence in financial statements and required an overhaul of regulatory standards. The legislation came into force in 2002 and introduced major changes to the regulation of financial practice and corporate governance. Named after Senator Paul Sarbanes and Representative Michael Oxley, who were its main architects, it also set a number of deadlines for compliance. Some sections of the act are more pertinent to compliance than others such as: Sections 302, 401, 404, 409 and 802.

The Health Insurance Portability and Accountability Act (HIPAA)

It was passed by Congress in 1996. HIPAA provides the ability to transfer and continue health insurance coverage for millions of American workers and their families, when they change or lose their jobs; reduces health care, fraud and abuse. It mandates industry-wide standards for health care information on electronic billing and other processes; and requires the protection and confidential handling of protected health information.

The HIPAA Privacy regulations require health care providers and organizations, as well as their business associates, develop and follow procedures that ensure the confidentiality and security of Protected Health Information (PHI) when it is transferred, received, handled, or shared. This applies to all forms of PHI, including paper, oral, and electronic, etc. Furthermore, only the minimum health information necessary to conduct business is to be used or shared.

The Gramm-Leach-Bliley Act, 1999 (GLBA)

GLBA first established a requirement to protect consumer financial information. Financial services regulations on information security, initiated by the GLBA, require financial institutions in the United States to create an information security program to:

- Ensure the security and confidentiality of customer information;
- Protect against any anticipated threats or hazards to the security or integrity of such information;
- Protect against unauthorized access to/use of customer information that could result in substantial harm or inconvenience to any customer.

The Gramm-Leach-Bliley Act requires financial institutions and companies that offer consumers financial products or services like loans, financial or investment advice, or insurance to explain their information-sharing practices to their customers and to safeguard sensitive data. The Act consists of three sections: the Financial Privacy Rule, which regulates the collection and disclosure of private financial information; the Safeguards Rule, which stipulates that financial institutions must implement security programs to protect such information; and the Pretexting provisions, which prohibit the practice of pretexting (accessing private information using false pretenses). The Act also requires financial institutions to give customers written privacy notices that explain their information-sharing practices.

The UK Data Protection Act

This Act sets out rules for processing personal information. It gives certain rights to individuals and it also says that those who record and use personal information must adhere to eight data protection principles. The

Data Protection Act controls how your personal information is used by organizations, businesses or the government. Everyone who is responsible for using data has to follow strict rules called *data protection principles*. They must make sure the information is:

- used fairly and lawfully
- used for limited, specifically stated purposes
- used in a way that is adequate, relevant and not excessive accurate
- kept for no longer than is absolutely necessary
- handled according to people's data protection rights
- kept safe and secure
- not transferred outside the UK without adequate protection

There is stronger legal protection for more sensitive information, such as:

- ethnic background
- political opinions
- religious beliefs
- health
- sexual health
- criminal records

The Fair Debt Collection Practices Act (FDCPA)

FDCPA, became effective in March 1978, was designed to eliminate abusive, deceptive, and unfair debt collection practices. It also protects reputable debt collectors from unfair competition and encourages consistent state action to protect consumers from abuses in debt collection. A creditor may seek to collect an outstanding debt in several ways. For example, the creditor may attempt to collect the debt through direct communications with the debtor, by filing a lawsuit against the debtor, by seeking to take possession of or to sell property securing the debt, or by hiring a debt collection service. Faced with "abundant evidence of the use of abusive, deceptive, and unfair debt collection practices by many debt collectors, The FDCPA applies only to the collection of debt incurred by a consumer primarily for personal, family, or household purposes. It does not apply to the collection of corporate debt or debt owed for business or agricultural purposes.

The FDCPA broadly prohibits a debt collector from using 'any false, deceptive, or misleading representation or means in connection with the collection of any debt. The FDCPA provides debtors with a means for challenging payoff demands, and for determining the validity and accuracy of asserted debts.

The US-EU Safe Harbour Agreement

It is a streamlined process for the US companies to comply with the EU Directive 95/46/EC on the protection of personal data. It is intended for organizations within the EU or US that store customer data, the Safe Harbour Principles are designed to prevent accidental information disclosure or loss. US companies can opt into the program as long as they adhere to the following seven principles[2] outlined in the Directive:

Notice: Individuals must be informed that their data is being collected and about how it will be used.

Choice: Individuals must have the ability to opt out of the collection and forward transfer of the data to third parties.

Onward transfer: Transfers of data to third parties may only occur to other organizations that follow adequate data protection principles.

Security: Reasonable efforts must be made to prevent loss of collected information.

Data integrity: Data must be relevant and reliable for the purpose it was collected for.

Access: Individuals must be able to access information held about them, and correct or delete it if it is inaccurate.

Enforcement: There must be effective means of enforcing these rules.

Most of these relate to Indian BPOs' biggest clients located in the US and the UK. Although the percentage of Indian BPO companies that are compliant with these regulations is not many, the majority of them are partially compliant on the technology front.

As regards India, the main law or regulation that affects BPO companies is the Indian IT Act, 2000. Other legal regulations that affect this sector are:

- The Indian Penal Code
- The Consumer Protection Act, 1986
- The Indian Contract Act, 1972
- The Specific Relief Act, 1963
- The Indian Copyright Act, 2000
- The Patent Act, 2005.

The required technology compliance for BPO companies is limited to copyright, patents and data security. These are easily fulfilled as most of these companies comply with BS 7799 and ISO 17799, that have the required mechanisms built in.

Each regulation requires a different strategy to handle it, due to the differing levels of complexity and coverage areas. There is no single all-encompassing strategy. However, the basic strategies followed by these companies are similar. The first strategy is to have clearly documented policies and procedures. This helps satisfy the client and the certifying or regulatory authority. It also helps the organization approach new business opportunities with a greater degree of confidence and comfort.

2. http://export.gov/safeharbor/, EU Directive 95/46/EC on the protection of personal data.

The knowledge of compliance policies has to go right down from the top management to the operational management. Organizations can achieve this through regular training and other means like online training over the Intranet, poster campaigns, awareness programmes, etc.

BPO companies emphasize data security and integrity. Extensive security policies and proper configuration right from access level control for data to configuring firewalls and IDS systems is essential here. These are complemented by regular audit and review mechanisms. Audits need to be done at regular intervals by the internal IT team as well as by third-party auditors. Reviews and modifications of the policies are also required to be done regularly. The specific compliance initiatives of most BPOs basically include the following:

- Assessing internal controls
- Managing and optimizing financial reporting processes
- Consolidating information for managing business performance
- Improving business intelligence
- Providing models for managing high-risk operations
- Improving records management and auditing process
- Ensuring fraud detection and prevention.

Some of the main certifying authorities or agencies used by Indian BPO organizations are:

- BSI (British Standards Institute)
- DNV (Det Norske Veritas)
- STQC (Standardization Testing Quality Certification), Government of India
- KPMG
- Ernst & Young.

In terms of technology regulations and certifications are largely built on ITIL, which forms the basis of most BPO infrastructure. Therefore, compliance should not be too difficult for most of these organizations.

The first technology framework becoming mandatory is COBIT (Control Objectives for Information and related Technology). It includes the best practices for IT governance, control and assurance. There will be increasing adoption of COBIT in the near future. BS 15000 is yet another standard that shows signs of becoming mandatory soon. This is the first global standard for service management, and it is basically an integrated set of management services for service provision. It will be required by BPOs that cater to European clients. Many of the Indian BPOs are already gearing up to achieve BS 15000. CISP (Cardholder Information Security Program) will soon be required for BPO firms that handle credit card information.

DOT RESTRICTIONS

The guidelines recently instituted by the Department of Telecom (DoT) for new long-distance licences and amendments to the existing ones have incorporated specific restrictions on remote access, traffic and transfer of any information outside India. These guidelines have created concerns for the rapid-growth BPO sector, and prospective telecom network operators are worried that these unprecedented conditions would turn India into a "blind spot" in the global communications network map. DoT recently cut entry barriers for STD, ISD by reducing the entry fee from ₹125 crores to ₹5 crores and revenue share from eight per cent to six per cent. It abolished roll-out obligations. It also combined virtual private network licences with long-distance ones. However, the new restrictions defeat the idea of encouraging greater investment and entry of new operators.

The guidelines lay down restrictions on traffic between two subscribers within India being hauled to any place outside India and transfer of accounting, network or user information. Remote access for networks to any equipment manufacturer or agency outside has also been prohibited, except during catastrophic software failure. The latter condition is similar to the one imposed earlier in 74 per cent FDI guidelines. With these restrictions in place, the operations of call centre companies will be impacted as the core of their work involves information exchange regarding international subscribers with Indian BPOs. The entire call centre value chain is integrated with global networks and sees round-the-clock, seamless transfer of information. These steps could also halt the business that companies like Reliance Infocom, Bharti and VSNL conduct in conjunction with global service providers. Most foreign investors, BPOs and Indian banks use high-speed telecom networks that are integrated in their global network plan. However, Indian companies possessing long-distance licences in other parts of the world, including the USA, do not face any such restriction.

CUSTOMS RULES FOR EOUs AND IT PARKS

The government has simplified customs procedures for registration of export-oriented units (EOUs), electric hardware technology parks and software technology parks for clearance of imported goods. The finance ministry has issued a circular under which these units and technology parks will now be required to submit only six documents instead of the earlier twenty five, along with the application for registration. The circular requires the customs authorities to grant registration to EOUs within five working days from the receipt of the application. This provision would considerably reduce the time-period of granting registration from the present period of nearly one month. The certificate of registration would be issued by the assistant commissioner or the deputy commissioner. The ministry has also done away with the formalities of repeated registration of these units with various ports, as is the practice at present. These measures would help EOUs in early registration with the customs authorities and in simplification of procedures.

PROPERTY TAX SOPS FOR IT FIRMS FOR ROAD PROJECTS

In an effort to boost infrastructure development within India's emerging Silicon City, Pune, the Pune Municipal Corporation (PMC) has become the first municipal body in the country to offer property tax sops to IT companies if they invest in road development. Under the IT policy adopted by the state government in 2003, local municipal bodies have been given freedom to provide rebate in property tax to the IT sector, provided it invests in the city's infrastructure. Taking advantage of the policy, PMC is offering a 75 per cent rebate in property tax to the developers of all the IT parks if approved by the state government as an IT park. Under the scheme, promoters of an IT park can undertake the development of roads which are proposed in the development plan of the city and which will provide connectivity to the IT park.

INCOME TAX

To make India as an attractive outsourcing destination hub for the foreign countries, the latest announcement by the Ministry of Finance is that foreign companies offshoring business process to India would not subject to income tax. The new circular details out the principle for taxation of captive ITES/ BPO units in India. As per the draft circular an Indian company is liable to be taxed at arm's length for activities performed by it, while no further income would be deemed to accrue or arise to the foreign principles irrespective of the nature of activities (incidental or core) performed in India.

PRIVACY LAWS

As there is no adequate protection in India to personal confidential information, this is a very critical issue in financial and accounting outsourcing to the service providers located in this country. This is particularly true when a large number of US citizens have started sending their confidential information like social security numbers, salary and income details, income tax returns or credit card numbers to the BPO firms in India during the last few years. Hence, there is a fear amongst the regulators in the USA that in absence of proper privacy laws in India, there is 'identity theft' resulting in rampant misuse of individual information, leading to huge risks in sending personal information to Indian BPOs. The US-based CFPs (Chartered Financial Planners) who are involved in financial and accounting outsourcing should tell their local clients that their sensitive documents are likely to be sent to the BPO in India for processing purpose. It is being made mandatory on the part of CFPs in the USA to reveal these facts.

REGULATIONS IN OTHER COUNTRIES

Due to the anti-outsourcing moves in the USA, a number of protectionist measures are under way to support Buy American Improvement Act 1933. So far, 60 anti-offshoring bills have been passed in 2002–03 by 20 US states for barring outsourcing of government contracts. It does not stop with state-level bills however; both the US Central Intelligence Agency and the General Accounting Office are working on reports to study how offshoring poses a threat to the economic and national security of the USA. The bills passed at the state level have not had much of an impact on Indian BPO business because government contracts, both state and federal, account for less than one per cent of the total outsourcing done out of the country. However, the impact may be much more if the US government decides to stop outsourcing in sectors like health care, energy, utilities, financial services and telecom. In a nutshell, the scenario is as follows:

- There is a tendency to give preferential treatment to local companies while bidding for government contracts.
- No total ban on Indian firms, but they will have to compete with 'preferred' bidders.
- Buy American Improvement Act is strangling offshoring of US jobs in manufacturing and services.

STANDARDIZED TEST FOR BPO JOBS

The BPO and IT-enabled services business in India will have its own standardized test soon.[3] The test is called the BPO Skills Assessment Test (BSAT). This has been devised and will be administered by an autonomous body called the Board for IT Education Standards (BITES).

The BSAT, which has been devised on the lines of standardized tests like GMAT and SAT, will assess various skills and turnout scores that could be used by BPO and IT-enabled services companies to rate potential employees. BITES is a non-profit society set up two years ago by the Government of Karnataka and the IT industry in partnership with the local academia, and comprises representatives from the government, educational and industry bodies, and the state's education secretary, IT secretary, Vice Chancellor of Visveswariah Technological University, Director of Indian Institute of Information Technology Bangalore, and Director of National Centre for Software Technology.

3. Priya Ganapati, www.rediff.com/money/2003/jun/12bpo.htm, June 12, 2003.

The BSAT test will check for communication skills, grammar, clarity, accent, logical reasoning, quantitative skills and keyboard skills. "Companies can ask potential employees their BSAT score and keep a certain score as the cutoff level for their organization. So only those who score above it can appear for the interview. This will greatly bring down recruitment costs for companies".

TAXING BPO

Business process outsourcing has seen an unprecedented growth in India. For further boost, this sector needs fiscal encouragement as well as political protection. The Central Board of Direct Taxes (CBDT), in a circular issued in 2004, laid down the circumstances under which BPO units will attract tax in India.

As per the circular, when a foreign firm outsources the whole or part of its core revenue-generating business activities to an IT-enabled entity in India, and the entity renders services to customers abroad, a considerable portion of the profit derived by the foreign firm from its customers abroad will be attributable to the activities performed by the IT-enabled entity in India. Such profit will be liable to tax in India in accordance with the Income Tax Act or the relevant tax treaty.

The circular, however, clarified that the question of tax in India would arise only when the BPO unit created a "permanent establishment" in India. The circular also said that if the BPO activity generated insignificant profit, which was difficult to determine, there would be no tax in India except on the direct income of the BPO unit. According to the circular, BPO activities in India should not attract any tax on the foreign company's income through the Indian BPO units, in the following cases:

- Where a non-resident carries on manufacture and sale of goods or merchandise or provision of services outside India, but outsources some of its incidental activities;
- Where a foreign firm manufacturing computers abroad, and also selling such computers to customers abroad, engages or sets up a call centre in India to procure orders from or concludes contracts with customers abroad and to answer sales-related queries on telephone.
- Where a foreign insurance firm insuring risks in countries other than India appoints or sets up a call centre in India to attend to calls from customers outside India, while actual policy issuance as well as collection of premium is done outside India.
- Where a foreign credit card company issuing credit cards to customers in countries other than India appoints or sets up a call centre in India to attend to the calls of customers, while the actual card issue, the delivery of the card and collection of charges is done outside India.

In these cases, no effort will be made to allocate any profit derived by the foreign enterprise from its customers abroad to the Indian BPO unit, provided that the charges paid to the Indian BPO unit for its services are at arm's length or fair market price. The Indian BPO unit will of course be liable to pay tax in India on its direct profits.

On the other hand, the CBDT considers that a considerable portion of the profits derived by the foreign firm from their customers abroad will be attributable to the activities performed by the IT-enabled entity in India for services relating to travel agents, software developers, software maintenance, investment consultants, and debt collection.

The circular, however, specifies that tax in India will become chargeable only where the foreign firm outsources the whole or part of its core revenue generating business activities to India, and further, if the Indian BPO unit constitutes the foreign enterprises' permanent establishment in India as per the provisions of the relevant tax treaty.

TAX DEDUCTION AT SOURCE (TDS)

Large manufacturing companies having patents and copyrights and outsourcing their manufacturing activities need to have tax deduction at source (TDS). The goods manufactured under an outsourced contract cannot be treated in terms of simple purchases. Similarly, companies getting their packaging material or labels manufactured under their brand names also come under the TDS clause of the Income Tax Act.

REGULATIONS—AMENDMENTS

The following have been permitted under the "Other Service Provider (OSP)" category, effective November 2, 2005:

1. The use of Internet telephony by the call centres is allowed to the extent it is permitted by the ISPs. The call centre operator may or may not use Internet telephony depending on their business considerations.
2. Sharing of the common infrastructure between domestic and international OSP centres has been further liberalized. The following are the main features:
   - No turnover restriction has been imposed. The company shall have 50 seats or more set up for the call centre.
   - Condition of "non-captive use" for the sharing of infrastructure has been removed.
   - OSP will have two options for sharing of common infrastructure:
     - Option 1: Separate and independent EPABX to be used for international and domestic OSP centres with sharing of the same operator position.

- A bank guarantee of ₹2.5 crores.
- Only one call shall be offered to the operator position at a time (be it domestic or international, incoming or outgoing).
  - Option 2: International and domestic OSP centres to share the common EPABX with logical partitioning.
- A bank guarantee of ₹5 crores
- The company shall submit a certificate from the vendors of the EPABX that the software is capable of logically bifurcating the common infrastructure into two separate and independent environments for the domestic OSP and international OSP centres.
- In case of violation of OSP terms and conditions, the following actions shall be taken:
  - Cancellation of OSP registration held by the company will be carried out. The company shall be debarred from obtaining OSP registration for 3 years from the date of cancellation of such registration.
  - The Directors of the Board of a company violating OSP terms and conditions shall be debarred for 3 years from taking, directly or indirectly, OSP registration.

3. Stand-alone domestic tele-marketing centres, i.e., those without any leased-line connectivity, have been permitted to make outgoing calls without any bank guarantee. The company would ensure that it does not infringe on the privacy and cause annoyance to the public at large and will follow the law of the land in this regard. Further, the marketing calls may be made only during normal working hours and in case a person does not want to be called, the company may enter such numbers in their database and ensure that calls are not made to such numbers.
4. Department of Telecommunications has agreed to permit, on case-to-case basis, subject to the submission of a bank guarantee of ₹10 lakhs in favour of the Department of Telecommunications, making outgoing calls from a domestic call centre using the local PSTN connections through the PABX of the domestic call centre. Leased lines will not be used for making outgoing calls.

   (*Note:* The above arrangement would facilitate the making of outgoing calls by the call centre agent, using the separate local PSTN line which is permitted to be terminated on the EPABX of the domestic call centre. This local PSTN line which will be used for making outgoing calls will not be connected in any way to the leased lines of the call centres or the incoming-only lines.)

5. For the foreign-end connectivity in the international call centre, use of ATM/MPLS/Frame Relay-based Managed International Networks is permitted in addition to the existing provision of connectivity through point-to-point IPLC. In order to make available to the Indian call centre industry the benefit of the latest technology, thereby making business more cost-effective and giving the industry an edge over other countries, the following has been permitted:

   To allow the international call centres to have foreign-end connectivity through ATM/MPLS/Frame Relay-based Managed International Networks in addition to the existing provision of connectivity through point-to-point IPLC. Accordingly, Para 1.2 of Part (1) of the terms and conditions of the registration for international call centres (Department of Telecommunication, Government of India) is being amended to:

   > The International Call Centre set up by the Other Service Provider (OSP) will be connected to foreign end Point of Presence (POP) by International Private Leased Circuits (IPLCs) and/or using technologies like ATMs/Frame Relay/MPLS in Managed International Networks provided by Authorized Service Providers.

De-constraining

Earlier, some regulatory restrictions prevented BPOs from claiming tax benefits when serving both international and Indian customers. Restrictive regulations such as these have now been removed. One of the enabling aspects of the India's regulatory environment has been de-constraining the Factory Act by allowing female workers to work at night shift. The emphasis of international regulations has mainly been on the privacy and data security aspects of the BPO business. The no-call list in the USA and the HIPPA standard for the health care industry are two prime examples of this regulatory trend.

IT MANAGEMENT STANDARDS

Amongst the IT Management Standards COBIT is a major one. It identifies certain control parameters and dependencies on IT resources, and puts certain practices in place. Any organization becoming more complex from the IT point of view needs to have some kind of COBIT compliance. However, one may not replicate the exact COBIT standard in the organization. Many IT vendors are now creating information structure management software compliant to these standards. For example, HP Open View is based on the ITSM COBIT standards.

The quality standards that Indian BPOs have adopted represent a mix of issues that the BPOs must address. Some are standards that directly affect the quality of service offered by the service providers, including COPC, ISO and Six Sigma. In addition, Indian BPOs have adopted standards that create a more enabling agenda, though peripheral to the quality of the final service offered. Under this category are the ones such as COBIT, ITSM and BS7799. Furthermore, many organizations are adopting procedures such as 'Whitehat Hacking', in which ethical hackers hack and test security. Third-party BPOs have been using these audit reports to highlight their security compliance to their customers.

As standards mature and BPOs realise the intrinsic value of each standard, there is a likelihood for some realignment in the standards that will be followed in future. Two mutually exclusive trends in the markets for standards are now seen. The first is in process compliance and the second is in outcome compliance. Standards such as COPC prescribe best practices, and root cause analysis templates specific to the BPO industry are creating increasingly complex situations that BPOs face today. Others such as the ISO standard may not be specific to the BPO industry; however, they prescribe the process and documentation aspects of ensuring quality. While there is a commitment to quality standards and regulation, an equally important aspect that BPOs must appreciate is that of cost and the extra management bandwidth that compliance demands from management. Hence there is a need to strike a balance between what the external world is demanding from BPOs and the intrinsic gains that BPOs can seek from adopting quality.

CYBER LAWS

The IT Act, 2000 is still somewhat opaque on the data protection front. There is a need for increased recognition for these standards of the BPO environment, and to create laws to prevent loopholes. Amid calls for tightening BPO regulations and more effective cyber laws, the country's call centres are busy taking adequate security measures on their own.

SUMMARY

As BPO business depends on outsourcing from customers in international markets, it is essential that Indian BPOs should focus on the issue of compliance to quality standards and also prevailing government regulations in both the countries. In business process outsourcing, service providers have to abide by the regulations that their clients follow. The BPO industry is driven by technology. The technology component of BPO will only increase as the industry moves from low-end services to high-end ones. The BPO outfits are normally expected to comply with the Sarbanes–Oxley Act, HIPAA, COBIT, GILBA, BS 7799, ISO 17799, UK Data Protection Act, etc. In fact, the compliance initiatives of most BPOs basically should include assessing internal controls, managing and optimizing financial reporting processes, consolidating information for managing business performance, improving business intelligence, providing financial models for high-risk operations and programmes to manage risk, improve records management and audit trail, ensuring fraud detection and prevention, etc.

Review Questions

1. Which regulatory compliances are needed for BPO service providers to get an outsourcing contract?
2. Discuss the various regulations that a BPO vendor in general has to comply with in the global context.
3. What are the restrictions imposed by DoT on BPO operations?
4. Discuss the various taxation regulations and their implications on BPOs in India.
5. Explain the standardized test for BPO jobs and discuss its acceptance by Indian BPOs.

Chapter 9

Service Supplier Selection

With every project, planning is key to the successful outcome. The requirements that the supplier must fulfil need to be identified, clarified and prioritized to provide a checklist against which Supplier Capability Evaluation (SCE) can be carried out to select the right supplier.[1]

Proficiency drives performance and competitiveness in the marketplace. The result of proficiency is that corporations are more successful in their marketplace and more profitable. Typical among the highest-performing companies is that they have enterprise strategies designed to support their corporate goals. One of the strategies is selection of service providers, which are best of the breed, helps business corporations to achieve their goals. Business process outsourcing promises cost savings, use of shared resources and greater process efficiencies resulting into competitiveness which is greatly impacted by supplier selection. Good BPO vendors provide reliable services by designing their solutions around client requirements and industry best practices while setting clear expectations.

INTRODUCTION

With globalization and the emergence of the extended enterprise of inter-dependent organizations, there has been a steady increase in the outsourcing of parts and services. This has led firms to give more importance to the purchasing/outsourcing function and its associated decisions. One of those decisions which impact all firms' business areas is supplier selection. Strategic partnerships are becoming more common today for firms. These new types of partnerships permit firms to compete more effectively in today's global market. Because of these new types of strategies, buyers and sellers are moving from the traditional arms-length, adversarial relationships to those based on communication and cooperation.

The cooperative relationship between business buyers and sellers has led to the reduction in the number of suppliers for some firms. As the supplier

1. Ravi Aron, Wharton Professor of Operations and Information Management.

base is reduced, the task of supplier selection becomes increasingly more important. This importance is magnified because the purchasing agent has fewer alternatives when a supplier cannot adequately perform its function. Hence, the buyer must depend more on the reliability and credibility of each individual supplier. However, selection criteria for suppliers extend beyond just these two supplier attributes. Therefore, the firm's supplier selection criteria are critical elements for business firms to succeed.

PLANNING FOR OUTSOURCING CONTRACT

The BPO contract will invariably involve multiple fears and anxieties even though the vendor choice is based on a competitive evaluation. In BPO contracts the transaction is unfamiliar and complicated, it involves critical business functions, and it goes on under top management's direct scrutiny. Hence, for the success of the BPO contract it is necessary that the contract should be more flexible and focused.

Uncertainty and anxiety are high when the vendor first takes over the outsourced function. A detailed transition provision will help to prevent early disaster and it will also lay the groundwork for a collaborative working relationship with the vendor.

It is essential that scope and service level agreements need to be defined in terms of realistic expectations and with a focus on the particular performance metrics where improvement will matter the most. In such a case the vendor will be more responsive to performance objectives that the customer has set carefully. The further changes in contract are normally incorporated in a phased manner at negotiated prices at the appropriate time.

In the planned contract, a non-adversarial and escalating dispute resolution process will keep the inevitable operational issues contained at the operations level. However, only disputes that affect the relationship as a whole should be managed with extra care. Focusing on core needs and providing in the contract for flexibility to adapt to operational disputes improve chances of a satisfactory completion of the contract.

The evaluation criteria should be based on empirical data as well as terms and conditions designed to address the most common outsourcing issues. This will help in identifying key areas of disagreement between vendor and customer.

In the mature business models, standardization can result in a formula-like approach to both vendor selection and subsequent negotiations between the parties. Such an approach can cause the parties to quickly lose sight of the inherent nature of an outsourcing relationship as a long-term strategic alliance to achieve specific business goals. A failure to address an outsourcing relationship in a collaborative way can have unpleasant consequences, resulting in damage to the relationship forever. Hence, it is necessary to include clarity, flexibility and realistic goals in an outsourcing agreement. Each requires that the parties communicate, collaborate and come to mutual agreement as to the purpose of the relationship.

A failure to describe the services in sufficient detail and with clarity will result in pricing issues, impacting the ultimate success of the project. Hence the parties should establish a practical governance model for regular communication on operational, financial, and performance issues, as well as the resolution of disputes. The most effective governance model is one that uses incentives to encourage the parties to resolve disputes in a timely manner and avoid unilateral personnel changes. The managements from both sides should empower team members to make timely decisions, with a certain accepted level of mistakes. The parties should define clear and objective metrics that reflect the underlying business goals but are stated in a manner that is time-based and quantifiable. Benchmarking may be used as a tool to provide necessary flexibility to environmental factors.

EXPECTATIONS FROM VENDORS

For remaining competitive in the industry, one needs suppliers or service providers that are the best in their particular industry. Flexibility is one component of a successful relationship. It is, therefore, critical that service suppliers are able to respond accordingly, particularly when the demands are fluctuating. For supporting an outsourcer, suppliers should take ownership of all aspects of the products and services that they provide and to show a willingness to provide support, responsiveness, and expertise as and when required.

The vendor should continually strive to increase quality and service while lowering costs. Vendor should share awareness and thus demonstrate that their processes and procedures support a lower total cost of ownership to their customers.

Vendors should have commitment to environmental conservation while implementing internal processes. Thus will result in the conservation of natural resources. The following key factors need to be considered when selecting a supplier or service provider:

- Quality of the product or service provided
- Competitive prices
- On-time, cost-effective delivery of products
- Technology infrastructure
- Demographics
- Financial strength
- Experience
- Environmental consciousness.

In those cases, where the complexity and the amount of money involved in the intended outsourcing project are high, bidders should make a formal presentation before a cross-functional selection team of the customer.

PERFORMANCE: MEASURES AND TARGETS

Performance measurement is essential for management control. This is a critical area of the process that drives the BPO project where one can benefit from the use of vendor's services to save time and cost, and minimize risk. It starts with defining exactly what the customer wants from the supplier, followed by measurement of their success and agree to it before the contract is drafted. This should include not only the technical requirements, but also time scales, milestones, budget, contingencies, rewards and penalties for any failure to deliver on time or delivery before the time schedule. The contract must draft out clearly the duties and responsibilities of both customer and vendor.

Prior to outsourcing, the organization should measure its own performance in terms of productivity, quality, and speed of delivery, so as to:

- Compare with potential suppliers and industry benchmarks
- Specify service level requirements
- Agree on targets with suppliers.

Measurement of the nature and quantum of service to be delivered and problems to be solved drive the predictive models and must be comparable with benchmark data. By estimating the functional size and likely performance of potential suppliers, independent estimates can be developed of:

- Cost
- Quality
- Staffing profiles
- Optimum delivery schedule
- Impact of delivering in shorter time scales.

Supplier Capability Evaluation is a proven method for gaining insight into the capability. It is a valuable, almost essential, decision-making tool for the management of outsourcing, because it provides a practical view of the relative merits and abilities of competing vendors. In other words, it gives a client a quantitative assessment of the risk involved with the placement of a contract.

REDUCING RISK IN BPO CONTRACT

Business process outsourcing (BPO) is always associated with risks, whether local or offshore. When one makes a decision to outsource a business process possibly involving layoffs—bringing it back in-house if it doesn't work as needed is an expensive proposition. This doesn't even take into account the public relations impact or the effect it will have on the careers of people involved in such decisions. Reducing these risks is essential to the success of the outsourcing effort. There are three kinds of risks in outsourcing:[2]

- **Operational risks.** Due to failure on quality, cost and execution time period
- **Strategic risks.** Due to intellectual property security and privacy
- **Capability risks.** Due to in-house incapability to execute such business processes.

Managing operational risk is an on-going activity that needs to be performed continuously. Strategic and capability risks to some extent can be tackled and reduced by contract terms and operational controls. However, BPO metrics provide a good framework for continuous monitoring, reporting and management of operational parameters. Factors that introduce operational risk can be broadly classified as people, technology and process risks. These factors are also highly inter-related. Good or bad performance on one front dictates good or bad performance on others. Hence a framework is proposed for identifying all related factors and then, by using appropriate metrics, mitigating these risks.

People Risks

Attrition rate affects the conduct of business processes to a great extent. So employee turnover is a key factor that predicts the success or failure of an outsourced business process. Call centres engaged in business processes like phone-based helpdesks depend upon employees showing up on time and handling their processes. Thus, high absenteeism is an important factor in enhancing the risk of increased waiting time. Also, if turnover is of concern, a constant stream of new recruits being trained is of great importance. Training also becomes essential in this case.

Technology Risks

Technology risks need to be mitigated for good operations management. It is almost always that technology integrating a company's systems with those of the service provider is involved. Service providers could be using the buyers' internal systems through a dedicated network link. Many outsourced business processes involve scanning and digitization of paper documents that are manually processed at onshore or offshore destinations. In these cases, unless a seamless computing and communication infrastructure is maintained at high levels of availability, business process execution suffers.

Service providers could have their own systems, networks and applications for providing process services. An example of this is outbound

2. Ravi Aron, Wharton Professor of Operations and Information Management.

telemarketing services, where the deliverables are qualified prospects; the service provider may invest in technology shared among many buyers of such services. Technology parameters such as system uptime, network uptime and application uptime need to be measured, so that business processes can be executed without interruptions. If a customer calls and the service provider can't access the customer relationship management system, the firm's business process suffers.

Process Risks

Process risks are a set that needs to be managed properly for ensuring minimal operational problems. Each business process has its own set of factors that are important to the buyer as well as the vendor of these services. To the BPO service provider, overall high customer satisfaction is the goal of customer-facing processes. However, other risks may be important, but are less important to the customer satisfaction goals.

The BPO vendor is interested in making sure that process risks covered by contractual obligations are addressed properly. This is because many contracts include provisions for incentives and penalties related to meeting targets. Other factors that will help them ensure that the business process is executed properly could also be monitored, irrespective of whether or not they need to disclose these to the customers. They know that if these metrics aren't met consistently, the entire contract may be in danger at some point of time.

The process risks are broadly classified into qualitative risks and quantitative risks. Qualitative risks may deal with customer satisfaction issues and are measured usually by the BPO client using customer satisfaction surveys. In non-customer-facing processes such as financial accounts finalization, qualitative risks may be linked to an assessment of how well the services were provided.

Quantitative risks broadly deal with efficiency and effectiveness of the process. They can be dealt with appropriately through appropriate choice of control parameters. Efficiency usually deals with time-related aspects of a business process. Average handle time and average hold time are good examples of efficiency metrics that deal with telephone support. Efficiency metrics may also include such items as number of loan cases handled per hour or number of claims handled per hour.

Effectiveness deals with outcomes of business processes which involve outbound or inbound selling. The percentage of outbound calls that resulted in a sale is a good example of effectiveness. Process-related factors are usually few in number, but highly relevant to the business process in question. These factors directly hit the bottomline performance of business processes such as credit card issues or insurance claims handling.

APPROACHES TO VENDOR SELECTION

There are two types of approaches—*collaborative* or *non-collaborative*—to vendor selection. The selection framework is structured in five main steps:

- Type of relationship,
- Evaluation criteria,
- Vendor selection,
- Negotiation, and
- Contracting.

However, due to vendor selection complexity, companies consider multiple criteria, either by using managerial intuition and preferences, or more formally by deploying some of the multi-criteria analysis methods.

Collaborative Approach

In the collaborative approach there is absence of preliminary formal documentation between the client and the vendors. This approach can be pursued by the client that looks for a vendor, or by a vendor that approaches a possible client. Actually, a more collaborative approach in seeking and selecting the vendor is emerging in consequence of the growth in strategic outsourcing arrangements. This approach has significant implications in the field of innovation, since the client can explore and evaluate vendor capabilities and promote common innovation. The collaborative approach can lead to the creation of the new growth platforms where strategic outsourcing becomes the link between the growth and innovation.

However, this solution requires high relationship investments and participation in the vendor selection phase for both the client and the vendor. The collaborative approach as an attempt of the client and the vendor of achieving the excellence across many parameters. This approach gives the chance to the vendor to adapt and optimize his internal business and service, while giving the client a real idea of vendor capabilities and scope for improving margin.

Non-collaborative Approach

In the *non-collaborative approach* client sends the formal request to the vendor submitting proposal. This also called *Request for Proposal* (RFP). In this way, there is no active interaction between the possible partners. This is typical transactional outsourcing arrangement to find an appropriate partner. This method is adopted since many client organizations may not have the specialized talents and capabilities to be involved in a more complex and time-requiring collaborative processes. Therefore, they prefer to use a RFP.

This is beneficiary to the client because they can compare the proposals by using a common format, hence making the vendor selection much easier.

This approach has limitation when the outsourced process becomes strategic for the client. In this case, the vendor selection phase becomes particularly critical and many times determinant for the whole outsourcing activity success. In consequence of that, a more collaborative approach with vendor is needed to share risk and promote vendor participation.

CHOOSING THE RIGHT CONTRACT PARTNER

Business process outsourcing promises cost savings, use of shared resources and greater efficiencies. However, only by having an appropriate set of choices can one ensure that the organization fully realizes the benefits of outsourcing. A systematic approach with a planning framework enables organizations to select the right factor and implement proper monitoring and analysis of business processes. In the age of outsourcing, it is critical to engage in business relationships that assure successful partnerships. Hence, high on the list of factors that result in successful BPO relationships is choosing the right partner to support an organization's business needs.

For example, FedEx has a unique supplier selection process. At FedEx, high standards for service quality from suppliers are never compromised. FedEx practices supply chain management for focusing on the lowest cost, speed-to-market, flexibility for achieving highest customer satisfaction from supplier's supplier to customer's customer. The supply chain decisions are based on total life cycle cost. FedEx identifies five principal attributes of supply chain management. These are strategy, resources, processes, optimization and globalization. FedEx selects its suppliers on the basis of their ability to meet stringent quality requirements and their ability to serve as a supply chain improvement partner. Before contacting FedEx to be a supplier, they will have to answer questions such as: Do I have a product to supply? Do I have resources to meet the quantity required? Do I have service support infrastructure? Can I bring sufficient value to FedEx to reduce total cost?[3]

Generally speaking, companies know their business needs and challenges. However, successful BPO relationships, defined by the vendor's positive impact on their customer's ability to meet their goals, is somewhat elusive in today's evolving BPO service industry. However, a failed relationship can result in millions of dollars of lost revenue, market share, and eroded customer base. Hence, it is critical to have clear criteria on which to base the decisions about partnership.

In terms of meeting clients' needs in such a relationship, it is necessary for vendors to understand those core characteristics that businesses must consider when selecting a BPO partner. Towards this end, a BPO relationship should

3. http://www.fedex.com/us/supplier/selection.htm.

be viewed as a highly strategic business partnership requiring a deep union between businesses. However, in deciding upon the appropriate partner, the corporate 'culture' becomes a very real and tangible aspect of the relationship to consider. In essence, the right cultural match is likely to result in a long-term relationship characterized by contract renewals, increased revenue for all and positive corporate images within their respective industries. The reverse is equally true for a poor match.

The firm must describe those business traits that characterize the "right partner" for corporate clients. Again, the fact is that corporations are organizations of people who need to be able to maintain a high level of communication and teamwork, and be capable and willing to negotiate differences.

Integrity

A vendor company should have integrity as one of their core values. This is an indication to prospective clients that the vendor will meet a company's business needs in the most ethical and legal manner. In establishing a partnership of trust, commitments must be made by those representatives who can assure delivery on promises and are decision-makers. Face-to-face communication and regular executive involvement helps to establish the relationship that is to be formed. Open discussion of the issues and challenges on both sides of the relationship is required. Honest assessments of what is required to meet a client's needs will drive customer confidence and establish a vendor as having integrity.

Commitment

In cases where vendors are uncommitted, performance goes down, revenue slides, frustration develops and the relationship is strained. The vendors who are able to keep up the core values of the company they support and deliver the services for which they have committed are able to generate customer satisfaction, increased productivity and revenue. Furthermore, this level of commitment enables BPO partners to trust them, which serves as support when times are bad.

Willingness to Listen

When engaging clients in BPO activity, it is critical to understand the business circumstances and drivers that has made them seek this relationship. To do this, vendors must allow clients to describe their perception of their issues and challenges in detail. A good vendor partner will take the time to gather the required data that will accurately represent the corporation's business needs and requirements. The best-of-breed vendors use their industry experience to bring forward additional considerations that should be made by their customers. Successful BPO vendors provide reliable services by designing their solutions around client requirements and industry best practices while setting clear expectations.

Responsiveness

Business customers need vendor companies to have the ability to respond to client requests and needs expeditiously. Additionally, vendors must demonstrate the ability to predict potential issues, which will prevent a lot of relationship conflicts. However, when issues do arise, good BPO vendors know the importance of understanding the impact of an issue for their client and taking swift action by communicating this fact to their client. Having processes and contingency plans in place to resolve issues demonstrates a vendor's ability to react to unforeseen problems in a controlled manner. This will enhance the customer's confidence in a vendor's ability to maintain a reliable service.

The clear difference between BPO vendors is in terms of identifying potential opportunities and risks for client companies. As the business environment changes, so must rules, processes and models. Vendor companies must proactively help clients take advantage of changes in the business environment with an eye on long-term gains. Vendors who respond to contractual relationships by simply reacting to client needs do to their clients a large disservice. Vendors who provide clients with regular industry insights, updates on changing technology, market insight, and business strategy drive have taken relationships to more successful positions.

Value Addition

One of the main reasons that companies join BPO relationships is that they understand that the business function they are outsourcing is not a core competency for their organization. As such, it should be the vendor's core competency and as a result should be able to produce increased efficiency through increased innovation and process improvement. Vendors who simply replace resources and maintain existing processes are not adding enough value to the customer's organization.

Innovative vendors must evaluate and challenge existing modes of work to establish the best possible work processes for the organization they service. Given the protective tendency that clients may have about these processes, it is important to clearly understand these processes and present service improvement recommendations.

Corporations expect and desire technology innovations from BPO vendors. Vendors who recommend unproven technical solutions must recognize the risks that they bring to their client's business. Therefore, it is critical that vendors invite clients for evaluation when recommending technology solutions that address business needs.

Vendor Soundness

Long-term BPO relationships tend to be maintained with the same vendor. Vendor facing financial instability bring an increase risk to the client in the case of being acquired, business downsizing, or in the worst case, going out of business. Vendors who are financially unstable are less likely to invest in innovation, resource training and client relationship-building activities. Financial responsibility also extends to business activities that vendors take on their clients' behalf. Good vendor partners strive to keep costs of business low and demonstrate appropriate accounting procedures for the business they support.

Proficiency

World-class BPO vendors maintain resource pools which can address their customer business requirements on a daily basis. This requires vendors to continually acquire talent and train staff to meet the challenges of their clients' businesses. Having workers who are certified or hold degrees in specific areas of expertise will provide a standard of knowledge that will benefit the client. Good vendor partners will work with their clients to identify and develop those skills that make workers competent for the roles they have to perform. Demonstrating interest in the client's business further strengthens the client–vendor relationship.

SUMMARY

A company which has decided to outsource a critical business function should clearly define its business objectives. It should approach the transaction as a strategic relationship rather than a stand-alone commercial transaction, making sure the vendor has similar approach and commitment. While this approach will require a greater investment of time at the outset, the parties will establish the key building blocks necessary for a mutually beneficial and ongoing relationship. This relationship should be structured with clarity, flexibility and an agreement as to the objectives in order to achieve success.

The vendors need to demonstrate that they are the "right partners" by exhibiting consistency in corporate traits. BPO relationships are strategic partnerships; it is critical to understand corporate cultures and establish relationships that are founded on principles that support business goals. With a foundation built on these traits, BPO relationships have a greater chance in establishing long-term business relationships. Hence such contracts will provide measurable value in terms of increased competitiveness, efficiency and profit in today's challenging and diverse marketplace.

Review Questions

1. What are the expectations of business clients from BPO vendors in general?
2. What are the risks associated with BPO contracts and how are these risks addressed during contract formation?
3. Discuss the various factors which are most relevant during the selection of a right BPO service provider.
4. What is the role of performance measures and targets in the BPO contract?

Chapter 10

Service Level Agreement

Service Level Agreements bring true accountability to vendor–client relationships. They validate the expectations of vendors and clients and set parameters for accurately measuring project success.[1]

Business process outsourcing involves the transfer of responsibility from an organization to its service provider. The management of this new arrangement is through a contract that may include a Service Level Agreement (SLA). The contract may involve financial penalties and the right to terminate, if SLAs are consistently missed. Setting, tracking and managing SLAs is an important part of outsourcing relationship management. SLAs involve the definition of service level requirements and related metrics. The SLA contents should be jointly developed and agreed upon by the service provider and the service recipient. Key factors to develop an SLA which is manageable and support successful long-term outsourcing relationships are risk and reward sharing, flexibility, and mutual benefits. For preparing an SLA the parties have to identify key indicators focused on the service recipient's business needs and objectives. Hence the logical steps in an SLA are to first define service level objectives, followed by setting target metrics with clearly defined service elements, and then establishing accountability for the achievement of the service-level objectives.

INTRODUCTION

Service Level Agreement (SLA) refers to the minimum level of service that must be provided by the service provider (vendor) to the customer. Due to characteristics of back-office operations based on Information Technology platform, it is extremely necessary for the client to ensure that the said services are provided by service providers with the minimum stipulated requirements as indicated by the client.

SLAs are an effective means to quantify the services to be delivered to users and to continuously improve those services. SLAs are critical in case

1. White paper on "Keys to Successful Service Level Agreement: Effectively Managing Enterprise Demand", http://www.syntelinc.com/uploadedFiles/Syntel_SLA(1).pdf.

of external outsourcing engagements, because they form a vital part of the contract. Further, the quality of the SLA is one of the pillars of a healthy long-term outsourcing relationship.[2]

Normally, the SLA is different and distinct from a BPO contract. This is so as the scope and ambit of the two kinds of contracts are different. BPO contract deals with the terms and conditions of providing the outsourced services by the vendor to the client. It incorporates within its ambit all relevant terms which constitute the terms between the parties.

The SLA is a very specific agreement. It specifies in detail the minimum level of service that must be performed as desired by the client. SLA incorporates evaluation, which enables both the parties to evaluate the quality and level of service provided. The parties go for one comprehensive contract—the BPO contract—which also incorporates the terms of the SLA. Practical experience often shows that such an exercise becomes extremely cumbersome and hard to manage. The SLA refers back to the main BPO contract and determines the most crucial and critical aspect of the service. SLA defines technical support or parameters that a BPO service provider would provide to its clients including measures for performance and consequences of failure.

CONTENTS OF SLAs

SLAs include various contractual binding clauses and terms which document the performance standards and service quality agreed upon by the client and the vendor. These terms specify and clarify performance expectations of the client, establish accountability, standards and procedures, and detail the remedies or consequences if service quality performance standards are not met.

The terms in SLAs include inter alia service levels, service response time cycles, service security, infrastructure uptime/downtime, network performance, reporting, client and client customer satisfaction, end-to-end performance of service features, scalability and acceleration processes.

The objective of any SLA is detailed statement of the following parameters:

- Types of service(s) available to customers
- Quality of service expected by the customer
- Time-frame for SLA contract
- Way to deliver the service
- Way to monitor service quality.

For 'Draft Service Level Agreement' please refer to 'Appendix E'.

2. "Outsourcing Road Map: Service Level Agreement", http://www.euroitx.com/content/sla_2004_01.php.

SLA ADVANTAGES

Service Level Agreements (SLAs) are an essential component of all outsourcing projects. It helps the customer and vendor to measure the productivity and service quality improvements provided by the outsourcing firm. An SLA helps to set expectations and establish targets for measuring the achievement of contract and business objectives. The answer to more effective outsourcing engagements involves an SLA that considers both short- and long-term objectives and integrates business with technology strategy. With a continual focus on service levels and risk, as well as cost reduction and efficiency, organizations can realize improved efficiency, reduced risk from unplanned events, greater assurance that service-level objectives will be met, and better overall responsiveness to the needs of business users will be shown. SLAs provide customers with a competitive advantage by offering the ability to:

- Compare real-time measurements against historical baseline trends, so that organizations can detect deviations and take timely corrective action.
- Predict potential problems associated with infrastructure (e.g., availability and performance) before they become bigger issues.
- Align service and business objectives for the maximum return on investment.

METRICS FOR SLA

The outsourcing contracts are governed by terms and condition stipulated in a contract document and terms and conditions stipulated therein. In general, a Service Level Agreement (SLA) covers the scope and limitations of the functions and services vendor is offering to his client. It includes nature and volume of work, quality acceptance levels, delivery time frame, error corrections, recovery time, etc. SLA is a documents which sets expectations for client and vendor, stipulated in the performance measurement metrics. The performance metrics is normally used to measure the service provider's performance against the committed targets. SLA metrics measure the right performance characteristics and gives the vendor an opportunity to meet its client requirements. However, selecting a proper metrics to judge vendor's performance is a critical step in the contract. The performance metric should motivate the service provider. The caution here is that the wrong metrics may break the relationship. Best way is to test the selected metrics. The metrics should be objective in nature as subjective metrics may be interpreted by different people leading to disagreement on achievements.

In SLA, achievements service provider's ability to meet objectives is dependent on an action from the client. Hence, client's role and actions needs to be defined and measured. For both vendor and client the select metrics should produce information that can be collected, analyzed, interpreted and understood to take decisions. The metrics must be set to reasonable and attainable performance levels.

Another factor which is critical in delivering targeted performance level by vendor is shortcoming (in the client's system) existing in the customer's system. These shortcoming or errors should be agreed upon, addressed and removed before vendor implements the outsourcing contract. In addition, client should evolve the SLA performance metrics to his business process in a way to reflect key factors as follows:

Scale: Flexibility in volumes/contract size.

Quality: Deliverables and its quality level against the acceptable industry standard.

Recovery: Time frame for system recovery after failure or error.

Service: Up/down time for service window.

Customer satisfaction: Speed to market, access to service and backlogs.

The metrics which are used to measure and manage performance to SLA are critical success factors in contract. Hence, any lack of experience in the use and implementation of performance metrics may cause problems for clients as they set the metrics to support their SLA strategies to achieve organizational goals.

SLA GUIDELINES

There are various options available for drafting SLAs according to the specific requirements of the parties. The SLA should start with an overview, describe the agreement, and should further include the agreement's duration. It should also identify the client, key stakeholders and owners who are responsible for managing each service and ensuring that service agreements are met. The key guidelines for an SLA are:

Service description

The SLA is dedicated to performance of services; therefore, it is essential that the SLA must give the detailed description of services and the relevant negotiated service agreements associated with it. Further, for each service, certain given service parameters should be incorporated in the SLA, including:

Description: There is a need for incorporating a clear, unambiguous and prescribed description of the service that is to be performed, measured, monitored and reported.

Time frames: The agreements should specify measures of time in terms of days, dates and time when service measurements are being made. It is necessary that the SLA must elaborate in detail the time-frame in terms of days, weeks and months over which appropriate measurements of the service are to be made. This is necessary so as to enable the client to determine if the service agreement is exceeded, met or not specified.

Rules: The agreements need to specify the exact role and responsibility of client and vendor. These need to be duly stated and both parties need to comply with the service agreements. The SLA needs to identify the party responsible for making each measurement and how each measurement is validated. Further, the primary and secondary points of the contract, for both the client and the vendor, need to be duly incorporated in the SLA for the purpose of maintaining clarity and transparency.

Service-level metrics: The SLA should detail the various measurements and measurement ranges for the contracted service, including service availability or response times. In cases of critical assets, service level must be individually identified. If the parties agree to a specific service level range, then it would be prudent that parties consider the desired service level as well as the minimum acceptable service level. The prudent approach would be to normally attach rewards and penalties to such service levels.

Measurement formula: The SLA should incorporate the mathematical measurement formula or equation to be used for performance monitoring and measurement. If parties agree upon any performance monitoring or measurements tools, then such tools also need to be specifically mentioned in the SLA.

Shared services: In case the vendor has multiple clients, there are chances that overconsumption of resources by one client may affect the performance of another. Normally, such issues and concerns are addressed with the vendor providing a specific guarantee of adequate capacity and implementation of blocking when demand exceeds established limits.

Data sources: In case the parties agree upon collection of measurement data, the SLA should specify the kinds of data to be collected and from what source, as also who is responsible for collecting it and how the same is to be stored.

Escalation of activity: Most SLAs include within their ambit the provisions for escalation of the services as and when the same are desired by the client in the interest of business expediency. The focus of the SLA is on service-level management; so it is essential that the SLA must document various processes necessary for managing service levels. These processes include measurement tracking and reporting; problem escalation and dispute resolution; service change requests including renegotiation; service measurement terms; implementing new services and service levels; and service level review process.

Approval process: When drafting an SLA it is important that various service attributes be specified in detail. These include not only service levels and performance standards, but also the client's responsibility in supporting them as well as reporting requirements. Considering the essential and critical nature of outsourcing, the SLA must also stipulate responsibilities and troubleshooting, problem escalation, continued improvement provisions and the consequences and remedies of non-performance.

In addition, the SLA needs to specify whether the concerned service has to be performed with some limitations or has to be on a 24×7×365 basis. The SLA must specify the Guaranteed Response Time (GRT). This is a specified response time when a service outage occurs and service is not available. Normally the focus of the SLA is on service level management; so it is essential that the SLA must document various processes necessary for managing service levels. The SLA has to incorporate the service architecture, and the service hardware and software. The SLA should define and describe the following factors relating to specific service level performance requirements:

- Response time (speed of notification attempts);
- Service processing time;
- Frequency of monitoring;
- Timeframe to problem resolution;
- Supporting analysis activities;`
- Specification of the manner in which emergencies will be handled; and
- Specification of the manner which special client requests are handled, including additional costs and turnaround time.

The SLA needs to be a flexible document. It should also describe in detail the process to be followed if a client would like to make changes to the service, to add new service, modify current service, or combine multiple services.

Often, parties prefer to describe the same as "emerging technology considerations and provisions of replacing or reducing or adding service based on technology changes."

Clarity in Roles and Responsibilities

The SLA should describe the general and specific roles and responsibilities of all parties which are not covered by the service level definitions. The roles and responsibilities so stipulated should be of the client, the service provider, any sub-contractor, any monitoring committee, as also of the key stakeholders managing the contract. Usually, clients prefer to provide comprehensive details of their infrastructure, architecture and network environment where the service providers have to perform complete the assigned job.

In addition, clients should also provide timely and comprehensive information about necessary client changes and problems such as network configuration upgrades, problems with Internet connectivity, major discovered vulnerabilities (security and otherwise), and unusual network activity.

OTHER ISSUES IN SLA

Since the SLA stipulates various details about the contracted service, it is also necessary that the SLA should address details about security. Before signing the SLA, it is necessary that there must be a review of the existing security policy, procedure and practices of the client, as also of the service provider. In case there is a conflict between the two policies, then the parties should resolve this conflict in the SLA. This is necessary so as to prevent any unforeseen security breach that may impact the contracted service in future.

Contingency Planning, Operational and Disaster Recovery

In an SLA, the service provider often provides stipulations requiring operational recovery, recovery time objectives and recovery point objectives. These objectives cover the time-period needed to recover and what information may have been lost. In the event of any disaster or similar emergency, the service provider often provides in the SLA the minimum and maximum limit of recovery time frames associated with the providers and the client's competing assets.

Access Control

The SLA should also determine which data belongs to the client and which data requiring client access belongs to the provider. For this purpose, the parties may agree upon any specified requirements for use of encryption, maintenance of keys, or other related infrastructure or requirements.

Backups

Since data is of critical importance in any outsourcing transaction, it is important that data must be duly backed up. For this purpose, it is imperative that the SLA defines what kind of data backups are necessary and also should stipulate the responsibility of data backup. The SLA should include guidelines for backup frequency (for weekly full backups and for daily partial backups) and time for restoration. The SLA should also stipulate the guidelines to be followed by the service provider for full life cycle data protection, including creation, use and destruction of data.

Incident Management

Both the client and the service provider need to agree on the various requirements and processes for handling incidents. This agreement needs to be put into writing in the SLA. The SLA should specify as to what constitutes an incident and its level of severity. The SLA needs to stipulate the following:

- Identifying what constitutes an incident and its level of severity;
- Actual or attempted user log on violations and access violations;
- Penetration attempts on provider systems and networks;
- Penetration attempts on client systems and networks;
- Logging of all incidents;
- Circumstances under which the service is shut down;
- Automated notification (e.g., via alerts) of serious incidents and to whom;
- Logs being provided to the responsible party for review;
- Time lag between the incident and verbally notifying the client;
- Requirement for notification based upon the severity of the incident.

The SLA should also stipulate the level of incidents or events that the service provider can handle, and at what level of the concerned event is it required to be turned over to the client. Similarly, the roles and responsibilities of the service provider are stipulated in the event of such an attack.

Client Satisfaction

The SLA should aim to ensure client satisfaction with regard to the contracted service. In the SLA, parties often resort to various parameters for the purposes of determining satisfaction. These parameters relate to the level of client service support to be provided by the provider to the client. This includes the following:

- Level of client service support to be provided including hours of service;
- Use of automated methods;
- Problem resolution times;
- Guaranteed time for call-back.

Sometimes, the SLA stipulates to the service provider to periodically conduct a client satisfaction survey and report the results to the client. This report should contain the following:

- Service availability and response time;
- Ease of use;
- Quality of customer service support;
- Training; and
- Acceptable downtime, including cost or impact.

Independent Evaluations

Since the client wants satisfactory performance of outsourced services, it often insists upon independent evaluations to determine the nature and quality of services being provided by the service provider. In that regard, the client often insists upon including a separate provision in the SLA. By placing such a provision, the service provider agrees to regularly provide the client with the results from various evaluations, including full system checks, audit, security risk evaluations, vulnerability assessments, and penetration tests performed by a mutually agreed third party.

Penalties and Rewards

The SLA should specify the necessary course of action to be taken by the parties in case if the terms are not met by either party. The SLA should provide for penalties for substandard service. Normally, clients insist that the service provider should absorb a penalty of up to 100 per cent of its charges in a given reporting period as compensation for service level failures.

Deficiency in Service

Detailed provisions relating to any deficiency in the performance of the outsourced service must be duly incorporated in the SLA.

These days, in the context of outsourcing, client insist upon 99.99 per cent uptime. This is so because any changes in the decimal can have a tremendous impact on business. For example, 99.99 per cent uptime really means only 5 minutes of downtime for a month, whereas 99.95 per cent uptime provides for 45 minutes of downtime.

The SLA must stipulate the downtime period and the penalty and rewards concerning the same. This is so because 15 minutes of downtime during daytime peak hours represent huge problems for the client, rather than 15 minutes of downtime late at night, which can possibly be of lesser consequence.

SUMMARY

Service Level Agreement (SLA) is a part of the service contract which formally defines the level of service. In practice, the term SLA is often used to refer to the contracted delivery time (of the service) or performance. An SLA results from formal negotiation between two parties—the provider and the recipient—and defines their relationship. It is a contract existing between customers and their service provider, or even between service providers. It is a record of the common understanding about services, responsibilities, guarantees, priorities and as such, collectively the level of service. For example, it may specify the availability levels, serviceability, performance, operation, or other attributes of the service like billing and even penalties for violation of the SLA.

The steps involved in the documentation in the SLA are: identify and define the customer's needs, provide a framework for understanding, simplify complex issues, reduce areas of conflict, encourage dialogue in the event of disputes, and eliminate unrealistic expectations.

The SLA embraces a wide range of issues such as the services to be delivered, performance, tracking and reporting, problem management, legal compliance and resolution of disputes, customer duties and responsibilities, security, IPR, confidential information, and termination.

Technical specifications in an SLA are described commonly through either a Service Level Specification (SLS) or a Service Level Objective (SLO). An SLS is meant to be an operational guideline for service implementation, and an SLO—a subset of an SLS—contains some service parameters and goals to be achieved through the SLS.

Review Questions

1. What is Service Level Agreement (SLA) and how does it differ from the BPO contract?
2. Discuss the contents of a typical BPO Service Level Agreement.
3. Explain the advantages of a well-framed SLA.
4. Discuss the various guidelines for drafting an SLA for creating a 'win-win' situation for both client and BPO vendor.
5. What are the various issues to be taken care of in the SLA for avoiding disputes during the tenure of the contract?

Chapter 11

BPO Legal Contract

Every outsourcing agreement should be modified as applicable under different circumstances. One brush should not paint all the painting.[1]

An outsourcing contract provides a comprehensive road map of the duties and obligations of both the parties. A properly drafted contract minimizes complications when a dispute arises. The contract acts as the reference for all terms and conditions agreed to between the parties. While negotiating a BPO contract, every concerned party must insist upon getting the entire contract and its terms vetted in complete detail by their lawyers. This is necessary so as to prevent unpleasant problems cropping up in the future, in which case either of the parties may have to pay heavy liquidated damages, face legal action, or even wind up its operations.

INTRODUCTION

Outsourcing is the contracting out of a company's non-core, non-revenue producing activities to expert. It differs from contracting in the sense that outsourcing is a strategic management tool that involves the restructuring of an organization around its core competencies.

Two common types of outsourcing are Information Technology (IT) outsourcing and Business Process Outsourcing (BPO). BPO includes outsourcing related to accounting, human resources, benefits, payroll, and finance functions and activities. Knowledge Process Outsourcing (KPO) includes outsourcing related to legal, paralegal, and other highly skilled activities.

A good outsourcing agreement provides a comprehensive road map of the duties and obligations of both the parties, i.e., buyer and seller of services. A well-planned and drafted agreement minimizes complications when a dispute arises. However, many a time, people neglect to pay attention while drafting an outsourcing agreement.

Before finalizing an outsourcing agreement, the terms and conditions should be discussed, negotiated and agreed upon to avoid any misunderstanding

1. Outsourcing Agreements, Madan & Co., www.madan.com

and dispute arising thereof at a later stage. The following issues must be properly addressed before signing a BPO agreement:

- Duties and obligations of the outsourcer
- Duties and obligations of the service provider
- Security and confidentiality
- Legal compliance
- Fees and payment terms
- Proprietary rights
- Auditing rights
- Law applicable to outsourcing agreement
- Terms of the agreement
- Events of default and how to address them
- Dispute resolution mechanism
- Time limits
- Location of arbitration
- Number of arbitrators
- Interim measures/Provisional remedies
- Privacy agreement
- Non-compete agreement
- Confidentiality agreement
- Rules applicable
- Appeal and enforcement
- Local peculiarities
- Survival terms after the termination of the agreement
- Jurisdiction.

CONTRACT COVERAGE

A comprehensive BPO contract should cover the following:

Scope: The contract should state the exact scope of the services to be rendered. The customer needs to state his expectations from the provider, and that will form the basis for the scope of the contract.

Confidentiality: The information that is provided by the establishment under an outsourcing contract may be highly confidential. Therefore, the contract should ensure that there is an obligation on the part of the service provider to hold the same in strict confidence and not to disseminate, transfer, or copy the same to any unauthorized person or organization.

Security: For any disaster recovery, it would be advisable for both the parties to provide for back-up plans, business-continuity planning, and contingency planning.

Intellectual Property Rights (IPRs): It is possible that some of the information provided by the establishment would be the sole proprietary information of such establishment, and that the establishment has intellectual property over the same. These IPRs should be honoured.

Time schedule: As the nature of the work is time-bound, it would be advisable for the customer to clearly provide the time schedule by which he wants its completion.

Exclusivity: It is pertinent for the contract to have an element of exclusivity. Hence the parties should keep in mind that the regulations are not violated.

Taxation: The taxation liability needs to be spelled out and whether the same be included or excluded from the consideration of payment should be mentioned.

Force majeure: This clause is a must to safeguard the interest of the parties concerned in the event of any act beyond the parties' reasonable control.

Risk management: The primary liability of the establishment is to its customers and same cannot be delegated. However, the establishment could seek indemnity for business losses, etc. from the provider due to any negligence or dysfunctional service. The establishment could also require the service provider to maintain insurance of a requisite sum to counter all risks.

Termination: It would be advisable for the parties to state in clear terms when and how a contract could be terminated, and if there should be any quantified damages payable for the same.

Personnel: Due to stringent labour legislation, it is advisable that the contract stipulates that the employees, consultants and retained personnel used by the provider shall be those of the provider, and that the provider shall be responsible for them, including payment of their statutory dues.

Miscellaneous: The contract should also cover additional issues concerning education and job experience for those suited for the project, the specifics of training to be incurred, and quality of service. In the event the work requires foreign travel, then the contract should provide for compliance required in that regard.

Payment: The contract should be very specific as to the payment terms, whether payment should be as per phase of completion of contract, or would be in lump sum or in instalments. Further, it would be advisable to specify the mode of payment as well.

Jurisdiction: As parties might be located at different places, it is always advisable for the parties to mutually agree on the places of jurisdiction.

Dispute Resolution

It is also advisable for the parties to choose arbitration as an effective method for dispute resolution as it is less time-consuming than litigation in India.

ESSENTIAL ELEMENTS OF BPO CONTRACT

Whenever any entity enters into an outsourcing contract or a BPO contract with any vendor, there are various issues that need to be kept in mind by it. These issues are critical for both the parties, as they impact both of them as also the delivery of outsourced services under the contract. Both the foreign company granting the outsourcing contract and the Indian BPO vendor need to keep the following important issues in mind whenever they enter into negotiations for formalizing a BPO contract:

Third-party agreements for BPO: Here the client and the service provider are independent third parties and are not related to each other in any manner whatsoever.

Captive agreements for BPO: In such agreements, the client and the service provider are related parties. In a majority of cases, the service provider typically is a subsidiary of the client company.

Build–operate–transfer (BOT) agreements: In these cases the service provider builds and develops the BPO operation for the client and at a future date transfers the entire BPO operation to the client.

Contract in General Terms

Whenever a party enters into a BPO contract, it is extremely important and crucial that they focus strongly on the terms and conditions. The contract acts as the reference for all terms and conditions agreed to between the parties. While negotiating a BPO contract, every concerned party must insist upon getting the entire contract and its terms vetted completely by its lawyers. This is necessary for preventing unpleasant problems from emerging in future.

It is a rule that the BPO contract should, as far as possible, be worded in general and broad terms and principles. This is a must for the purpose of business and administrative convenience, apart from increasing the comfort level of the parties. The BPO contract must have an inherent flexibility so as to incorporate additional services, charges, changes and responsibilities within its ambit. This is necessary as the parties do not normally want to enter into separate contracts for every new service agreed upon and rather prefer to work within the ambit of their existing contracts. Hence, while drafting the contract in broad terms, it is necessary to provide this flexibility to the contract by drafting it, at the relevant places, in general terms. It is, therefore, necessary that the parties develop and mutually arrive at such pricing mechanism that would accommodate changes in terms of the volume of services consumed by the client.

It is necessary to ensure that changes to the services do not give rise to any additional charges, reduction in charges or renegotiations of the charges. There is an inherent need in the BPO agreement to state specifically that performance of services would require the parties to make an adjustment in pricing. The adjustment in pricing is calculated on a mutually beneficial basis and should be mutually agreed to by the parties.

Training and Infrastructure

While negotiating the BPO contract, it is essential that the vendor, as also the client, keep in mind various important factors which have a legal bearing. The client should normally ensure and get ascertained that the service provider has a team of dedicated persons to handle the specified transaction. The client should also ensure that the service provider renders services of such nature and quality which are in conformity to the service requirements and expectations as stipulated in the contract. The client should insist upon the requirement of mutually accepted training terms which need to be imposed upon the persons working on different transactions, so as to ensure the highest level of performance. In addition, the client should ensure that the latest technology and the proper infrastructure at the vendor's site are in place.

Scope of Service

The important part of any BPO contract is inclusion of the scope of service. The parties must agree on terms in this regard and put them into writing. Thus, it is absolutely essential that all the necessary specifications and requirements of the outsourced service to be performed by the vendor must be specified by the client. These services are invariably specified by means of detailed schedules and service level agreements (SLAs), which provide the details in terms of the performance parameters.

SLAs incorporate the needs of clients, the compliance of which is critical for the performance of the relevant outsourced services. The particulars in each contract would vary from case to case and the outsourcing project or assignment. It is essential that the provisions and the schedules relating to the scope of services must be elaborated in minute detail to avoid disagreement in execution stage. As the BPO industry is getting competitive, the vendor must insist upon the following:

Terms

The BPO contract should cover in detail the terms of the contract. Invariably, clients go for negotiation for short-term contracts with renewal rights. This is a good approach and provides a win-win situation for both the parties.

In contracts, there should be a termination clause which enables any party to terminate the contract by giving the stipulated notice in this regard to the opposite party. This provision enables any dissatisfied party to come out of the contract at a reasonable price at a reasonable time. The dissatisfaction may arise out of deviation in agreed service or the quality of service provided by the vendor.

Jurisdiction

In a BPO contract, it is essential that parties agree upon the common jurisdiction of the courts, which alone would be authorized to take cognizance of the dispute. Normally, clients insist that the jurisdiction needs to be that of their own country where their principal businesses are located. This is done so as to save the client from running and being forced to litigate in a foreign jurisdiction where the service provider is located. In a BPO contract between an UK client and an Indian vendor, the UK client insists on the insertion of the UK courts for jurisdiction, so as to ensure that litigation will be carried out only in UK courts in accordance with UK law. This provides a comfort factor to the client and also encourages the vendor to give the best possible output in order to prevent any possible litigation in the UK. However, a case in the UK can be extremely problematic and cumbersome, apart from being economically unviable, from the Indian vendor's perspective. This is also true for the client in India.

Dispute resolution

Whenever any contract is entered into, the parties are aware of the probability of disputes arising under the same. Consequently, any contract, including a BPO contract, must provide for dispute settlement mechanisms. Disputes can be settled within the ambit of the governing law of that country whose jurisdiction is agreed to between the parties.

The parties may also resort to alternate dispute resolution mechanisms, including arbitration, mediation and conciliation, instead of resorting to the traditional legal systems. This is so because in traditional legal systems and dispute resolutions, there is high cost and time lag involved.

Mechanisms for timely payment

The BPO contract must specify, in clear terms, the exact payment to be made by the client to the service provider. However, such payment schedule would be specified in the contract to prevent any potential dispute, which could arise later on. The contract must also specify the consequences of non-payment of the stipulated duties and the remedies available to the other party for securing payment.

The contract should specify the mode of stoppage of services if payment is withheld or delayed beyond stipulated time by the client. Similarly, in some situations, clients insist upon a clause that mandates payments in accordance with quality of services rendered. Thus an efficient payment mechanism in a contract is critical to the success of any BPO project. This is essential to avoid bad debts and delayed payments.

Consequences and liability for breach

There is always a chance that BPO agreement may be breached. It is essential for parties to specify in the contract the significance of breach of the contract.

It may so happen in some cases that the service provided by the vendor may not be of the required quality or standard as per the expectation of the client. This becomes a major problem when standards of services are not stipulated in the contract. In such a case the vendor, by not providing service of the expected quality, does specifically stand in breach of the agreement. Hence, it is essential that the agreement should specify the consequence that shall follow in case one party or the other breaches the agreement. These consequences may be in the form of liquidated damages or any other form as agreed. In many cases, breach of the contract in itself can mean termination or expiry of the contract.

Limitation of liability

Delivery of service in the BPO contract is valuable, critical and of great importance for both client and vendor. In case if there is a failure in the delivery of such services on the part of any party, there arise issues of liability to the other party. Hence, in the contract the liability issues should be appropriately addressed and limited to a particular specified maximum amount.

In a BPO contract, the vendor tends to insist upon the inclusion of a clause that helps in limiting its liability in the event of specified exigencies. This is true in case the outsourcing process is a multinational process, where fluctuation of currency can have impact on payments. Therefore, the vendor must insist that his liability be limited to a stipulated amount, as specified in the terms of agreement, and no more. This helps in putting a limit on the damages that can be recovered from the vendor. Thus, this clause further helps in contributing to the long-term sustainability of the business.

Restrictions on subcontracting

Normally, after a lot of deliberation, the foreign company zeroes in at a specific vendor for the purpose of outsourcing its business processes to the service provider. Choosing a vendor is itself a tough task and takes a lot of time, money and energy of the client. It is only when the client is satisfied about the capability and capacity of the vendor in providing quality level services expected by the client that the BPO contract is assigned. Clients do not want the vendor to subcontract his contract to other subcontractors, as the quality of the promised services may suffer. Often the client insists upon inclusion of a clause in the BPO contract which restricts the vendor from subcontracting the assignment to any other subcontractor.

Permission for subcontracting

In case the client does not have any objection for the vendor to subcontract the service, the client and the vendor are required to enter into the contract a clause that grants written permission to the subcontractor.

Non-competition

In a BPO contract, the issue of non-competition becomes an important issue for inclusion in the terms of the contract. Firstly, foreign clients, who outsource their business processes to different countries, want to ensure that their BPO vendor does not enter into any contract with any other company which is their competitor. This is necessary to avoid leakage of important and confidential data belonging to the client to its competitor.

Secondly, the clients often insist on clauses in their agreement to the effect that the vendor shall not for a specified period enter the same field of activity as that of the client company, or that the vendor shall not compete with the client in respect of the services of the client. This is done to prevent the vendor, who has gained knowledge about the confidential business practices and data of the client company, from competing with the client company. A period of 5 to 6 years is usually the time-period for which such restriction is imposed upon the vendor.

Thirdly, when a client outsources a specific service to a vendor, he wants to ensure that during the contract period, the vendor should not work for any other company which is a direct competitor of the client company.

Asset ownership

It may so happen that during the contract a number of intellectual property assets are likely to be created. In such cases, the BPO contract must be able to identify such potential assets and provide for their ownership. The contract should describe how assets will be transitioned at the end of the outsourcing contract, and whether the ownership of the assets is to be retained by the vendor or be under the client's control if the use of such assets is required. These assets include software licences obtained by the service provider on the client's behalf. Hence, the contract should have provisions to transfer data, including all Intellectual Property Rights, so that the client can use them in future.

Data ownership and confidentiality

In many cases the vendor may generate a lot of data or information during contract execution, in performance of the services as part of normal business practices. In some BPO services, clients require vendor to capture data which is to be used for the purpose of future use.

Normally, the clients insist that this data belongs to them. Thus, often a clause is inserted in the BPO contract to the effect that the said data collected by the vendor during the course of its performance of outsourcing services is the property of the client.

Client data handling by vendor

The vendor, during the course of providing services, handles a lot of client data. A provision must be made in the contract that the service provider's use of client data, either for data mining or for any other purpose than the services directly contracted for by the client, is not permitted without the express, written, unequivocal and clear permission of the authorized client data owner.

Intellectual property rights (IPR) protection

In any BPO contract, the client always wants to protect his Intellectual Property Rights by means of some provisions. These are necessary in order to avoid any conflict that may arise in future. The client must seek the representations and warranties, or both, from the vendor that there is a valid right to use such software, which vests in the service provider. In case if the vendor claims ownership of all software, the client would require representation and warranty.

In addition, in BPO contracts the client insists on non-use of pirated software by both the parties. The contract further needs to say that in case, at any point of time during the validity period of the BPO contract, it comes to be known that the service provider is not the owner of the particular software, the vendor would indemnify the client for all loss that may be incurred due to the false representation.

During the course of the contract, IP may be developed by the vendor. In such cases, client will not be under any legal obligation to make any additional payment for the creation of such intellectual property and will also keep ownership of the same.

Change management

In BPO operations, change is the only constant factor. Clients are extremely sensitive as to how the vendor would be able to manage changes, which are often rapid in nature. The clients insist upon insertion of appropriate provisions in the BPO contract, detailing the elaborate processes and procedures to be adopted by the vendor in relation to change management.

Legal compliance

In any BPO contract, it is essential to ensure that there is compliance with law on the part of the client. This is necessary to ensure that the entire BPO transaction is legal and comes within the ambit of law in the destination jurisdiction at which the outsourced services are targeted.

Protection and security of data

In BPO transaction, data is very crucial. The client is concerned about that data that it sends for back-office operations in India should be secure and protected. Therefore, any BPO contract must stipulate specific provisions to the effect that the data of the client shall be protected, as agreed between the parties. The contract should mention the mechanisms, processes and procedures adopted by the vendor to ensure protection of data provided by the client.

Privacy and confidentiality

In any BPO contract, the foreign client is invariably concerned about ensuring the privacy and confidentiality of information that is collected and processed during the course of back-office operations. A large number of companies outsource those business processes which deal with collection of customer details, credit card details and other confidential personal or banking information. It is the utmost concern of the foreign client that such confidential personal or financial information should be protected and should not be leaked or sold for any consideration whatsoever. Therefore, in a BPO contract, appropriate provisions are provided for the same.

Disaster recovery

Clients prefer no interruption of delivery of services. That is why BPO clients and vendors negotiate provisions relating to disaster recovery management. In case the country where the outsourcing has been done faces a disaster of one or the other variety, the client does not want such a disaster to obstruct the free flow of service provided by the BPO service provider.

Compliance with laws

In the BPO contract, service providers need to ensure compliance with all laws that are applicable for the time being in the country of its operations. Vendors need to ensure compliance with local labour, employment and IPR laws. In addition, it is necessary that the client protects itself against any local laws relating to life tenureship of the vendor's employees.

The BPO vendor needs to understand that for the sake of its foreign client, it has to necessarily comply with all relevant foreign laws, rules, regulations, byelaws, notifications and other legislations which impact the outsourced service in question. This is necessary so as to enable the foreign client to fulfil the compliance requirements under the laws prevailing in the jurisdiction where its principal business is situated. In the BPO contract it is imperative for the vendor rendering services to foreign companies to ensure compliance with laws in those countries.

Exit provisions

The contract should be able to provide appropriate exit provisions so as to enable either party to come out of the contractual relationship in an easy manner, without causing much financial loss or disruption of the outsource-contracted service. Normally, termination of the contract can be done for specified causes including breach of contract, inability to perform to the accepted standard, breach of security, confidentiality, integrity or availability. A BPO contract is different from other contracts as it deals with the performance of specified contractual services; thus it is necessary that the contract provides for the responsibilities of the outgoing vendor.

The contract should stipulate client responsibility in such a scenario and also provide for the procedure to be followed in case of such termination. The issue of evaluation of key assets including data, software, hardware and tools has to be appropriately addressed in case of termination of contract.

For 'Sample Contract on Outsourcing Services' please refer to Appendix 'D'.

SUMMARY

The BPO contract should, as far as possible, be worded in general and broad terms and principles. This is a must for the purpose of business and administrative convenience, apart from increasing the comfort level of the parties. The BPO contract must have an inherent flexibility so as to incorporate additional services, charges, changes and responsibilities within its ambit. The contract should cover clauses on duties and obligations of client and vendor, security and confidentiality, legal compliance, fees and payment terms, proprietary rights, auditing rights, laws applicable to outsourcing agreement, terms of the agreement, data protection and security, IPR, dispute resolution mechanisms, time limits, location of arbitration, terminations and jurisdiction. A well-drafted contract will help in developing a long healthy relationship between client and vendor.

Review Questions

1. What should a comprehensive BPO contract cover in general?
2. Discuss the essential elements of a BPO contract.
3. What, according to you, are the major issues that a client should address in a BPO contract.
4. What are the issues, as per the point of view of a BPO service provider, that need to be addressed in the BPO contract?

Chapter 12

BPO to KPO: Up in the Value Chain

The key success factor for the 21st century will be Knowledge Management. Harnessing the advantages of KPO (Knowledge Process Outsourcing) will be critical, as high-end knowledge work in fields such as Biotechnology and Pharmaceutical research, Intellectual Property and Financial Analytics, etc. are being outsourced to India.[1]

KPO is the upward shift of BPO in the value chain. Old BPO companies that used to provide basic back-end or customer care support are moving up this value chain. Unlike conventional BPO where the focus is on process expertise, in KPO the focus is on knowledge expertise. KPO is involved in services like valuation and investment research, patent filing, legal and insurance claim processing, clinical research, etc.

INTRODUCTION

The quality of employees available with the vendor and technology used has a profound impact on the value of offshore IT jobs done by the BPO service provider. There are certain activities such as para-legal and medical transcription which require low-quality human capital. However, activities such as data mining and analysis, engineering design and e-learning, which are mostly IT-enabled and require high-quality human resources. Other services such as legal consulting, intellectual property research and strategic consulting require the highest level of human capital and are the least dependable on IT enablement. Companies in the BPO space need to shift to KPO space and climb up the value chain. They thus need to make the transition from offering services that require low human capital quality and low IT enablement to those that require a high degree of human capital and IT enablement.

For example, Evalueserve,[2] with its headquarters in Bermuda and main operational centre in Gurgaon (near Delhi) in India supplies a range of value-

1. Marc Vollenweider, CEO and co-founder, Evalueserve, www.evalueserve.com.
2. www.evalueserve.com.

added services to clients in the KPO domain. The clientele includes a large number of Fortune 500 companies and many global consulting firms. They provide services like patent writing, legal advice, evaluating investment opportunities and training people to communicate in multiple languages.

Activities considered for offshoring have moved up the value chain and begun to touch core functions such as highly analytical processes. More complex customer services are substituting simple data processing and call centre activities. The higher-end functions being performed offshore include information research, financial portfolio analysis, customer data mining, statutory reporting and inbound insurance sales, among others.

WHAT IS KPO?

In the BPO space, the focus is on executing standardized routine processes. However, KPO involves processes that demand advanced information search, analytical, interpretation and technical skills, as well as some judgment and decision-making ability. Examples of KPO functions are intellectual property or patent research, R&D in pharmaceuticals and biotechnology, data mining, database creation, and a range of analytical services such as equity research, competitive intelligence, industry reports and financial modelling. Many of these activities lend themselves to remote execution from anywhere.

Typical users of KPO services include market research and consulting firms, investment banks and financial service institutions, industry associations, media, publishing and database firms, corporate planning departments of large Fortune 500 companies, and pharmaceutical companies for conducting clinical research.

KPO vs. BPO

KPO is a step ahead of BPO. BPO has its own way to solve a particular problem. The BPO market is long-term in nature as compared to the KPO market. With every passing day the BPO market base is expanding and so is the number of processes outsourced through it. BPO undertakes

- Data processing
- Basic data entry
- Setting up of bank account
- Department outsourcing
- Technical support
- E-mail support to customers.

The fundamentals of outsourcing apply to knowledge-based services as well. A shortage of trained professionals shoots up the cost of maintaining such services in the host country. However, the same job can be done with similar precision and quality and at less than half the cost abroad. Standardized technical education is now widely available to all in the developing countries. This trained manpower is also accessible at very low cost as well. It, therefore, makes sense to utilize their services. Outsourcing to KPO firms can provide the following benefits:

- Valuable cost savings that can be utilized elsewhere
- Standard operational efficiency
- Trained professionals at work
- Savings in time and management energy
- Increase in profits
- Option to recruit a larger workforce without raising costs.

The following skills form the basis of knowledge-based firms and their workforce:

- Analyzing data and information to produce meaningful documents
- Researching information from various sources
- Converting raw technical data into presentable documents
- Use of high levels of conceptualization and theoretical knowledge
- Proficiency with various advanced software and hardware devices
- Maintaining workflow, meeting deadlines, and applying quality controls.

Table 12.1 presents the difference between BPO and KPO.

Table 12.1 BPO vs KPO

BPO	*KPO*
In BPO client engages the third party service provider to perform some of their business process. The purpose of outsourcing to cut cost, as the expert performs the process without error or redo which is based on his past experience.	KPO is outsourcing of core functions of the client. This is done mostly for value addition and necessarily for cost benefits.
The business processes outsourced are for back office (related to finance or HR) or front office (related to service to customer) operations. (BPO may be for back office or front office operations.	KPO is technical in nature and for outsourcing complex business processes where technical or domain knowledge/ expertise is primarily required, which will be expensive or client do not have the expertise to do the same in-house.
Classified as off-shoring (location of vendor is outside the country of client) and in-shoring (location of vendor is the country same as of client's).	KPO Competitor research – Engineering Designing in Mechanical, Structural, Architectural and Civil – Legal Process Outsourcing – Technical Writing and Communications – Remote IT infra-structure Management – Animation, 2D, 3D modelling, etc.

Even after the entry of KPO in the Indian market, BPO will continue to exist for performing certain jobs which do not require any specialized knowledge base. KPO specializes in various challenging sectors, namely business research, clinical research, intellectual property research, etc.

KPO Partnership
GLOBAS, is a leading KPO service provider specializing in providing high value services to its clients. They helped MICA build flexibility into their supply chain operations to optimize product delivery and enhance service delivery levels. MICA are service providers to Airlines wherein there are number of back office process which are non-core in nature, but affects the productivity through low degree of responsiveness and also enhances the cost though extended time frame to perform the same. To overcome this, MICA partnered with GLOBAS for creating responsiveness and streamlining product and service delivery to the airline clients. The other services extended by GLOBAS were telesales, managing accounts payables, customer order management and new product launch. In addition, GLOBAS provided support for IT application, project/service management and, business analytics. GLOBAS standardized and consolidated MICA's supply chain knowledge management process worldwide in six zones. Benefits accrued were; increase in sales by 40 per cent, savings through debt collection by 20 per cent increase in on-time delivery, multiple new product launchings, one sixth reduction in the customer handling time.

BPO TO KPO: DRIVERS

The gradual shift from BPO to KPO in some offshore countries is expected to change the dynamics of skill development and job migration. The factors that drive transition from BPO to KPO are:

More Savings in Outsourcing Higher-end Process

Buyers of outsourcing services save more at the high end of the value chain, compared to the low end. Hence, the current low-cost destinations will become a logical choice for companies for outsourcing their high-end processes.

Scarcity of Specialized Talent Pool

Developed economies such as the US, the UK, and western European countries are already facing a shortage of highly trained and specialized professionals in some knowledge-intensive high-skill sectors such as R&D in VLSI, engineering design, IT, and financial risk management. One way to meet this problem of skill shortage is to source talent from low-cost countries, which produce highly educated scientists and professionals. This has been the practice in the USA for the past several decades. The USA permits emigration of engineers, scientists, and medical doctors from developing countries such as India and China. However, with tightening visa regulations in the developed countries and cost-reduction pressures on MNCs, outsourcing of high-end services to low-wage countries to tap the existing talent pool in a cost-effective manner is a viable and lucrative option today.

Evolution of Outsourcing Vendors to Higher-end of Value Chain

The evolution of outsourcing vendors in low-end destinations to the higher end of the value chain, aided by the maturity of the processes, will result in BPO organizations moving up the value chain to provide KPO services. Commoditization of BPO services will further boost this transition, and the better margins expected at the higher end of the value chain might act as a deterrent for companies in accepting low-end work. The barriers to entry in the KPO industry are also higher, and therefore offshoring companies may not have the same competitive pressures as are there in traditional BPO.

Increasing Number of Professionals in Offshoring Industry

The number of professionals working in the offshoring industry is expected to increase as more and more companies decide to become involved in BPO and KPO. This will further drive the trend towards the migration of low-end service providers to high-end services, especially as offshore service vendors gain substantial experience and capabilities to provide high-value services.

KPO—OPPORTUNITY AND SCOPE

The experts estimate exponential growth in the near future in the following high-end service areas of the KPO sector:

- Intellectual Property (IP) research
- Equity, financial, and insurance research
- Data search, integration, and management
- Analytics and data mining services
- Research and information services in human resources (HR)
- Business, market and competitive intelligence research
- Engineering and product design services
- Design, animation, and simulation services
- Legal content and services
- Medical content and services
- Remote education and publishing
- Pharmaceuticals and biotechnology clinical research
- Research and Development (IT and non-IT areas)
- Network management
- Decision Support Systems (DSS).

In the following critical areas, the nature of the research required will be as follows:

Intellectual property research (IPR)

It will cover drafting and filing of patent applications with the patent and trademark bodies. In addition, IP asset management, IP landscaping of technology domains, IP licensing, IP docketing, and IP commercialization services are some other services that can be outsourced to low-cost destinations in a similar manner. Apart from patents, the services can be outsourced for trademarks, copyrights and industrial designs.

R&D in pharmaceuticals and biotechnology

Contract research organizations are being widely used by pharmaceutical companies. This covers developing crude molecules at low-cost destinations and passing these on to developed country destinations for final processing. The other emerging areas within this sector include clinical research, lead optimization and improvement of manufacturing processes. The cost of drug development is \$800 mn in the USA while in India it may cost \$200 mn. Therefore, companies such as Astra Zeneca and Glaxo-SmithKline have set up drug discovery centres at low-cost destinations, thereby offshoring their R&D.

Analytics and data mining services

Companies can save significantly—as much as 60–70 per cent—by offshoring data mining, analytics, and inventory management work to low-wage countries. Similarly, demand and channel planning, manufacturing scheduling, and transport planning are examples of some supply chain management solutions that require the use of mathematical programming, statistical analysis, and computer-aided simulations. These require highly specialized knowledge and can be offshored.

Search engine optimization (SEO)

Here, primarily the focus is on the search engine marketing business. The marketing methods employed are SEO, direct site promotions, affiliate Internet marketing, PPC search engines, site membership mailings, etc.

Legal services

Writing legal briefs and memos need not mean hiring costly professionals, as the same quality documentation can be done with a KPO firm based in India. The work gets done at reduced cost in India.

Accounting services

From simple bookkeeping to auditing, KPO firms can provide trained professionals who offer cheaper services with standard quality.

Journalism and content development

English-speaking trained writers from a KPO firm are good candidates to help newspapers and journals with their editing and copywriting work. This sector has recently seen a good growth with the rise of content development firms.

Architectural and engineering services

A large pool of trained draftsmen can provide expert CAD/CAM services to clients.

Other key KPO areas

The areas of KPO services are as vast as the field of business and industry itself. These include programming, software development, English-language services, content development, and website design and promotion.

KPO CHALLENGES

KPO calls for outsourcing of knowledge-intensive business processes that require specialized domain expertise. Unlike BPO, which follows pre-defined and structured processes that can be performed by virtually anybody, KPO processes demand advanced analytical and specialized skills of knowledge workers who have specific domain proficiency. Therefore, outsourcing of knowledge processes faces more challenges than BPO. The usual list of challenges of any offshore activity like political, infrastructure, and legal issues still exist. But the advent of KPO will bring along a few additional challenges, which are unique to the industry and are from both the internal and external environment. These are:

- **Internal challenge:** Recruiting and retaining the right talent
- **Customer challenge:** Demand for quality, data security and compliance
- **Competitor challenge:** Other countries and global KPOs operating in India
- **Industry challenge:** Information infrastructure and branding.

In the future, the requirements of a successful KPO business would involve recruiting and training the right professionals, developing domain expertise, creating value for clients by offering highly differentiated services, providing dependable quality over time, and building credibility alongside competing countries. To achieve these, many steps need to be taken at the strategic and operational levels by both the government and the individual KPO.

In a BPO, clients provide the business process requirements, and the outsourcing service provider in India follows the needs of the client. KPO is significantly higher on the value chain and involves processes that demand advanced information search, analytical, interpretation and technical skills as well as some judgment and decision-making. For example, a financial services KPO usually deals with areas such as insurance underwriting, fund management, risk assessment and actuarial analytics, debt collection and recovery, equity research, financial data mining, corporate and market research. Cost savings, operational efficiencies, access to a highly skilled workforce and improved quality are the major drivers behind knowledge process outsourcing to India.

Unlike a BPO which deals with low-end, pre-defined processes, knowledge creation and codification cannot be turned into a process and subsequently outsourced. In the case of knowledge, there is often no pre-defined process or structured, rules-based manner to reach a conclusion or to solve a problem. Instead the term *KPO* can be interpreted to mean outsourcing of knowledge-intensive business processes that require specialized domain expertise. For example, a few of the prominent Indian players in the financial services KPO domain are 'Office Tiger', 'Smart Analyst', and 'The Smart Cube'. In addition to these, a number of MNC KPOs such as EvalueServe, GE Capital as well as captive arms of global firms such as JP Morgan, HSBC, Reuters, Fidelity, Morgan Stanley and Citigroup also operate in India. KPO in India is a sunrise industry and the challenges before KPO are:

Internal challenges

KPO services in India are set to have exponential growth in next few years. To grab a sizable market share in the KPO sector, Indian companies will need to recruit a significant number of highly qualified employees with very strong academic backgrounds. Unlike a BPO where fluency in English is all you need to get in, the work in a financial services KPO requires expertise in specific domains such as financial analysis and equity research. Access to a large, high-quality skill pool is a precondition for successful KPO operations. But the requisite skill pool is not easy to get because:

- High competition exists for access to a limited pool of skilled people.
- Successful players attract better people with very high compensations.
- High attrition rates exist due to poaching by competitors and frequent job hopping by young employees looking for better job opportunities.
- There is lack of domain expertise as the graduates in India may not be aware of the client's business requirements, e.g. the US system of accounting (US GAAP).

Customer challenges

The major customer challenges are:

Demand for quality: In BPOs, there is a pre-defined way to solve a problem which the employees can be trained to learn. Clients have an OLA (Operation Level Agreement) or SLA (Service Level Agreement) with the outsourcing company where both parties decide on certain metrics for quality adherence. For example, a customer service call pick-up time should be less than ten seconds. In contrast, KPOs require keen understanding of how a client works and what his exact needs are for each assignment. No pre-defined process can be created and replicated each time there is an assignment, since every project is unique. As a result of this, defining an ideal metric to measure the quality of work can be quite a difficult task. For example, an analyst may target twenty factors of importance for a market research study, whereas another analyst may shortlist just five. The client may be pleased with the preciseness of the latter, though the number of factors seem inadequate compared to the former. Thus, the difficulty lies in accurately determining whether you met client expectations or not. Ultimately; the client in a KPO will not look at money, but will be mainly concerned with quality of services.

Concern over data security and client confidentiality: Offering sophisticated information security provisions and practices provide a competitive advantage because security has become a critical selling point today. The data and information a KPO business works with is extremely sensitive. Clients such as banks, insurance companies and corporations trust KPO providers with company financial data, treasury and cash management functions, and investment portfolio decisions. Thus, KPOs are privy to information that is otherwise not public knowledge. Thus, clients often hesitate to offshore research and processing of sensitive financial data and information involving strategic decisions. A big challenge is to convince clients that their confidential data will be treated with extreme caution and will not fall into the hands of unscrupulous or unauthorized individuals. Thus, the fundamental and near-term challenge facing Indian companies is to provide the necessary security and data protection while working on client data. To keep up with increasing demand from clients to maintain information security, KPOs will need to balance the escalating costs of maintaining global security standards while staying competitive in a cost-driven market.

Compliance and corporate governance: With legislation such as Sarbanes–Oxley (which requires company executives to provide personal assurances as to the completeness and accuracy of the financial figures they publish), companies that outsource finance functions are facing increasing business risk. A greater emphasis on governance and greater direct control of finance processes, as compared to previous times, is acting as a barrier in the way of decisions to outsource finance functions. The client concern is that outsourcing might lead to a loss of control, which might in turn lead to weakening of corporate governance and subsequent breaches of compliance with regulatory requirements.

Competition

Countries such as China, Philippines, Mexico, and Ireland are fast emerging as alternative KPO services destinations. Although, according to McKinsey analysis, India is comfortably placed in the Location/People attractive metrics, other countries like China are fast catching up. A positive foreign investment climate, favourable government policies and an educated yet low-cost workforce are encouraging foreign financial firms to offshore their KPO needs to these countries.

Industry challenges

Information infrastructure KPOs need 24/7 Internet connection to collect data, perform secondary research and transmit data back and forth, either nationally or internationally. According to the Telecom Regulatory Authority of India (TRAI), Internet bandwidth prices account for almost 40 per cent of a KPO's total costs, thus being a critical differentiator between its success and failure. Although major reforms have been undertaken by the government to spur the growth of IT infrastructure, there are a few significant roadblocks such as:

- **India's high international bandwidth prices:** Leased line is the most preferred mode of Internet connectivity due to its permanent continuous connectivity, reliability and speed. Unfortunately, India's international bandwidth prices are the highest in the world, the main reason being market control by a few players such as VSNL, Reliance, and Bharti. In contrast, in highly competitive Western and East Asian markets (e.g. 14 players in Korea and 32 players in Germany and the USA), a large number of players force prices down and keep bandwidth charges minimal.
- **High entry fee for Internet Service Providers (ISPs) supplying Virtual Private Network (VPN) services:** This is a viable alternative to leased-line connectivity. The entry fee for the cash strapped ISPs is around ₹10 crores for an all-India licence, apart from an annual revenue-share licence fee of 8 per cent.
- **Low cost-low quality image:** India's unique positioning as a low-cost, low-down-the-value-chain service provider, due to its BPO operations, has turned out to be a double edged sword. It is a cash cow for Indian firms, but when it comes to the choice of knowledge processes outsourced to India, Indians seemingly cannot shed their 'cost-effective service provider' image. Foreign companies also worry about the quality of work that a low-wage country can

deliver. Thus, more and more foreign companies contemplating outsourcing to India consider outsourcing only the trivial back-office operations in order to cut costs, simply because they do not know any better. Thus, organizations are finding it increasingly difficult to migrate from their cost-effective standardized service offerings to a more differentiated financial service offering, which commands a premium price. This is also the roadblock that existing BPO companies may face as they try to scale up their operations and move higher up the value chain to offer KPO services. To avail of the KPO opportunities, the service providers will have to face formidable challenges in the path of their development, which include the following:

- **Higher quality standards:** Processes executed within the KPO domain require higher quality standards, because the stakes for the clients are high. The clients are likely to be apprehensive about the quality of services delivered. In some cases, investment in KPO infrastructure is expected to be higher than that in traditional BPO. For example, the contract research organizations are likely to require higher amounts of capital because of the large time-frame required for success as well as the domain knowledge and expertise required. The lack of a good talent pool for the execution of projects may often prove to be a hindrance in many countries.

KPO projects require a higher level of control, confidentiality and enhanced risk management. Laxity in any of these parameters will not only jeopardize the KPO services being provided, but may also affect the entire business conducted by the client.

- **Attracting talents and facing attrition:** KPO companies are faced with the challenge of hiring the best talent and imparting continuous training to these professionals.

Another key challenge in the management of KPO is the identification of performance criteria. This involves setting the right expectations with the help of the end-client as well as its professionals, continuous assessment and monitoring, constructive feedback, appropriate coaching and mentoring, and identification of the right career path for the company's professionals.

KPO: INDIAN SCENARIO

After the great success of Business Process Outsourcing (BPO) in India, it is now KPO's turn to make its presence felt. BPO success in India is encouraging overseas companies eyeing the Indian market for outsourcing their high-tech knowledge-based jobs. Operational cost saving, pool of talented workforce, infrastructure improvement and favourable government policies are the major factors which are responsible for Knowledge Process Outsourcing (KPO) in India. The KPO industry, unlike BPO, provides domain-based processes and business expertise. KPO is more like a challenge as it demands advanced and expert skills on the part of its employees. BPO, on the other hand, is more or less like a commodity business which relies comparatively more on Information Technology and its various sectors.

The Indian workforce is highly literate and well-versed with English language due to the Indian educational system. Every year, India is producing hundreds and thousands of English-speaking, trained professionals in the fields of IT, engineering, education, law, science, finance, architecture and other competitive fields.

The Indian advantage primarily lies in the educational and technical qualifications of its workforce. A survey conducted by NASSCOM (National Association of Software and Service Companies) showed that an Indian ITES–BPO centre in the banking and financial services sector performs better than US and UK-based ones. It has also showed in the survey that 45 per cent of Indian KPO service providers have the highest quality certification like Six Sigma. BPOs or KPOs in India are getting more quality-conscious and they are striving to attain standards that are internationally accepted. They are in the process of acquiring highly acclaimed quality management standards from the International Organization for Standardization (ISO) such as ISO 9002, ISO 9001, ISO 9001:2000, ISO 9001:2001, and from the Capability Maturity Model (CMM) framework as well as the new Capability Maturity Model Integration (CMMI) framework.

Indian KPOs promise to provide the next surge of growth to the service sector in India. Many of the firms engaged in providing BPO services are now migrating to KPO services. Though the two industries look similar, there is a significant difference in terms of the service offerings. KPO is much higher up in the value chain and Indian firms will require specialized skills and a unique business model to be successful in this arena.

India clearly has the first mover advantage. By the time other countries ramp up their facilities and gain expertise to get on par with India, Indian firms can move up the value chain to ensure continuous growth in the long run. India as an attractive KPO destination can be explained with Porter's Diamond Model (see Figure 1.3) for competitive advantage.

Factor Conditions

The critical factor conditions responsible for India as the source destination for KPO jobs are as follows:

Human resources

India has a highly talented workforce. There is a large pool of English-speaking and computer literate manpower. There are many qualified professionals including engineers, doctors, finance graduates, CAs and lawyers. More and more professionals are choosing the outsourcing industry as a career option, because the pay is more lucrative compared to other sector jobs, and the growth rate is much faster.

Physical infrastructure

India's infrastructure is not so conducive to BPO or KPO business, as the poor roads and connectivity do not make it an instant choice for businesses for the clients. However, of late, due to change in government policies towards privatization in telecommunication and infrastructure sector, opening them up for FDI has boosted the business in the last few years.

Information infrastructure

With improved communication systems in place, distance is no longer a disadvantage to Indian companies serving clients around the globe. Indian firms can share information with their clients in various countries on a real-time basis through Internet and audio or video conferencing. In addition, India has good intellectual property rights and excellent data security procedures.

Scientific and technological infrastructure

Many MNCs have set up R&D centres here. About 2000 recognized R&D institutes operate in India. India has the world's largest number of scientific and technological training centres after the USA.

Demand Conditions

With a booming economy, Indian manufacturing and services companies, like their counterparts abroad, have adapted IT to improve their capabilities. They are looking to outsource a lot of their high-end work to KPO vendors. The demand from different industry segments is expected to rise rapidly as global players feel confident about outsourcing their high-end work to India.

Related and supporting industries

India has around 3,000 software-services companies. These vendors are leaders in IT services and BPO sector, which leverages India's KPO sector. India has 5 cities that act as information technology clusters where thousands of Indian and multinational service providers are operating at cutting-edge technologies. The huge base of doctors, pharmacy graduates and engineers is boosting the domain expertise that firms need in various verticals.

Firm strategy, structure and rivalry

India has the highest number of CMM-certified companies in the world. Indian vendors have internationally accepted quality standards and processes.

Many of them have garnered international recognition and a global clientele. With global giants like CSC, Accenture and EDS entering the Indian market, competition has increased and margins have reduced. The increasing wages threaten to nullify India's low-cost advantage. In the global competition context, the Indian KPO may have to face the following challenges:

- Enhancing manpower quality
- Understanding the market
- Building domain expertise
- Conforming to international quality standards
- Branding.

Even though most of the Indian KPOs provide world-class offerings, they are not big brands globally as an IBM or an Accenture is. Sufficient effort needs to go into creating the brand image abroad, that will help reinforce the superior quality image of Indian vendors.

PPO: An Emerging Trend

PPO means *person-to-person outsourcing*. This terminology was coined by Alok Aggarwal, chairman of Evalueserve Inc. PPO services are being used in small offices, home businesses and even individually run business everyday through various means such as online tutoring and home and landscape design services. Many of these PPO professionals work from their homes with a broadband connection, and given the low overhead, vendors and freelancers can charge fairly low rates. PPO services would include payments made to utility service agencies, educational or other institutions, and purchase of simple items such as movie tickets, personal computers, and electronics equipment. PPO services follow two business models:

- The first one is the direct interaction model, where the individual client signs a contract directly with a vendor in a low-wage country, whose employees (tutors, administrators, etc.) work on a full-time or part-time basis, or as subcontractors.
- The second is the online marketplace model, where the vendors providing PPO services enrol in an online marketplace by paying a monthly subscription fee plus a fixed percentage of the revenue if they win the project through this marketplace. In this model, the online marketplace typically earns between 5 to 15 per cent of the contract price in return for an assurance of a minimum service level from the vendor, thereby reducing the risk for the client.

As per research conducted by the KPO major Evalueserve, there are currently more than 90 online marketplaces on the World Wide Web, and the projects that they have involve over 500,000 vendors and freelance professionals who are providing these services from low-wage countries. A few prominent players in the PPO space are Guru.com (the largest marketplace with more than 625,000 registered vendors and freelance professionals), California-based Elance.com, Florida-based RentACoder.com and GetAFreeelancer.com, owned by Sweden-based Innovateit.

SUMMARY

Knowledge process outsourcing companies are those service providers that have strong domain expertise, clear focus on the high-end space, a proactive solution orientation and a collaborative mindset. The Indian KPO industry needs to scale greater heights by leveraging on domain knowledge and augmenting human resources. Another challenge is to attract and retain a multi-lingual workforce spread across various locations across the globe. The Indian government has realized that the outsourcing industry can provide jobs to thousands of educated youth and is supporting the industry. It has announced various tax holidays for players and work is on to improve the infrastructure facilities, which are the major barriers to growth. Simultaneously, the firms need to evolve their business models to gain a larger chunk of the global KPO business. Apart from location-based cost arbitrage, factors such as domain expertise, risk mitigation techniques and effective marketing will help KPO companies to create a competitive advantage.

Review Questions

1. Differentiate BPO and KPO in terms of their objectives, features and operations.
2. Which are the drivers for BPO firms to shift from BPO space to KPO space?
3. What is the opportunity and scope for KPO firms in future?
4. Discuss the scenario for the KPO industry in India and its scope for growth in the country by using Porter's Diamond model.
5. What is PPO services and how it is beneficial to new startups and small businesses?

Chapter 13

HR Challenges in BPO Industry

The key to success in ramping up talent in a BPO environment is a rapid training module. The training component has to be seen as an important sub-process, requiring constant re-engineering.[1]

Customer-companies tend to demand better results from outsourcing partners than what they could actually expect from their own departments. When the job is being done 10,000 miles away, demands on parameters such as quality, turnaround timeliness, information security, business continuity and disaster recovery, etc. are far higher than at home. The challenge before a BPO company is how to be more efficient than the original, and that depends on talented manpower available with the organization. Hence recruitment, training and retaining the manpower requires certain benchmarks in HR policies.

INTRODUCTION

The challenges for HR professionals in 21st century are immense. Most of the big companies' values are tied up in intangible assets. The study of intangible assets breaks them into three components. The first is business processes, second is customer based and third major one is workforce and investment made on employees. Processes are important for any industry and they should manage their processes well and derive maximum results out of them. Secondly, companies should focus more on driving maximum value for existing relationships with their existing customer base. Thirdly, with the workforce and the investment made on the employees, the challenge is ROI (Return on Investments) to get the expected output. 'People are our biggest assets' has become the buzzword for all organizations and 'how are these great assets managed' is real challenge before the HR professionals. Today, HR challenges may span from attrition rate, staff motivation, employee

1. NASSCOM Report, 2004.

engagement, managing diversity, restructuring, change management, work life balance etc. However, the priority of HR challenges keep changing from time to time. With changing times, the leaders will have to adopt a more participative approach in dealing with subordinates. HR practitioners will have to understand the changed psyche of the new generation and conduct leadership programs in line with that for seniors. HR professional will have to find out and understanding the tangible and intangible benefits that employees seek and appreciate. They will have to standardise compensation plans by not only comparing with the industry but also other relevant industries. However, HR challenges keep changing from time to time.

HR PRACTICES IN BPOs

To retain the experienced professionals in the midst of growing demand for trained manpower, many business process outsourcing (BPO) firms opt for a competency-based framework for selection and promotion of its key personnel. The idea is to fill up a majority of the leadership positions from within the organization instead of recruiting talented people from outside. Through this policy, it is also attempted to keep out bias in the system and increase transparency. Normally, the programme is performance-driven and puts in place a scientific process which matches employees' knowledge, skills and attributes with the role requirements.

Apart from compensation, developing managerial talent from within the organization is considered to be an important retention tool. The skills of the middle management level would be critical as operations are growing. Hence identifying talent and building capabilities to enable them to handle larger teams and develop new skill-sets that drive business capability are needed in today's business environment.

The work culture and value system are the key foundations and enablers in creating a unique workplace. There is a strong emphasis on skill and behavioural training, leadership development and e-learning. These practices are benchmarked by the entire industry.

HR DELIVERABLES

Basically, there are two HR deliverables in BPOs. The first is stable and high talent staffing. This deliverable has several dimensions. For one thing, the BPO staff must have the unique competencies as defined by say a hi-tech firm and must demonstrate those competencies at the highest level. These competencies combine cutting-edge technical knowledge with the specialized product demands defined by the high-level technology. Thus they are not influenced by in-house professional development efforts. Moreover, because these competencies are specific to high-level technology and require several years of firm experience to develop, the company must keep its R&D staffing turnover very low.

The second HR deliverable is optimal staffing levels in the BPO unit. Both of these deliverables have clear implications for the firm's overall performance. One contributes to revenue growth, while the other influences profit growth.

Performance Work System

Once the HR deliverables have been clearly defined, then it is time to go for identifying and measuring the foundational High-Performance Work System (HPWS) elements that help to generate those deliverables. In the case of a hi-tech firm, this means designing and implementing a validated competency model linked to every element in the HR system, and providing regular performance appraisals to all employees. There are a variety of ways in which this data can be represented. The most common approach is to present the proportion of achievement on each element, although it is also possible to indicate whether or not each element is either up to standard or below standard.

HR System Alignment

In the case of stable, high-talent staffing in BPO, one can assume that the firm has developed a validated competency model. At a hi-tech firm, selection into these positions must correspond to the existing competency model, and the quality of the hires should be at the highest levels. These alignment goals would strongly influence the particular sourcing decisions needed to produce those results. However, the sourcing decisions do not have to be part of the HR scorecard. BPOs also need to enact the kinds of retention policies that build experience in the enterprise. We need to note, though, that understanding that retention policies are a key or leading indicator is more important than the actual selection of policies, which are unique to each firm.

To achieve optimal staffing in manufacturing, HR must keep its recruiting cycle time short. The appropriate alignment measure can be a short recruiting cycle time, which would reflect progress towards that objective.

Identifying HR Efficiency Measures

A BPO vendor firm must be able to identify cost per hire as a strategic efficiency measure. For both deliverables, cost per hire will probably be higher than average. But the benefits of those hiring processes will also be well above average. The HR scorecard that BPO develops should highlight these links between important costs and benefits.

CHALLENGES IN BPO

HR challenges in recruitment and development are widening and getting complex with the passage of time. A HR professional handles heavy pressures in the BPO sector as the requirement keeps changing on an hourly basis. Intra-BPO poaching and supply versus demand gap were the main challenges in this sector. There is a lot of myth, gossip and misinterpretation about the industry with regards to night shifts and monotony of work. However, there are lots of jobs which involve regular shifts and repetition of the same work.

Exit interviews are great sources of information, and the person who leaves the organization can also be seen as its brand ambassador. Hence, policies need to be transparent and clear, and procedural delays need to be avoided. People don't quit an organization because they dislike it, but because they find it difficult to get along and work with particular people in it. Hence HR policies should be customized to brand-building. Human resources have therefore become human relations with more and more emphasis on emotional bonding.

Employee Safety

BPO companies should adopt the best HR practices for ensuring safety and security of their employees. Amendment to Section 25 of the Shops and Commercial Establishments Act permits IT and ITES companies to employ women in night shifts without stipulating requisite conditions with the government. However, the government should also ensure that certain conditions ensuring the safety and security of their employees are made compulsory for the BPO companies. All BPO and IT companies must install Global Positioning System (GPS) in their vehicles as has been done by GE in Hyderabad. The government should also make police verification of all drivers employed or outsourced by BPOs mandatory. Except for clarifying that he does or does not have a criminal record, this will, however, hardly throw any light on the kind of person he is. The security desk of the firm must act as an intermediary, and any change about transport schedules must be conveyed to employees much in advance.

Recruitment of BPO Employees

NASSCOM, the public body representing outsourcing organizations located in India, has developed the NASSCOM Assessment of Competence (NAC) programme for potential employees in the Business Process Outsourcing (BPO) industry. The NAC scheme has the aim of creating a talent pool within the BPO industry, as part of NASSCOM's commitment to raising standards within this field. Included in the aims of the NASSCOM (National Association of Software and Service Companies) initiative are the provision for a national-level standard for entry-level recruitment for BPO, and also the enabling of offshoring organizations to cut costs through a more speedy recruitment process.

NASSCOM assesses candidates in the areas of listening and keyboard skills, verbal ability, spoken English comprehension and writing ability, office software competence, numerical and analytical skills, mental concentration and level of accuracy. NASSCOM is also urging state governments to commit to the NAC to improve their recruitment programmes, attract investors to the BPO sector and forge ties between education and employability. The NASSCOM programme demonstrates a strong commitment to raising standards of the BPO industry.

Although the recruitment solutions market is somewhat underdeveloped at the moment, web-based software-as-a-service applications exist. These can handle much of the recruitment process very smoothly, but can also hand over charge to the regular HR application once a recruit comes on board.

High Rate of Attrition

The reason for high attrition rate is supposedly the unique working conditions at BPO centres. Most operating jobs at BPOs or call centres are in night shifts. The employees working at night shifts for a long period of time face health hazards because of change in biological cycle. So they shift to day jobs. Unless there is motivation or some concessions in duty hours, BPO workers do not stick to their jobs for much time. Secondly, the background of the employees is also responsible for the high attrition rate. The call centre employees are normally young people looking for a platform or some job to gain experience and then jump to better or stable jobs to suit their requirements.

The biggest challenge before the IT-enabled services (ITES) sector is the ever-increasing level of attrition. A recent study by NFO India and People Equity Consulting attempts to highlight the nature of this attrition. It provides the basis for evolving HR policies that could cope with the unusual demands of the BPO sector.

What causes this high level of burnout? Peculiar working hours, working days or holidays determined by geographic considerations, assuming pseudo identities, learning foreign accents, operating in an alien business environment and altered social and family life are some of the causes. Managing employees in a BPO industry with a different work environment involve high risk. What BPOs require is a focused HR policy that takes into account the peculiar needs of the workers as well as the industry.

Employee poaching emerges as a problem as most employees are reasonably well-qualified, though not qualified enough to find specialized jobs. Since BPO jobs are reasonably well-paid, they anticipate a rise in the salary and managerial step ladder, in turn, resulting in a rise in the social ladder. However, this does not always happen. Employees feel that they could get a better salary package elsewhere, and with the number of BPOs growing, it is often the case.

CULTURAL ISSUES IN BPO

India definitely enjoys the benefits of a vast pool of skilled workers who are proficient in English language. India produces the largest number of graduates every year, and most of these graduates have the knowledge of English language. Thus, language is one of those factors which attract MNCs to contract out their business operations to Indian BPOs and IT companies. Though there are competitors like China which have a large pool of skilled workers, but they don't have enough graduates who have command over the English language.

In addition to this, the Indian education system also places strong emphasis on mathematics and science. This has resulted in a large number of science and engineering graduates. Mastery over quantitative concepts coupled with English proficiency makes India one of the hot spots of the IT/BPO world. It has enabled India to take advantage of the current international demand for IT.

BPO companies particularly need to develop sensitivity towards this issue, but they must also make the client understand. The challenge facing cross-cultural adaptation and business success is about making these programmes mutually compatible. In today's turbulent world, there is a strong need to establish global communications. There has therefore never been a greater need to understand cultural differences. More misunderstandings and tensions arise due to cultural differences and prejudices than due to any other factors. Unfortunately, when it comes to international business, the same uncomfortable parameters apply, leading to both positive and negative consequences.

EXHIBIT 13.1

Transformation to Human Resources Face of Tomorrow

To help HR leaders embark on the journey, there are following three approaches or catalysts which aim to provide guidelines based on proven industry inputs:

Drive Technology-enabled Consolidation

This typically involves the enterprise-wide consolidation of Human Resource Management Systems (HRMS). It is a fact that most enterprises operate legacy and disparate systems for HR, which add to the administrative burden as well as lack of visibility and consolidated reporting of key HR parameters—even something as transactional as Payroll. Consolidating the HRMS strategy across organizations with clearly-interfaced ancillary systems and solutions enables processes to be harmonized and standardized across the organization where possible, immediately reducing the administrative focus. This also ensures the setup of a centralized or a regionalized shared services model, mostly in cost-advantageous locations, increasing the impact of the business case that will already be secured by HRMS consolidation. Taking this one step ahead, many large enterprises who want to focus on their core business and not really worry about managing and hosting HR IT systems or about compliance and upgrades, have taken the route of going the 'managed services' way. Here, one provider with their own partner network—as the need be—is responsible for delivering end-to-end HR services to the enterprise, which includes managing the technology aspect of the same. In such cases, quite a few enterprises have realized business cases leading up to 30–40 per cent savings over the period of the contract.

Unlock Analytics-empowered Decision-making

Model information and data to deliver meaningful insight—both predictive and diagnostic consolidation of HRMS and other technology warehousing tools have fared well as far as data integrity is concerned. The HR and HR-IT leaders of business are increasingly looking at this data which is stored, what it is; and if mined, what it can do for them. This data holds the potential to slice-and-dice recruitment and retention initiatives, compensation, workforce performance, and untapped skillsets. Whether it's a pre- or post-mortem analysis that is desired, analytics can deliver powerful predictive and diagnostic insights that prove invaluable to both front-line and higher management. The way to deliver this goal is to ensure the information needs and requirements are captured from the business and as well as senior HR leadership, and then create the necessary frameworks to be implemented. Once these frameworks—including predictive models—are created, deploying data to these models and frameworks will obtain the right information set to facilitate meaningful and strategic decisions.

Unleash Social Media-driven Outcomes

This is achieved by a combination of technology elements and policy decisions. Self-service is the first step towards this outcome—an intuitive self-service interface to the employee ensures greater adoption, ensuring minimal change management needs, as well as decreasing administrative burden on the part of shared services. More employee adoption means more alignment and immediate real-time feedback to HR. Once a large employee base begins operating in self-service mode, the doors to unprecedented employee productivity open up. One approach enterprises can take is to deploy off-the-shelf social media and collaboration tools where informal mechanisms help capture best practices across the organization on an as-needed basis. Such tools, which are built on the premise of employee engagement, also provide a forum for internal referral hiring which can reduce hiring costs. Other outcomes from such tools include collaborative innovation and crisis resolution, greater discoverability of resources and talent pools, re-enforcement of corporate values, and the creation of a "social enterprise" which is flatter, faster and smarter".

(*Source:* Maheedharan Thiagarajan, *Do More with BPO, Part I—Transform to the Human Resources Face of Tomorrow*, www.infosysbpo.com)

The changing world of IT

The IT outsourcing world has gone through a period of phenomenal change since programmers first stepped into that brave new world of onsite jobs.

Business patterns have been radically altered too, affecting offshore models significantly due to changing onsite-to-offshore ratios and the ever-increasing trend of relocation of jobs due to the BPO and call centre wave apparently sweeping across the region. Alongside these changes, a whole new IT generation has come to the forefront on both the software supplier and customer fronts.

However, throughout all this change, one factor has remained constant—the need to do business with people who understand people. Rather surprisingly, many of the earlier lessons learnt from the previous generation have not been passed down to the next, or have not been absorbed as intended. Thus, a growing chasm can be seen to develop between the mindsets of the customer and the supplier, which cannot simply be bridged by knowledge management principles alone.

Diagnosing the problem

In spite of its success, awareness of cultural differences within the Indian IT industry still remains at a disappointingly low level. Unfortunately, this problem starts from the CEO downwards. In large organizations, the well-travelled CEO may indeed be extremely 'culture-savvy', yet with a lack of direct interaction with the customers on a daily basis, the nuances in business communication are handed down the chain of command to the onsite marketing or resident managers to interpret.

Often, the problem begins even before the customer acquisition stage. This has resulted in many customers using outsourcing consultants to bridge the gap instead of themselves trying to manage the problem of cultural clashes. However, the negative side of this approach is that customers must then deal with these problems after the contract is signed and the outsourcing relationship has been initiated. At this late stage, many customers turn to management consultants who specialize in cross-cultural issues to make the relationship work. But by this time, much heat will have been generated as the overheads estimated during the planning of outsourcing budgets have greatly increased, with goodwill and understanding between the parties in short supply.

Importance of local knowledge

Currently, in many western countries there is seen to be the ever-present threat of 'taking jobs away', due to lack of growth and nourishment of latent local talent. Understanding these undercurrents and being able to provide strong arguments to both potential customers and the local industry at large requires a fair amount of maturity and cultural sensitivity. This lack of sensitivity, if left unchecked, will seriously dent the competitiveness of the Indian industry as a whole.

Cultural awareness as differentiator

Getting the right cultural fit is especially important for customers looking for suppliers in the BPO space. It is often accepted that suppliers already possess the right expertise in terms of technical infrastructure, domain experience, etc. However, the key differentiator or value addition which customers are looking for is the final piece of the jigsaw—the cultural understanding of doing business with foreign companies. It is therefore vital that marketing managers who interact with potential customers have high levels of cultural sensitivity and proficiency in dealing with international business, but are comfortable with local customs and traditions. Marketing managers become both ambassadors of their company and also their own home country, particularly if the potential business process has never outsourced to India. However, 'awareness' should not stop at the first point of interaction. It must permeate into the whole organization, creating a 'global perspective' in every individual employee that stands out as a competitive differentiator and gets highlighted during customer visits to India.

As BPO suppliers attain maturity and more companies enter the global market, there will be little to differentiate one from another. As margins become lesser and technology becomes increasingly commoditized, the softer issues will gain importance in attracting customers. This has already been true of the software services industry, and BPO/ITES is not going to be any different. For managing cultural differences, the following are some practical considerations for different functional areas:

Management

The management should recognize the importance of 'cross-cultural' differences in business. It needs to formulate globalization in such a way that it forms an integral part of the company culture and not a specilized function.

Human resources

HR needs to be responsive to feedback from employees at client sites. It should be ensured that HR has relevant experience of cultural issues. Strengthening of offshore teams by including people with overseas work experience is important. Listening to the client and watching out for hidden signals before things go wrong can be vital.

Training

Client teams need to be offered 'training programmes' on Indian culture and cross-cultural training programmes at all levels need to be conducted. Training programmes need to be tailored to function and country. Debriefing sessions on 'culture clashes' are of great use.

The benefits to supplier organizations in overhauling their policies in tune with today's global requirements cannot be understated. There should be a separate department for handling 'cross-culture management'. It will be one of the key determinants of success for the Indian BPO/ITES industry. Organizations are nothing but people in various roles, buying and selling to and from each other. The difficulty in selling will reduce if the cultural dimension is given its right place in the corporate structure.

HR OUTSOURCING (HRO)

In a knowledge-led economy, people are the foremost resource for any organization. HR has hence emerged as one of the most important functions for any enterprise. With hiring, recruitments and people management happening on an extensive scale, there is a need for streamlining HR-related business processes. This problem is further compounded by the concept of a global workforce—many multinationals hire and retain talent from around the world in order to gain strategic advantage, and hence an efficient method of managing and mobilizing a global workforce is a top priority.

Given the scale of HR operations and the related administrative and legal requirements, the HR function has huge cost incident as well. Hence a large number of organizations are looking at exploring HR business process outsourcing, in order to transform their HR processes by using technology, improve their service levels and save costs.

HR outsourcing (HRO) is generally defined as the administration of personnel functions, payroll administration, benefits administration, employee training and testing, compliance, relocation and recruiting by a third party. The HR outsourcing business in India is still in its infant stages. The erstwhile BPO focus in India (customer care, banking, insurance, etc.) has been built on a knowledge transfer model for primarily lower-order transactional work. In the HRO world, it is perceived that there is a lack of domain expertise, along with a lack of knowledge of specific legal, regulatory and compliance structures. This results in difficulty for potential Indian HRO service providers in moving into the field and becoming credible operators.

Aside from a general reduction in cost of 15 per cent to 40 per cent, the primary value of HRO is that it removes the burden of having to manage the administrative or back-office functions from corporate HR. This enables HR executives and their teams to focus their full attention on business processes and strategic initiatives. HR outsourcing areas are:

- Benefits administration
- Human resources administration
- Data systems (management, administration and hosting)
- HR process consulting
- Payroll processing

- Recruitment
- Training
- Employee records management
- HR helpdesk.

Key benefits of HR outsourcing include reduced effort in HR administrative work, focus on HR strategy, access to strong HR domain expertise, and process knowledge, legal and regulatory compliance on HR laws including HIPAA, FMLA and OSHA, improved HR service levels and turnaround time, higher employee satisfaction and substantial cost savings.

The human resources (HR) department is critical for employees' well-being in any business, no matter how small. Just as companies have realized the importance of customers and are taking proactive steps to ensure their satisfaction, they have also recognized the key role played by its employees in winning the battle of the marketplace. A motivated and innovative employee can work wonders for a company. Hence getting and retaining a motivated workforce has found its way on to the HRM agenda. Also, the slowing economy has forced the workforce to be productive; once employees become productive, companies want to retain them at any cost.

This has meant a shift in the focus of HR departments from routine activities to playing a more proactive role of constantly motivating and retaining employees. Usually, HR executives are busy with work related to employees; some of these activities are routine, requiring little imagination and creativity. Most of the time, the HR department does have activities 'of' the employees and not 'for' the employees. Some such mundane HR responsibilities include payroll, benefits, hiring, firing, and keeping up-to-date with state and central tax laws. Companies the world over are spending resources and time on critical activities (motivating and retaining the existing workforce) and hence prefer to outsource routine activities.

Reducing operating costs has been the main reason for outsourcing. However, access to best practices, latest technology, and faster turnaround are some of the other benefits that outsourcing provides. Outsourcing has now become an important element of business performance transformation, as this allows resources to be concentrated on core competencies. Outsourcing allows HR to make a stronger and formidable contribution to the growth and well-being of the company.

In human resource management, workers' compensation, dispute resolution, safety inspection, office policies and many of the other functions are outsourceable in nature. Over the past 20 years, the HR outsourcing marketplace has evolved beyond benefits administration. Companies are outsourcing more HR activities to achieve a fundamental shift from an administrative, tactical and compliance-driven function to a focus on the strategic acquisition, motivation and retention of talent. The transactional functions must be done right and can be handled with greater quality and efficiency by a provider who has the process and technology expertise.

According to analysts, cost reduction is usually the most crucial reason for HR outsourcing as it can lead to savings of 30–40 per cent for companies. The other reasons are:

- Cost-effectiveness
- Reduced administrative costs
- Capitalizing on technological advances or expertise
- Improved customer service
- Redirecting HR focus toward strategy or planning
- Focus on core business
- Reduced corporate overheads
- Provision of 'seamless' delivery of services
- Insufficient staff.

The process of outsourcing begins with identifying core and non-core activities, i.e., activities that the companies need to do in-house, as against outsourceable activities. The next step is finding a suitable vendor who can carry out such activities on behalf of the company. HR outsourcing service providers can fall into one of four categories:

- Professional employer organization (PEO)
- Business process outsourcing (BPO)
- Application service providers (ASPs)
- e-services.

A professional employer organization (PEO) takes legal responsibility for the employees. The PEO and business owner are partners, with the PEO handling HR aspects and the business owner handling all other aspects. BPO is a generic term and could refer to all fields and activities, but as far as HR is concerned, a BPO ensures that a company has access to the latest technology. Application service providers (ASPs) host HR software on the Web and rent it to users, while e-services are those HR activities that are Web-based.

HR outsourcing, though having started slowly, is now one of the fastest-growing BPO areas worldwide; in fact, certain HR activities such as payroll outsourcing were among the first activities to be outsourced. One of the reasons for the initial slowness is the nature of responsibilities of the HR department. This department is responsible for employee well-being in any business, irrespective of size, and any mistake here can lead to major legal problems as well as strong employee dissatisfaction.

HR MANAGEMENT CHALLENGES IN INDIA

Outsourcing increases the interaction between HR managers in the West and in India. Some insights into the common challenges that HR managers face may improve support and collaboration between managers in both locations.

Recruitment

The major challenge in an organization is recruitment. The number of people recruited at an entry level varies up to 500 people per month. This means lots of logistics as people come from different parts of the country as well as loads of paperwork. Once selected, they are trained to get them operational within four to five weeks.

Attrition

Recruitment reduces once the organization is able to keep the loyalty of the employees. Attrition remains an enormous challenge, as the average BPO attrition rate was 30–35 per cent in the last few years. A NASSCOM–Hewitt Associates survey shows that the cost of attrition is one and a half times the annual salary of an employee. Costs are due to loss of productivity, temporary replacement, loss of knowledge, and new recruitment and training. The attrition rate is linked to causes such as the average age of the employee and also to available lucrative career opportunities.

Research shows that the job is stressful as employees are moved from one process to another with little time to adjust. The work environment has rigid rules and strict monitoring, and employees become affected by sleep disturbances due to working irregular hours. In addition, the regular poaching by competitors contributes to employees leaving the organization for a better salary, a better position or career opportunities.

Salaries and Bonuses

In BPO industry, new hires are offered a competitive salary of anywhere between US$200 and US$300 a month, which is very interesting for Indian youngsters. Those who are capable and loyal to the company get a chance to move up within a reasonable period of time. There are financial bonuses for best performers.

Job Satisfaction

Job satisfaction is one of the most important factors for retaining employees. In order to manage the expectations of the recruit, the job description and the role of the employee in the organization should be clear when entering the organization.

An employee segmentation survey by Tesco, the British retail major, in 2005 indicated that there were five broad attitude segments of people in their workforce: 25 per cent were work-life balancers; 25 per cent wanted it all; 18 per cent were pleasure seekers; 16 per cent lived to work and 16 per cent worked to live. By understanding the drives and needs of each such segment, an organization can tailor the individual employment propositions in order to improve retention.

Training

The level of competencies and the job expectations of the recruits can be fully understood only once they have been inducted into the training programme. This programme should be followed with interpersonal and intercultural training at a later stage. Once people move up the ladder, there is little time for training. There is a lack of leadership training at the operational level, which is reflected on the work floor and consequently on the job satisfaction of the employee.

People Orientation

The reality and the challenges for HR managers in India are truly different from challenges faced in the West. Even though the attrition rate is high in India, HR managers are very people-oriented, while their western colleagues are far more process- and task-oriented. The happiness of the employee and consequently the well-being of his extended family are important to the Indian organization. The employee is given leave to take his mother to the hospital regardless of whether other siblings are available to do so. The employee is allowed to attend the wedding of a neighbour, or to go and mourn for a deceased family member on the other side of the country. The well-being of the employee on a personal level is of benefit to the organization.

Today, India is the hottest destination for any company which wants to outsource its business processes. But what can be the reason for India being so popular with the companies worldwide? The attractiveness of India can be contributed to three basic factors—cost, people and environment. India ranks first among a host of desirable nations in terms of cost (which includes employee cost, infrastructure cost, management cost and the tax structure).

It beats all its competitors on the people front as well. The people factor is evaluated on the lines of size of the job market, workforce education level, language barriers, past outsourcing experience and employee retention. When it comes to environment (which includes country risk, infrastructure, cultural compatibility, proximity, etc.), however, India lags behind countries like Canada, Australia and Ireland.

Challenges of Growth

The major challenges being faced by the ITES or BPO industry in India can be classified into internal and external challenges. The internal challenges include shortage of competent managers for the middle and senior management and the high attrition rates.

The external challenge is in the form of opposition from the US politicians and the UK labour unions against shifting of the BPO operations by local companies to India. The threat of real competition from other players like Philippines also exists, but doesn't seem to need our immediate attention.

The middle and senior level managers are being poached by the new entrants to the industry. Hence, large and established players face an attrition rate of 45 per cent against the industry average of 35 per cent. Everyone agrees that hiring from competition is a cyclical process and will not help the industry grow. But with very few options available, competitors resort to the easiest solution of poaching.

Attrition is not only loss of talent, but also includes the cost of training the new recruits. The attrition rate in the industry has been around 35 per cent, which is quite high for any industry. An average Indian call centre employee works with a company for 11 months, where as an average UK call centre employee stays in a company for three years. High growth rate in Indian BPO sector is one of the reasons for the high attrition rates. However, it is expected that the attrition rates would come down once growth stabilizes.

Creating Career Paths

Today, firms need to get creative with job titles and compensation practices to retain employees. If a firm has only 10 employees and little or no room for advancement within the company, HR needs to develop different "micro" job tiers for which employees can strive.

Performance Measurements for Individuals

Since performance measurements are usually tied to expectations and standards, this will raise issues about fairness. Consequently, there are about as many different sets of performance measurements and standards as there are call centres.

SUMMARY

India is called a BPO hub. One of the critical problems prevailing in the BPO industry is high attrition rate and how BPO should manage this talent. In addition, HR challenges in recruitment and development are widening and getting complex with the passage of time. A HR professional handles heavy pressures in the BPO sector, as the requirement keeps changing on an hourly basis. Intra-BPO poaching and supply versus demand gap are the main challenges covered in this sector. There is a lot of myth, gossip and misinterpretation about the industry with regard to night shifts and monotony of work. However, there are lots of jobs which involve regular shifts and repetition of the same work. HR outsourcing, though a slow starter, is now one of the fastest-growing BPO domains worldwide; in fact, HR activities such as payroll outsourcing were among the first to be outsourced. One of the reasons for the slow start could be the nature of responsibilities that the HR department has. The HR department is critical for employee well-being in any business, no matter how small, and any mix-up here can cause major legal problems for the business, as well as major employee dissatisfaction. In today's turbulent world of global communications, there has never been a greater need to understand differences in culture. More misunderstanding and tension arise due to cultural differences and prejudices than due to any other factor.

Review Questions

1. Discuss the HR practices in general in India as against in developed countries.
2. Explain the various facets of 'HR outsourcing' in the Indian industry.
3. Discuss the various HR management challenges faced by Indian BPOs and show how these are addressed.
4. What are the cultural issues in BPO organizations? How are these handled?

Chapter 14

Performance Evaluation in BPO

Benchmarks may be difficult to develop and administer, but they can play a major role in sustaining a satisfactory relationship between buyer and supplier in an outsourcing situation. However, they do not replace the trust, confidence and goodwill; those are the foundations of every successful outsourcing partnership.[1]

The BPO industry is characterized by very closely monitored service-level indicators of productivity, timely delivery and quality-related aspects. All customers in this industry demand prompt reporting on these performance metrics. Performance evaluations is addressed in order to provide clients' performance beyond their expectations using knowledge and expertise. The process is designed so as to give full satisfaction to the client, and smooth completion of the project is the main objective of the performance evaluation phase. Accurate and detailed performance measurement and management are pivotal to the success of any shared service or outsourcing initiative.

INTRODUCTION

According to H. James Harrington, "Measurement is the first step that leads to control and eventually to improvement. If you can't measure something, you can't understand it. If you can't understand it, you can't control it. If you can't control it, you can't improve it." When describing the performance measurement system, it can be best compared with the control panel on the machine or the dashboard on the vehicle. Irrespective of the size of operations, all the business organizations, however, small or big, need performance measurement and controllership for efficient and effective deployment of resources and track the health of business organization. A system of performance measurement and control, needs to be designed on the criteria of reward and penalty to the performers. However, a well-designed

1. Jan Duffy, Group VP, Solution Research, USA.

performance measurement system supported by information system will make cross-functional coordination and integration easier. The system performance is judged by its output with respect to the inputs. The higher output to input ratio is a measure of the system's efficiency and the effectiveness. However, the above ratio is also to be reviewed with respect to the time period. In the today's competitive environment the industries are being forced to focus on the effective and efficient use of the scare resources. Hence, it becomes necessary to monitor, control and improve the performance of the operations so as to attain the set goals of cost reduction and customer satisfaction. The performance measurement system helps in either reducing or eliminating the non-value added activities from the system. In today's competitive business scenario, the importance of accurately measuring and controlling the organizational performance cannot be denied as process competency has become more critical in enhancing the competitiveness of the business processes.

PERFORMANCE MANAGEMENT IN HR

After the economic reforms of 1991, India's economy became much more integrated with the world economy, which was the effect of liberalization in our country and of globalization worldwide. The concept of human resources has undergone drastic changes as far as the Indian industry is concerned. The age-old concept of Human Resource Management has changed to Human Resource Development. This change has come as a result of the change in industry from manufacturing in the public sector to information technology in the private sector.

The change in concept of performance management in the HRM model shows change of emphasis in organizations from command-and-control to a facilitation model of leadership. This change has resulted in recognition of the importance of the employee and his work performance to the strategic or long-term mission of the organization as a whole. The process of performance evaluation management provides an opportunity to the employee and his manager to discuss the development objectives and jointly create a plan for achieving those objectives. Development plans should contribute to organizational goals and the professional growth of the employee. For the success of this model, a flexible attitude in the face of constant change is essential. However, this change in environment offers many new challenges and opportunities to performance managers. This is, however, driving managers to become generalists in support of team objectives and goals.

Job Analysis

Job description is a process which involves systematically collecting, analyzing, and documenting the important facts about a job. Assignment of responsibility for the accomplishment of goals and strategic initiatives is related to the essential functions of the job description. A job description is completed before a job vacancy is advertized. After the employee is hired, this job description becomes the job assignment and forms the basis of the job function description on the Performance Evaluation Form. This process is called *job analysis*. The job analysis provides a basis for job-related selection procedures and performance standards. It specifies:

- Job functions and tasks
- Time typically spent performing each function
- Skills, knowledge and abilities required to perform the job
- Physical and mental skill requirements
- Special conditions of employment

Standards of Performance

Standards of performance are written statements describing how well a job should be performed. Performance standards are developed collaboratively with employees, whenever possible, and explained to new employees during the first month on the job. The performance standard provides a target against which to evaluate work performance.

Observation and Feedback

Observing employee performance and offering feedback about what you see should be a routine part of the way firm manage employee performance. If employee has confidence in the feedback process and its framework, it is most effective in reinforcing or improving work performance. From the standpoint of performance management, observation involves noticing specific facts, events, or behaviours related to work performance, and the results of work performance. Observations are the raw data upon which effective performance feedback may be based. The feedback should be used to help the employee be successful and continue to develop his or her skills, knowledge, and experience.

Performance Appraisal

Performance appraisal is a process resulting in improvement in work performance of an employee. Therefore the management should make every effort to obtain as much objective information about the employee's performance as possible. The most modern and widely used methods such as 360-degree appraisal should be used. The major sources from whom to get the inputs for the 360-degree approach are superiors, subordinates, peers, internal customers, external customers and a self-evaluation. For example, subordinate assessments of a supervisor's performance can provide valuable developmental guidance, peer feedback can be the heart of excellence in teamwork, and customer service feedback focuses on the quality of the team's results.

Evaluation

Evaluation by superiors are the most traditional source of employee feedback. This form of evaluation includes both the ratings of individuals by supervisors on elements in an employee's performance plan and the evaluation of programmes and teams by senior managers. The 'self-assessment' form of performance information is actually quite common, but usually used only as an informal part of the supervisor–employee appraisal feedback session. Peers are often the most relevant evaluators of their colleagues' performance. Peers have a unique perspective on a co-worker's job performance and employees are generally very receptive to the concept of rating each other. Peer ratings can be used when the employee's expertise is known or the performance and results can be observed. An upward-appraisal process, i.e. feedback by subordinates is among the most significant and yet controversial features of the performance evaluation programme. The managers being appraised as well as their own superiors agree that subordinates have a unique, often essential, perspective. The subordinate ratings provide particularly valuable data on performance elements concerning managerial and supervisory behaviours.

Continuous Learning

For the organization to remain competitive and to retain its reputation for excellence, employees should have up-to-the-minute information and the ability to use new technologies, adapt to organizational change, work in flatter organizations in which cross-functional skills and knowledge are required, and work effectively in teams and other collaborative situations. Hence it is essential for employees to continue to learn, so that they will be effective in their current jobs and able to move into other positions or accept new responsibilities as circumstances demand.

Performance Development Plan

An important component of the performance management process is development of employees' work-related skills, knowledge and experience. For that the organization should promote a climate of continuous learning and professional growth, helping to sustain employee performance at a level which meets or exceeds expectations. Performance development plans may be considered at each stage of the performance management process. The development process offers an opportunity to employees to work collaboratively to improve or build on his or her performance and to contribute to organizational effectiveness. In the performance management process, manager should discuss training, education or development opportunities with employees, identify the specific steps to be taken, and document a strategy for accomplishing these objectives.

PERFORMANCE MANAGEMENT IN BPO INDUSTRY

The BPO industry with its major thrust on knowledge workers offers a challenge to the Human Resource (HR) manager. The major challenges are:

- **Image:** The low image of BPO jobs makes it difficult to attract the best talent.
- **Pre-job training:** Due to the wide variety of the jobs, lack of general clarity on skill sets, etc. exists. There is no standard curriculum which could be designed and followed.
- **Benchmarks:** There are hardly any benchmarks for compensation and benefits, performance or HR policies. Everyone charts his or her own course.

In both pre-job training as well as in benchmarks, the role that performance management plays is not too small. Performance appraisals, whether they be pre/post-training, offers the company a quick glance through the effectiveness and the worthiness of a person in the organization and also helps in effective placements.

The key to success in building up talent in a BPO environment is a rapid training module and also in post-appraisal training. The training component has to be seen as an important sub-process, requiring constant re-engineering.

Performance appraisal has become a tool of much importance in today's management scenario. This could be used properly only with the help of objective and fair HR practices. The outputs of this could be used for organization development rather than for mere employee efficiency improvement. Firms are thus being forced to emphasize a participative but joint management by objectives, followed by a participative, joint-periodic appraisal, to bring more clarity into the system.

PERFORMANCE MEASUREMENT AND CONTROLS

Accurate and detailed performance measurement and management are pivotal to the success of any shared services or outsourcing initiative. If existing in-house process performance cannot be measured, how can its performance be determined or measured when outsourced or consolidated? Hence, measuring current performance first and then benchmarking it to others to understand, where that stands—good, better, or worse—is a must when transforming processes via shared services or BPO.

The productivity of a BPO outfit greatly depends on its performance measurement system. Many clients demand the implementation of

QA (Quality Assurance) programmes to regularly evaluate the service quality provided by the outsourcing vendor. Clients and vendors should also use clearly defined parameters that do not involve complicated measurements and thus reduce the possibility of disputes over service quality. Using parameters that enable performance measurement on an objective basis is the key to avoid complicated measurements. In BPO the performance evaluation normally includes the following areas:

- Activity monitoring process
- Performance of employees
- Performance of different teams
- Process integration
- Satisfaction to customers
- Technology set-up
- Functional and operational plan execution

Key Performance Measurements

A significant amount of information is required to effectively manage a BPO. For example, data on customer needs and expectations, customer's tolerance, the load on the system, agent activities and performance, cost components, the activities of other parts of the organization, and conditions in the external environment are equally important for managing a BPO.

Customer Satisfaction

Customer satisfaction is a top priority. Most BPO outfits conduct surveys via outbound calls to randomly selected customers. Some BPO outfits contract with outside firms to conduct surveys and prepare the results, while others do the surveys themselves. A growing number of BPOs are automating some surveys.

Service Level

Service level takes the form of 'X' per cent successfully completed jobs within a given time-frame and with acceptable quality standards.

Cost Per Unit Time

There are various ways to calculate cost. The basic formula is to divide total costs by time of completion and also the head counts involved.

Errors and Rework

A major theme of the quality movement is that good service pays for itself, because of the elimination of things that come with a lack of quality: doing work many times over, correcting mistakes, handling complaints, increased public relations costs, cancelled orders or subscriptions, costs of closing accounts, costs of inspection, and others. Errors and rework are often part of a performance cycle. For example, errors and rework consume valuable staff time, which can lead to insufficient staffing to handle the incoming workload; insufficient staffing tends to lead to high occupancy, unhappy customers and increased stress on the staff, which contributes to errors and rework. So, reducing errors and rework has a positive impact on service level, morale, customer satisfaction and costs. A reduction on errors and rework is a measure of the performance.

INCENTIVES-BASED PERFORMANCE FOR EMPLOYEES

BPO sector offers handsome initial salary, good growth and many other benefits to its employees. However, the attrition rates is very high in this sector. Hence, the performance measurement and appraisal processes are of extreme importance in BPO companies. The incentive schemes are often used as one of the tools for employees' retention. BPO employees have the advantage of getting performance-based incentives. Most of the BPO organizations today have well-designed schemes for awarding the incentives to the individuals and/or the teams as a whole based on their performance. The parameters for the measurement of employees' work performance are:

- Speed
- Accuracy
- Productivity

However, parameters measured differently (as given) for employees at different level depending upon level of responsibility and authority assigned.

- Average value generated
- Time and cost of unit work handled and completed
- Adherence to schedule
- Errors
- Work discipline and attendance
- Compliance

A recent survey shows that the pay for performance varies up to 25 per cent of the salary. Therefore, performance evaluation, reviews and appraisal play a vital role in the performance management in BPO sector. All the above mentioned parameters are used in performance appraisals to evaluate and review the performance of the employees. Commissions, incentives and bonuses, and piece rate pay help the employer to pay the employee according to their productivity and hard work. The process of performance-based pay involves:

- Clearly defined performance goals
- Evolving performance metrics
- Setting the target levels of performances
- Measuring the performance
- Rewarding employees with incentives and bonus

Organizations are also designing variable compensation plans for various roles and positions in the organization. Types of performance pay are:

- **Merit pay:** The first step to performance pay, and merit pay means setting some basic salary according to the position and the rank of the employee and the variable part of the salary is based on the periodic performance reviews.
- **Profit sharing:** Sharing the profits of the enterprise with the employees as bonus.
- **Performance bonus:** Rewards for special accomplishments or fulfillment of the targets set such as sales commission.

It has been proved through surveys that performance-based pay motivates employees to perform better and earn, and encourages learning, innovation, creativity, problem-solving and empowerment which can be facilitated through proper performance measurement and reviews.

SUMMARY

Performance measurement of BPO arrangements has evolved from measuring primarily service delivery to measuring a number of key "partnering" drivers such as quality and data security, conforming to industry standards and regulations, relationship values and value addition. The performance evaluation system sets the expectations and measures the achievement of those expectations. It transacts both the contract and the service level agreement to combine the expectations with monetary and service outcomes. It is a new way to continuously monitor the service provider and to ensure that long-term success is achieved. The performance evaluation system emphasizes the importance of defining the goals and objectives associated with any major outsourcing initiative prior to choosing a supplier and signing a contract. Obtaining the right advice, learning from the experience of others, and developing and applying appropriate benchmarks to the initial evaluation process are all-important steps.

Review Questions

1. Differentiate between performance management and performance appraisal.

2. Explain what is performance management and why this process should be in place in an organization.
3. How is performance measured and controlled in general in the business organization in the Indian context?
4. Discuss how the performance management process in BPOs should differ from other industry in general and why.

Chapter 15

BPO: Prerequisites and Precautions

Effective BPO solutions are built on a platform of outstanding quality. IT service delivery is built on the premise that customers need a partner that can integrate the enterprise.[1]

Business process outsourcing (BPO) is a process with a lot of risk. When the firm makes a decision to outsource a business process possibly involving layoffs, it becomes difficult to bring it back as in-house process. Then it becomes an expensive proposition, if it fails. Reducing these risks is essential to the success of the outsourcing effort. BPO metrics provide a good framework for continuous monitoring, reporting and management of operational parameters. To make sure that risks are mitigated in some way, a BPO metrics framework provides the answers. A systematic approach with a framework of metrics enables organizations to select the right metrics and implement proper monitoring and analysis of business processes.

INTRODUCTION

A few Asian countries are emerging as a preferred business process outsourcing destination. However, there is a voice of caution advising that BPO companies are long way to go in for requirements of domain and process knowledge. There are far fewer companies who can claim to have high-end expertise. And even in many cases the high-end work is a small faction of the total work, but it is critical to retain the customer. Customers in developed countries are increasingly looking for transaction-processing skills in areas such as HR, accountancy and finance. Most significantly, Asian BPO operators are mostly offering simple call handling services. But as the complexities of the transaction increases particularly in case of MNCs and TNCs, the BPO organizations have to assume a new role to meet the

1. Syntel White Paper, "The Keys to Successful Service Level Agreement: Effectively Meeting Enterprise Demands".

challenge of price competition at the low-value end of the work with domain and process knowledge.

THE ROAD AHEAD

BPO typically in India gives an impression that it is something which hires the college graduates for running the call centres. However, this image is changing slowly and today due to competitive pressure in the open economies of the countries across the world, the business corporations, for cost-effectiveness and system efficiencies, are looking towards destinations for outsourcing their business processes which are not so critical and not their core competencies. The philosophy is "Let experts do their jobs with least cost and maximum efficiency using their domain knowledge and past experience". As outsourcing is gaining popularity, the opportunities to outsource business processes have greatly increased.

PROCESS ANALYSIS BEFORE OUTSOURCING

An operation is composed of processes designed to add value by transforming inputs into useful outputs. Inputs may be materials, labour, energy, and capital equipment. Outputs may be a physical product (used as an input to another process) or a service. Processes can have a significant impact on the performance of a business, and process improvement can improve a firm's competitiveness.

The first step to improving a process is to analyze it in order to understand the activities, their relationships, and the values of relevant metrics. Process analysis generally involves the following tasks:

- Define the process boundaries to mark the entry and exit points of the process inputs/outputs.
- Construct a process flow diagram to show various process activities and their interrelationships.
- Determine the capacity of each activity in the process.
- Identify the bottleneck.
- Quantify the impact of the bottleneck.
- Use the analysis to make operating decisions and to improve the process.

Once the boundaries are defined, the process flow diagram (or process flowchart) is a valuable tool for understanding the process using graphic elements to represent tasks, flows, and storage. The symbols in a process flow diagram are defined as follows:

- **Rectangles** represent tasks.
- **Arrows** represent flows. Material flow by a solid line and information flow by a dashed line.

- **Inverted triangles** represent storage.
- **Circles** represent storage of information.

Box 15.1 shows the various symbols which are used while preparing the flowchart.

Box 15.1 Flowchart symbols

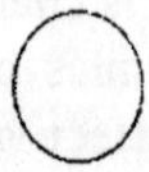	**Circles** represent data in most flowcharts. It is convenient to use different colours to identify various states of data: input, temporary, output, final product, and the like.
	**Lines with arrows** determine the flow through the chart. Flowcharts are usually drawn from top to bottom or left to right. Numbering shapes is optional.
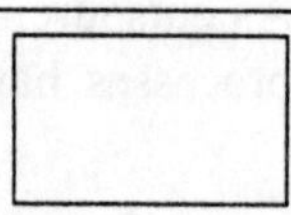	**Rectangle** is used to show a process, task, action, or operation. It shows something that has to be done or an action that has to be taken.
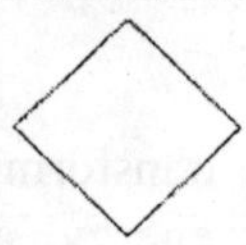	**Decision** asks a question. The answer to the question determines which arrow you follow out of the decision shape. Decisions can take place at points where results need to be evaluated before the process may continue.
	**Rounded rectangle** is used as an alternate process. The lines associated with the alternate process are usually dashed. It allows you to specify a process in a sharp cornered rectangle and an alternate process in a rounded rectangle.
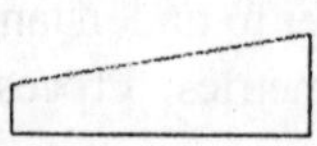	**Manual input:** The shape looks like a side view of a keyboard. It is used for entering data into a computer via a keyboard.
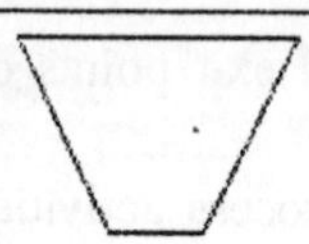	**Trapezoid shape** represents a manual operation. That is any operation or adjustment that has to be done by hand rather than automatically.
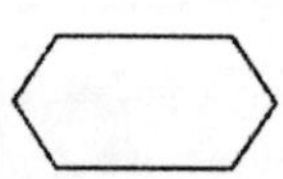	**Preparation:** This shape was originally used by IBM programmers to set a switch, modify an index register, or initialize a routine. It can be used to differentiate between steps that prepare for work versus steps that actually do the work.
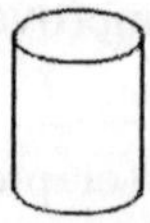	**Database:** A cylinder represents a data file or database. This shape can also represent the magnetic disc itself.
	**Parallelogram** is used to show input or output. Examples of input are receiving a report, getting an e-mail, getting an order, receiving data in some format, etc.
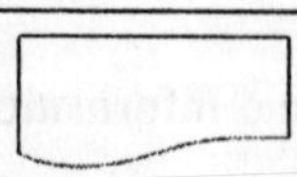	**Rectangle** with a curved bottom represents a document or report.

	**Terminal:** This shape tells you where the flowchart begins and ends. It shows the entry point of your flowchart and the exit point.
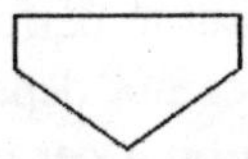	**Off-page connector:** This shape means the flow continues on another page. A letter or page number in the shape tells you where to go. It is an alternative to using a circle.

In a process flow diagram, tasks drawn one after the other in series are performed sequentially. Tasks drawn in parallel are performed simultaneously. Operations managers are interested in process aspects such as cost, quality, flexibility, and speed. Some of the process performance measures that communicate these aspects include:

- **Process capacity:** The capacity of the process is its maximum output rate, measured in units produced per unit of time. The capacity of a series of tasks is determined by the lowest capacity task in the string. The capacity of parallel strings of tasks is the sum of the capacities of the two strings, except for cases in which the two strings have different outputs that are combined. In such cases, the capacity of the two parallel strings of tasks is that of the lowest capacity parallel string.
- **Capacity utilization:** The percentage of the process capacity that actually is being used.
- **Throughput (flow rate):** The average rate at which units flow past a specific point in the process. The maximum throughput rate is the process capacity.
- **Flow/throughput/lead time:** The average time that a unit requires to flow through the process from the entry point to the exit point. The flow time is the length of the longest path through the process. Flow time includes both processing time and any time the unit spends between steps.
- **Cycle time:** The time between successive units as they are output from the process. Cycle time for the process is equal to the inverse of the throughput rate. Cycle time can be thought of as the time required for a task to repeat itself. Each series task in a process must have a cycle time less than or equal to the cycle time for the process. Put another way, the cycle time of the process is equal to the longest task cycle time. The process is said to be in balance if the cycle times are equal for each activity in the process. Such balance rarely is achieved.
- **Process time:** The average time that a unit is worked on. Process time is flow time less idle time.
- **Idle time:** Time when no activity is being performed, for example, when an activity is waiting for work to arrive from the previous

activity. The term can be used to describe both machine idle time and worker idle time.

- **Work-in-process:** The amount of inventory in the process.
- **Set-up time:** The time required to prepare the equipment to perform an activity on a batch of units. Set-up time usually does not depend strongly on the batch size and therefore can be reduced on a per unit basis by increasing the batch size.
- **Direct labour content:** The amount of labour (in units of time) actually contained in the product. Excludes idle time when workers are not working directly on the product. Also, excludes time spent on maintaining machines, transporting materials, etc.
- **Direct labour utilization:** The fraction of labour capacity that actually is utilized as direct labour.

The process capacity is determined by the slowest series task in the process; that is, having the slowest throughput rate or longest cycle time. This slowest task is known as the *bottleneck*. Identification of the bottleneck is a critical aspect of process analysis since it not only determines the process capacity, but also provides the opportunity to increase that capacity. Starvation occurs when a downstream activity is idle with no inputs to process because of upstream delays. Blocking occurs when an activity becomes idle because the next downstream activity is not ready to take it. Both starvation and blocking can be reduced by adding buffers that hold inventory between activities. The following list covers some of the ways that processes can be improved:

- Reduce work-in-process inventory—reduces lead time.
- Add additional resources to increase capacity of the bottleneck—an additional machine/resource.
- Improve the efficiency of the bottleneck activity—increases process capacity.
- Move work away from bottleneck resources where possible—increases process capacity.
- Increase availability of bottleneck resources—increases process capacity.
- Minimize non-value adding activities—decreases cost.
- Redesign the product for better manufacturability—improves process performance measures.

Flexibility can be improved by outsourcing certain activities. Flexibility also can be enhanced by postponement, which shifts customizing activities to the end of the process. In well-optimized processes, significant investment may be required to achieve a marginal operational improvement. Because of the large investment, the operational gain may not generate a sufficient rate of return. A cost-benefit analysis should be performed to determine if a process change is worth the investment or worth to outsource.

BUSINESS PROCESS MANAGEMENT (BPM)

BPM is a *discipline of modeling, automating, managing, monitoring, and optimizing business processes to increase profitability.* BPM is not a technology or a tool. It is not merely a software which can be purchased, installed and run to fix a business issue, but people play a significant role in business process management.

In a business process the activities may be performed by people or systems and are completed either sequentially or simultaneously to achieve desired goals. These can be done internally or outsourced to outside agency. BPM is a systematic approach to make an organization's workflow more effective, more efficient and more capable of adapting to an ever-changing environment. The goal of BPM is to reduce human error and miscommunication. It helps to optimize an organization's resources and core operations.

There are two different kinds of BPM frameworks available in the market today. Horizontal frameworks deal with design and development of business processes and are generally focused on technology and reuse. Vertical BPM frameworks focus on a specific set of coordinated tasks and have pre-built templates that can be readily configured and deployed. In general, BPM has five basic components:

- Process discovery
- Process modeling and design
- Business rules engine
- Work-flow engine
- Simulation and testing

When beginning with BPM, it is important to realize that processes vary greatly. The processes can be categorized in many different ways, including:

- Complexity
- Duration
- Volume
- Industry
- Department

The reason why this is important is because some types of processes are not well-suited to being managed within software. For example, while highly standardized, repetitive or regulated processes tend to be excellent candidates, highly unpredictable and unstructured processes typically are not. Business process management is a discipline consisting of basically five phases: Model, Automate, Manage, Monitor, and Optimize explained as follows:

Model

The first phase of BPM is to create a model. A model is an object created to represent something else. During the Model phase, a high-level diagram of the process is created. Initially, the goal is to gather just enough detail to understand conceptually how the process works and the main steps involved therein.

Automate

During the Automate phase, the model is expanded to create the specific set of instructions, form details, and rules needed to run the process. It is at this point where decisions about how to specifically implement the processes are made.

Execute

The Execute phase of BPM consists of interpreting the instructions created during the Automate phase to manage the flow of work from the beginning of the process until its completion. Within BPM software, the workflow engine is responsible for creating tasks and automatically directing them to the right people or systems based on the process rules. It is similar to a GPS system provides you with step-by-step driving instructions to reach destination.

Monitor

The Monitor phase is where process performance is measured, tracked and reviewed for potential improvements. From our example, identifying that travel time has increased by 30 per cent might cause you to test an alternate route to avoid the traffic signals.

Optimize

During the Optimize phase, managers use data and lessons learned from Manage phase as a foundation to change the process. Optimization may include such things as enhancing the data collection forms, adding or removing tasks, automating steps that were previously completed manually, or modifying the reports generated. The goal of the Optimize phase is to identify changes that will improve the process. From our example, identifying and test an alternate route to reduce travel time. In BPM further repeating the same cycle for continuous improvement in the changing environment of technology.

The reasons why BMP is necessary are:

- **Reduce waste:** Paper work elimination reduces time and money.
- **Returns on investments:** Get the most out of your IT investments.
- **Better customer service:** Process with compliance, speed and with few errors.
- **Time frame:** Tasks within deadlines given by customers.

- **Data quality improvements:** Through data validation and system integration.
- **Productivity improvements:** Deploying automation for repetitive processes.
- **System flexibility:** Possible to modify processes to adapt to changes.
- **Increase process efficiency:** Due to elimination of manual tasks and activities.
- **Process visibility:** Better process understanding due to measuring and tracking.
- **Cost advantage:** Lower costs, higher revenues satisfied customers.

Managing business processes comprises all those management activities aimed at the proper execution of each process of the company. This covers monitoring, provision of resources, improvement in subsequent executions of the process, resolution of incidents and problems associated with the process execution, the re-engineering of a process, etc.

BPM has a clear objective, to promote and facilitate continuous improvement (continuous projects). In BPM, the organization leadership and the participant have their defined role in managing the business process in given process architecture. It is a continuous activity to achieve improvement. However, before taking any outsourcing decision it is necessary for an organization to have proper BPM for all its processes to assess the benefits of outsourcing to vendors.

OUTSOURCING: A PREFERRED STRATEGY

Outsourcing is not new to business firms. The typical age-old outsourcing activity is transportation or warehousing for distribution of the manufactured products. However, due to the philosophy of 'hollowing of the corporation', which is being adopted by business houses, many business processes which were earlier exclusively performed internally due to the policy of business secrecy are now being outsourced. The non-critical business processes in functional areas like Finance, IT, HRM, Marketing, Advertising, Logistics and Supply Chain Management are today outsourced. Due to emerging business opportunities, there has been mushrooming growth of the service providers for generic business services, which are being commoditized due to cut-throat competition in the BPO industry. Even though the BPO success wave today is in the IT sector, many other industry sectors like automobiles, pharmaceuticals, engineering, health care, insurance and retail are going in for outsourcing their IT-enabled business processes to make their supply chain lean and efficient due to the following advantages:

- Achievement of cost reduction through process improvement, and reengineering by using technology

- Focus on the firm's core business or core competencies, while back-office operations performed by BPO vendors
- Reduction in wastage through better resource utilization
- Use of expertise of domain specialists from outside to do one's job cost-effectively and efficiently
- Business risk mitigation in changing environment
- Enhanced customer service and speed to the market.

The success experienced by BPO has encouraged many business firms to outsource their entire operational functions. However, as a caution, the following needs to be looked into before outsourcing any activity in any of the functional business areas (see Figure 15.1).

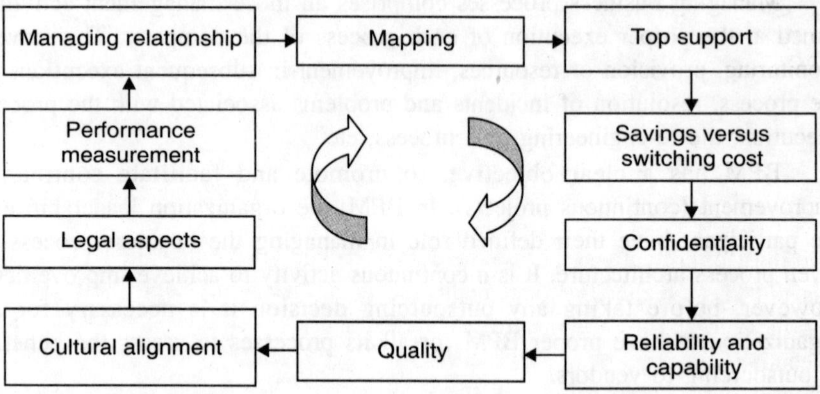

FIGURE 15.1 BPO risk mitigation framework.

Mapping Business Processes

The first step is to segment or divide the process into microelements or activities. This is to be followed by clearly demarking the non-core activities which can be outsourced to the BPO vendor. These non-core elements, wherein the firm lacks in efficiency and effectiveness due to technology advancement (which the firm does not have), or due to the organization's working culture, can be handled by the BPO vendors effectively.

Top Support

BPO policy decisions involve top management support and involvement. The sharing of information sometimes may lead to the risk of divulging business secrets. Therefore a clear-cut policy has to be evolved to decide the degree of sharing of information, and accordingly the contract terms may be framed.

Savings versus Switching Cost

Domain knowledge and process expertise is key to survival for BPO service providers. However, Indian BPOs have a long way to go in this high-expertise area. The Indian BPO outfits mostly (except in IT) rely on the expertise of their foreign principals. Therefore the contracts initially given are sometimes abruptly terminated, as the actual results are much below expectations. Secondly, due to killing competition, there is a price war to get a pie of the market. Therefore, in a bid to get business, the BPO service providers often ignore the implications. This results often in severance of the contract, which keeps the client in an uncertain state and results in heavy switching cost or loss of business for it.

Confidentiality

The other key aspect of BPO is confidentiality about the contract and the information, which is transferred continuously between the parties. The BPO vendor should assure the client that there is enough security for the information which is passed on to him, and he has adequate technology and equipment to deny access to information to unauthorized users.

Reliability and Capability of BPO Vendor

The most important task before the customer is to ensure that the BPO vendor has the latest technology and dedicated people to handle the particular job and the transaction. The customer should impose training requirements on the executives working on a transaction to get maximum level of performance. The reliability and capability of the BPO vendor will depend on the following things:

- Technology used
- Infrastructure
- Trained and competent people.

The most important point is that the customer should put some restrictions on BPO vendors to subcontract the job to any third party, and ensure that the BPO vendor is dedicating some resources to perform the assigned task.

Quality

The cutting cost is not the only reason for business process outsourcing. Outsourcing makes sense provided there is upgradation in the quality of the task. If it is not being done locally, the option is business process offshoring, which is considered a strategic option to get world-class quality. That is the reason why many clients abroad are offshoring the projects to BPO vendors. Such jobs include:

- Evaluating the commercial prospects of inventions
- Funds research on the financial statements of MNCs and TNCs

- Research and analysis of value chain segments of firms in IT and telecommunications
- Patent writing and evaluation
- Coding and billing procedures in health care sector
- Market forecast studies for over-the-counter (OTC) drugs.

Cultural Alignment

It is said that the mind is akin to hardware and culture is akin software. In a BPO outfit, people are hardwired but the programmes are quite dissimilar to the local culture. Because of globalization, the challenge before the BPOs is cross-cultural adaptation, so that the programmes run are compatible with each other. The need of the hour is to understand the differences between the cultures and move towards reducing the 'understanding gap' by:

- Offering training programmes to clients and vendor teams at all levels,
- Making country- and function-specific training programmes
- Conducting sessions on cultural clashes
- Being responsive to feedback from employees.

Legal Aspects: Contractual Obligations and Limitations

BPO is a contract between two parties, wherein a business firm (called as customer) transfers the ownership of internal functions of a company to a third party (called as vendor). This contract needs to be framed to the minutest detail to decide on the obligations and responsibilities of both the parties. Remedies have to be clearly spelt out for possible contraventions or violations of the terms. The key area is the jurisdiction, which needs to be mutually agreed and spelt out to avoid inconvenience. The precaution is to have a separate negotiation team, which consists of executives well-versed in the legal aspects of the areas of finance, personnel, marketing and operations. The contract document should cover issues like resources allocated, pricing, timely payment, delivery schedule, warranties, obligations, exit and termination of contract.

Performance Measurement and Reporting System

For any process, performance measurement is very important to understand the deviations or shortcomings and take corrective actions thereafter. The customer first sets the performance standards for the BPO vendor and then should insist on a proper reporting system, depending on the nature and criticality of the task which is outsourced. This may help both the customer and the vendor to take the corrective action much in advance before any major deviation takes place in the expected results.

Managing Relationship: Interface

BPO is B2B marketing, wherein customer relationship management has a major role to retain the customer by satisfying him on a continuous basis by using the following tools:

- Keeping knowledgeable interface for coordination
- Developing transaction processing skills through training
- Value additions in regular services
- Developing high-end process expertise and innovations.

SUMMARY

BPO involves a mix of decisions. However, growth for both customer and BPO vendor will come through partnership based on mutual trust, teamwork and innovations, resulting in a win-win situation irrespective of the BPO models being followed.

Review Questions

1. Why is outsourcing a preferred business strategy for many leading corporations in spite of the great risks in the outsourcing process?
2. How are corporations trying to mitigate the outsourcing risks?
3. What precautions should the client take in outsourcing its business processes?
4. "In outsourcing the firm should achieve a balance between resources, capabilities and distinctive competencies to create customer value". Explain.

Chapter 16

Service Quality Issues in BPO

Quality is a journey of continuous improvement and not a destination. Quality is therefore everyone's responsibility; everyone performs appropriately, on time, first time, each time.[1]

In manufacturing, the traditional quality control methods address physical measurements and processes. However, in the service sector, quality issues are mainly non-physical. Service quality is measured in the terms of time taken in the transaction process, its accuracy and completion, and finally customer satisfaction. Service quality requires the entire organization's orientation to quality delivery to get overall desirable business performance. The primary requirements that the client's executives have from the BPO are commonly acknowledged to be cost reduction, quality gain, innovation, risk reduction and the ability to concentrate on core business values. But many independent surveys regularly pinpoint dramatic failings, and differences between expectations and what is actually achieved. BPO will require an organization to change to achieve maximum success. In order to obtain these expected benefits, it is necessary to ensure that BPO is initiated, measured, reported and delivered in the correct way towards its service quality.

INTRODUCTION

As the Indian BPO industry is growing at a faster rate and increasingly grabbing bigger chunks of BPO jobs from developed countries, recognizing quality standards is a vital issue. Due to the success derived by US firms with the business strategy of offshoring, BPO has been gaining popularity over the last few years in India. However, companies that are looking to outsource non-core processes to third-party service providers are literally placing their fate in the hands of another company. A major concern and challenge for the adoption of an outsourcing strategy lies in ensuring that the high level of quality that has been achieved in-house, prior to outsourcing, is not diluted. In the absence of correct checks and balances, companies run the risk of

1. Corporate philosophy, http://www.datamaticstech.com/quality_systemapproach.htm.

straining their relationship with customers through the inability to provide good service continuously.

Manufacturers also have begun to recognize the importance of service quality as they add intangibles—value-added services such as installation, warranties, delivery and after-sale service—to their product offerings. In addition to preventing physical defects, quality in manufacturing means addressing all factors affecting business success. There are five dimensions of service quality such as:

- **Reliability:** Performance of promised service accurately
- **Responsiveness:** Timely help to customers
- **Assurance:** Developing trust and confidence
- **Empathy:** Outside-in view
- **Tangibles:** Physical facilities supporting intangible deliverables.

Uttarayan Bagchi, Professor in University of Texas at Austin, has developed a model[2] (see Figure 16.1) which explains the gaps in delivering service quality as generally applicable to service-based products.

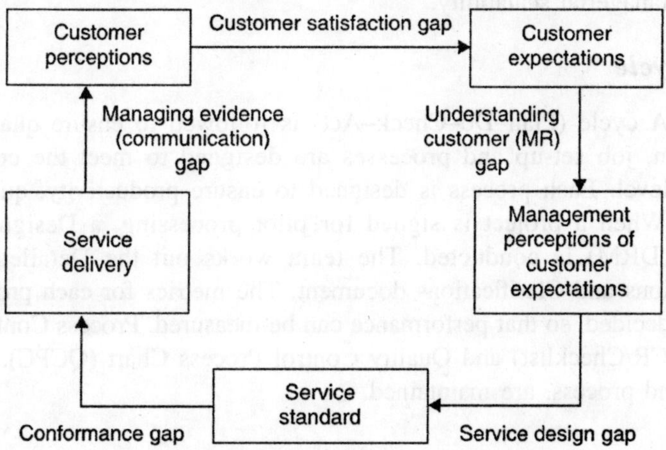

FIGURE 16.1 Service quality gaps.

The major gaps identified are in the area of understanding customer needs, designing an appropriate service, offering to meet customer needs, conformance to the applicable standards, communication for implementation, and degree of satisfaction amongst the customers.

QUALITY PRACTICES

Total Quality Management is the mantra today. Industry culture requires

---

2. James A. Fitzsimmons and Mona J. Fitzsimmons, *Service Management*, Tata McGraw-Hill, New Delhi, 2006, p. 131.

quality in all aspects of the company's operations, with processes being done right the first time and defects and waste eradicated from operations. In many BPOs, commonly the following quality practices are in use at every stage of the delivery process to build, improve, monitor and ensure quality.

TQM system

The TQM system helps plan and monitor daily work management. Every employee is either accountable for some results or directly responsible for them. For every result, there may be one or more success indicators or managing points. For every result, there may be one or more process indicators or checking points. These are integrated in a single place with the help of the TQM system, which enables:

- Visual representation of the actual results against set targets
- Faster and more effective decision-making
- Greater clarity in the individual's roles and responsibilities
- Up-to-date data which gives timely warning about problems
- Managerial scalability.

PDCA cycle

The PDCA cycle (Plan–Do–Check–Act) is followed to ensure quality. The application, job set-up and processes are designed to meet the committed accuracy level. Each process is designed to ensure productivity, quality and delivery. When a project is signed for pilot processing, a Design Review Meeting (DRM) is conducted. The team works out the Detailed Project Specifications and Clarifications document. The metrics for each process and person is decided, so that performance can be measured. Process Conformance Report (PCR/Checklist) and Quality Control Process Chart (QCPC), both for product and process, are maintained.

Training

The training programme for any new recruit should be designed in such a way as to ensure quality. The induction programme should include training on TQM concepts and other QC tools. Existing employees undergo training programmes on Six Sigma, ISO 9000 and testing.

WIs and SOPs

A set of Work Instructions (WIs) and Standard Operating Procedures (SOPs) are defined for each process and there is no deviation acceptable to the instruction or specification. Exceptions should be handled immediately to avoid bottlenecks.

Stage inspection

Stage inspections are carried out during each process and final inspection is done for the whole product or process. When a new project is started, Quality Assurance check should be done to ensure that client's specifications are met.

Quality audits

Quality audits are carried out periodically for each department to ensure that SLAs are met, processes are followed, and required documents are maintained. If there is a customer complaint or non-conformance on the part of any process or people, a detailed causal analysis is done to identify the root cause and come up with a preventive action plan. Audits should be conducted by a team of trained Internal Quality Auditors. The auditors are identified on the basis of their experience and qualification. The HR team identifies the training requirements and sends the team for quality-related training like Six Sigma and ISO 9000.

EXHIBIT 16.1
Quality Assurance though BPO

The DORAB is a leading consumer durable products company with over ₹20,000 million in annual revenue. It places a strong emphasis on customer services and satisfaction. Online sales account for a major portion of its sales. DORAB launches campaigns for best offers on its products across its global markets in various formats. The DORAB has, over a time built large Web applications for efficient global sales delivery and management. Web applications service DORAB's retail customers, campaign managers, sales representatives, and distributors. Though there are different channels of order processing, the Web applications system processes 69 per cent of the total orders. Thus, productivity gains in this channel directly impacted the bottom-line of the business. DORAB further needed a robust tested web application system for efficient performance during millions of simultaneous online sales of its products.

DORAB had many issues such as their IT staff was occupied with building new systems and enhancing the existing systems to serve the fast-growing needs of its customers. There was a clear gap between the development of new systems and successful implementation of the same. The online application has a simple outlay for users, but has complex business logic built into the system through various user roles, privileges, geographical parameters, campaign information, etc. The projected cycle with daily builds used to take longer than expected during manual testing days. Despite long cycle, the outcome was not encouraging mostly because of the volume of testing required. Due to the complex nature of Web applications, frequent changes to front-end layout and back-end business logic required laborious re-work in updating of test cases and re-testing of the same.

BPO vendor was identified to develop sustainable Quality Assurance (QA) process to ensure quality expectations of the Web application and optimize the post development to UAT cycle time by developing an automated process for testing the system. BPO vendor specialized application Quality Assurance team did a thorough system, environment, and requirements study and designed the QA Solution. They delivered robust automated test scripts and also paved the way for effective and fast regression testing with minimal manual intervention to scripts required.

The results was improved resource management. The gap between the development of new systems and successful implementation of the same to serve the fast-growing needs of users was bridged. This was experienced by vendors as they supported testing of its business-critical applications on a 24×7 cycle with increased visibility and predictability in software testing process. The DORAB moved towards automating all its testing process. This enabled the DORAB to reduce the time required for testing as well as to remove the bugs that might be introduced during manual testing and bug fixing cycles. The updated builds are tested again in the night. This drastically reduced the regression cycle as well as built efficiency into the testing process. The manual intervention reduced by 85 per cent. This automation component reduced the test updating by 85 per cent. With outsourcing partnership the DORAB's IT staff has been able to focus on its core business and on building more efficient systems, while still ensuring complete customer satisfaction.

ADDRESSING SERVICE QUALITY ISSUES

There are three alternative quality strategies that could be considered, such as: to achieve the strongest client loyalty by delivering the best customer experience; to achieve the highest customer satisfaction by reducing cycle times, waste, and process errors; or to minimize the cost of bad quality.

The BPO vendor chosen must match the quality strategy. Some BPO groups deliver extraordinary client experiences, some focus on efficient and effective processes and some crank through high-volume service interactions for the lowest possible price. It is impossible for any one firm to deliver some measure of each strategy; they can only do one well or all poorly.

Quality outcomes are impacted by the way people breathe, the way the restrooms are cleaned, the CEO's smile or frown as they walk past the desks. Nothing in your contract, no matter how lucrative, is going to alter those irreducible elements in the short term. Once this strategic match has been established, the tactical management approach must also be aligned. The companies and their BPO vendors, aiming for high levels of satisfaction and efficient processes, are tightly integrated around service contracts and monitor outcomes continuously. However, they do not link at the level of principles, values, and culture. These relationships take into account the total cost of quality at the process level and attempt to optimize enterprise costs over the short term. The basic concepts that can be applied to increase customer value and contribute to the organization's competitiveness are:

- Continuous improvement
- Cost of quality

- Customer satisfaction
- Problem-solving
- Process view of work
- Quality assurance and quality control
- Supplier quality.

The BPO's job is to reduce the cost of transaction processing irrespective of the total cost of quality. This is never stated explicitly because of the tacit assumption that there will not be an adverse impact on the cost of quality. These relationships still make good economic sense overall, but they are almost always calculated in a manner that optimizes the appearance of local savings versus the true enterprise-level savings.

With the client firm carefully aligning quality strategy and tactics with a BPO relationship that supports the company's market segmentation, there is an attractive opportunity to gain flexibility, expansion capacity, and value-added capabilities. The risk premium associated with BPO, if done well, should be value-neutral to the shareholders in the worst case and offer significant opportunities in the best case. The challenge is how to quantify the true cost of poor quality as well as the true financial benefit of improved quality. There are several elements to consider:

Vendor management

In the event the BPOs are struggling with quality, clients often find themselves burdened with unexpected overhead and management costs. This will result in requirements of additional and unplanned management staff to track and manage vendor quality issues. This staff group may also be needed to deal with internal management escalations that result from quality issues, errors, or mishandling by the vendor. This will quickly eat into the expected savings achieved by outsourcing.

Training costs

If a BPO vendor does not excel at QA, clients will face persistent, uncorrected quality issues that ultimately will require more hands-on training. This can result in unplanned hard costs related to international travel and even hiring of additional training personnel.

Customer satisfaction

Poorly treated customers will desert the firm with a negative opinion of the company. They are less likely to transact again in future. They are likely to share that negative experience with their friends and colleagues. Hence a pleased customer supports interaction, cements loyalty and increases future revenue-generating activity.

The preceding points highlight the three clear ways in which a vendor's quality can directly impact the financial benefits of the outsourcing venture. Note that this runs in both directions—not only can poor quality increase cost in unforeseen ways, but quality improvements can also provide measurable incremental financial benefit as well. Companies that identify these cost risks, quantify them, and factor them into their overall outsourcing analysis, including vendor selection, will be much more likely to enjoy sustainable financial benefit from their offshore programmes.

QUALITY GOVERNANCE

For addressing the quality issues, the BPO vendors need to establish quality philosophy at the grassroots level by defining quality policy, defining organization structure, identifying key processes, establish a clear roadmap for COPC and hire people with proper skills. The documentation is prerequisite to quality governance. The documentation will enable verifications, validations, testing, auditing, and status review, so as to address the deviations at the right time. Figure 16.2 illustrates the typical quality system documentation.

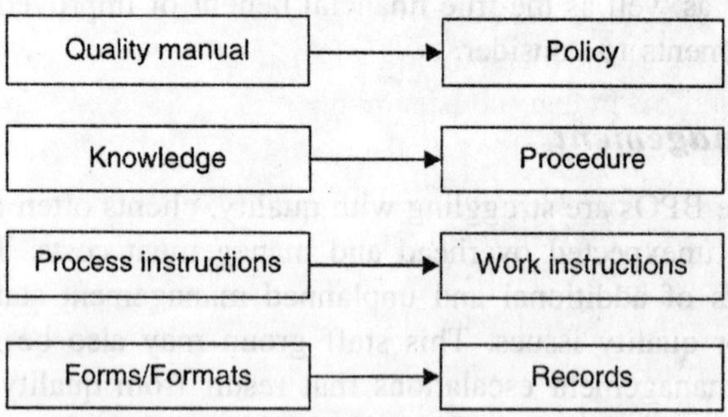

FIGURE 16.2 Quality system documentation.

In Figure 16.2, each level of documentation serves a different purpose and answers different questions concerning the quality system. The information content (i.e., procedural details) increases as one moves down the levels. Each level also typically cross-references documents in levels below. As a system, it consists of quality manuals, procedure manuals, standards, checklists, guidelines, templates, forms, etc.

Introducing a quality assurance standard is a fundamental way of measuring the efficiency of business processes. A quantifiable benchmark enables problems to be pinpointed and can assist companies in identifying ways and means of improving their processes. It also encourages adoption of best practices in relationships with customers, suppliers and employees, for which a number of standards exist. Companies can work towards achieving them. The most-recognized and widely used include ISO 9000, Total Quality Management, and Six Sigma—a data-driven methodology based on a measurement strategy, focusing on systematic process improvement and variation reduction, through the application of powerful statistical tools. The following techniques are normally used to address the quality issues in BPO:

- Malcolm Baldrige National Quality Award Process (in the USA)
- Benchmarking
- ISO 9000 and other standards
- Lean
- Six Sigma
- Total Quality Management.

Each of these standards has been designed not only to eliminate defects, but also the root causes of defects in business processes, in order to work towards greater efficiency, productivity and accuracy. These quality systems follow different methodologies, each of which has its strengths and weaknesses. Any of these can be applied to improving quality, and therefore it is important for an organization to understand these nuances when considering the introduction of a practice to benefit outsourced business processes.

ISO 9000 is a family of standards maintained by the International Organization for Standardization remains the most basic quality standard sought by new BPO and outsourcing players and among the most common standards adopted by Indian industry players. It is developed in 1987. In fact, their consistency in terminology and content through the years has resulted in ISO reaching a stage in maturity where they are considered to be almost generic quality standards. Although, originally developed for the manufacturing sector, ISO standards are applicable across industries and sectors have been adopted by BPO industry players. ISO standards deal with the management systems. They are used to design, produce, deliver and support products and services. They are based on the following major principles:

- Customer focus
- Leadership
- Employee involvement
- Process approach
- System approach to management
- Continual improvement
- Facts-based decision-making
- Mutually beneficial buyer-supplier relationships

The above eight principles are incorporated into the ISO Certification which covers:

- A standard set of procedures and policies covering all key processes.
- Monitoring processes to ensure that procedures are effective and followed.
- Adequate record keeping.

- Checking for defects and taking appropriate to correct any.
- Regular review of processes and the system itself to ensure continual effectiveness.
- Continual process improvement.

The latest ISO revisions (ISO 9001:2008) adopted a more process approach where emphasis is placed on measuring process performance, process effectiveness and process improvement through objective measurement.

The principal benefit of the ISO 9000 quality standard is that it is globally accepted and hence its core requirements have the same meaning worldwide. The ISO 9000 standard looks at every area of a business where quality problems or defects can potentially occur, including order entry, procurement, training, and document and process control. Because the rationale behind ISO 9000 involves the whole organization, the certification process and the speed of implementation tends to be fairly lengthy, as employees across the board have to adjust to newly introduced changes in process. The certification process itself can take anything from six months upwards. It is also difficult to track tangible results with the ISO 9000 standard because of its focus on the organization as a whole entity.

TQM is an organization-wide management philosophy that encompasses planning, directing and assuring quality at all levels and works particularly well when tasks are routine and repetitive. The philosophy behind TQM is attributed to the work of William Edwards Deming and others in Japan following World War II. In fact, TQM in Japan incorporates the Kaizen philosophy of "continuous process improvement" as one of its four process steps.

After ISO, TQM has become the next stage in the quest for quality. In fact, implementation of ISO will put 80 per cent of the necessary steps for TQM in place. Hence, TQM is almost be considered as an add-on to ISO. Hence, Indian BPO and outsourcing organizations, in particular, have increasingly adopted TQM as a standard management philosophy.

Unlike ISO 9000, which looks at all areas of a company, the primary focus of the Total Quality Management (TQM) standard is on process management. It aims to solve quality problems by involving everyone who is part of a particular process in the analysis and correction of any defect. It is based on studying past data to help encourage continuous improvement. However, it still remains difficult to measure tangible results from the introduction of a TQM standard. This is because there are a number of TQM definitions and the onus for implementation falls on the internal personnel who are championing the initiative. TQM requires no external audits, documentation or record-keeping, unlike ISO 9000. It also takes a notoriously long time to implement because of the huge level of analysis, evaluation and confirmation of buy-in across departments for a successful implementation.

Today, in outsourcing industry, in addition to ISO as a quality standard and TQM as a management philosophy, Six Sigma has increasingly become a standard tool to fine tune, perfect and improve outsourced business processes. It was first originated and implemented at Motorola in the mid-1980s. Six Sigma incorporates TQM along with the work of other quality pioneers such as Deming. It uses a simplified performance improvement model known as the DMAIC (define, measure, analyze, improve, control) that contains five parts:

- Define the objectives of the improvement activity.
- Measure the current system in order to collect relevant data.
- Analyze to eliminate the deviations between actual performance and goals.
- Improve or optimize the system through data analysis techniques.
- Control the system that was put in place.

The Six Sigma model is designed to force systematic change and to identify and resolve problems that are preventing an organization from achieving its goals. In BPO industry Six Sigma model is considered to be a tool that helps to devote more attention to the Voice of the Customer (VOC) as automated feedback systems are put in place. It can also help in assigning the right person for the right job.

Six Sigma, however. tracks tangible results very effectively because it is based on a statistical process that guarantees a 99.99966 per cent level of perfection, which is currently as close to flaw-free status as possible. Specific processes are evaluated and no more than 3.4 defects per million opportunities are allowed to occur. Six Sigma can be used to monitor either a single process or a range of processes, from anything as specific as a line of code or an administrative form to any aspect or transaction within the business.

The Six Sigma methodology is completely flexible; each individual company can define what it considers a defect and then go about resolving the defect to ensure that the standard is achieved. If a third-party provider uses this methodology, an organization will be able to outline the defects that it would like to track at the Service Level Agreement (SLA) stage, ensuring that they are monitored. The SLA will then include all critical issues that need to be addressed, no matter how small the detail.

Six Sigma is self-policed because of the detailed data-driven approach that it is based on. An organization can involve the most relevant people in its implementation, so that those involved in the process are responsible for its success. If a third-party provider uses a recognized quality standard, it is a reasonable expectation that outsourced business processes will be in safe hands. The accreditation to ISO 9000 and the practice of TQM standards reflect a dedication to high-quality service. Six Sigma, being a process-oriented methodology, is a disciplined approach that fits in well with the needs of both the client and the processor and complements internal quality assurances already in place.

The other approach to quality is Capability Maturity Model Integration (CMMI) which is a process improvement approach that is specifically intended for the software engineering organizations. CMMI was released in 2002 as the successor to the Capability Maturity Model (CMM) that was developed by Carnegie Mellon University's Software Engineering Institute (SEI) from 1987 into the late 1990s and widely implemented by the Indian software industry. CMMI is different from traditional quality management programs as organizations are appraised rather than certified. Depending on the type of appraisal, an organization can be awarded one of five maturity levels:

Maturity Level 1: Initial unpredictable processes that are reactive and poorly controlled.

Maturity Level 2: Managed processes are often reactive.

Maturity Level 3: Defined processes are proactive tailored for projects on adopted standards.

Maturity Level 4: Management processes are measured and controlled on quality.

Maturity Level 5: Optimizing process improvement focus.

However, CMMI is focused on what processes should be implemented and not so much with how these processes can be implemented.

Further, eSourcing Capability Model for Service Providers (eSCM-SP) was developed by Carnegie Mellon University's IT Services Qualification Center (ITSqc) specifically for IT organizations, but it is focused on improving relationships between them and their customers. Currently, eSCM consists of two capability models, the eSourcing Capability Model for Service Providers (eSCM-SP) which was released in 2004 and the eSourcing Capability Model for Client Organizations (eSCM-CL) which was released in 2006. eSCM-SP capability model contains six basic capability areas for IT industry:

- Relationship Management
- People Management
- Knowledge Management
- Technology Management
- Performance Management
- Risk Management

For each of these capability areas, there is a list of activities and guidelines for establishing a policy, procedure, program or action plan.

The next one is People Capability Maturity Model (People-CMM) which focuses exclusively on continuous improvement of the management and development of an organization's human capital. It was first released by the Software Engineering Institute (SEI) at Carnegie Mellon University in 1995 and eventually published in book format in 2001.

People-CMM seeks to help organizations determine the maturity of their Human Resources (HR) practices, set priorities for improving workforce competencies, integrate the growth in competence with process improvement and to establish a culture of excellence among the workforce. It has five maturity levels:

- **Initial:** Workforce practices applied without analysis of impact.
- **Managed:** Managers take responsibility for managing and developing their people.
- **Defined:** Develop workforce competencies to align with the overall business strategy.
- **Predictable:** Empower and integrate workforce competencies manage quantitatively.
- **Optimizing:** Continuous improvement.

People-CMM is a relatively new model. However, organizations that have implemented it have experienced improvements in their human capital management capabilities, lower attrition and turnover and improved employee satisfaction. People-CMM basically acts as a roadmap for organizational growth that is combined with other quality improvement programs.

At the end, BPOs and outsourcing organizations need to tailor their capabilities for each of their clients and no quality model or tool can effectively do this. Furthermore, no quality model or tool can replace deep industry and market knowledge and once such a level is reached, process costs are generally low and of high quality. Nevertheless, the adoption of global quality standards, certifications and philosophies has clearly enabled BPOs and clients to become leaders and establish the global benchmark for quality in outsourcing. However, maintaining a leadership position in the industry will depend upon how well a provider can balance the competing demands of cost and quality along with maintaining a long-term relationship and having the ability to provide innovative solutions to clients.

QUALITY CERTIFICATIONS

The issue of quality has assumed great importance for companies in the BPO industry. Indian BPO companies are acquiring these certifications to improve their quality and attract business from abroad. Most BPO firms operating in this industry conform to one or more of the leading quality standards in use across the globe. Currently, the quality models that are popular among BPO organizations include the following: ISO 9001: 2000, SW-CMM version 1.1, CMMi version 1.1, P-CMM version 2.0, MBNQA 2002, COPC 2002, and so on.

While having a certification may not help one to get business, not having a certification may be a good reason for the prospective clients to reject an organization. Certification is a useful way to advance a BPO's contact centre business or evaluate how the centre performs against competition. There are several certifications applicable to the BPO/call centre world, and these are classified into two broad categories—organizational certifications (for employer) and individual certifications (for employee). NASSCOM is planning to introduce certification programmes for HR personnel and also for BPO firms, which can become an industry standard in India.

Organizational Certifications

The prominent ones are:

ISO 9001: 2000

It is a certification for quality assurance. It was developed initially for the manufacturing industry and only later interpreted for the service sector and for software development This is the recent quality management standard that can be applied to both product- and service-oriented organizations to achieve standards of quality that are recognized throughout the world. However, to apply it in the ITES sector, there are certain limitations. Some of the shortcomings of this standard as revealed by the NASSCOM study are as follows:

(a) It does not address the overall issues of risk, confidentiality and security or personnel performance management.
(b) It is deficient in capturing, analyzing and disseminating organizational experiences or in covering critical pre-contractual issues such as negotiation, pricing, proposals, contracting, and technology upgrading and licensing.

SW-CMM version 1.1

The Capability Maturity Model for Software (SW-CMM) is a model used by the software companies to identify the best practices that are useful in helping them increase the maturity of their processes. CMM was upgraded in 2000 to Capability Maturity Model Integration (CMMi). This standard too has its deficiencies. The study brings to light the following shortcomings:

(a) It does not cover service deployment, delivery and enhancement stages in the contract–execution phase.
(b) It does not address issues of relationship management, risk, confidentiality and security, and critical pre-contract and post-contract requirements.

COPC-2000

COPC stands for Customer Operations Performance Centre. COPC certification is issued by COPC, the world's leading authority on service-chain operations management, including performance improvement for buyers and providers for customer service, customer contact centre and BPO operations. It was founded in 1995 to focus on improving call centre operations, monitoring best practices in call centres and training contact centre vendors for certification. COPC, as the study showed, lacked adequate focus on managing appropriate technology and knowledge base to improve the service capability of a company.

eSCM

eSCM will assess the capabilities of service providers to serve customers in the IT-enabled BPO business sector.

BS 7799 security standard

It is the most widely recognized security standard in the world.

P-CMM

P-CMM stands for People Capability Maturity Model. This provides guidance for organizations in crucial areas such as attracting, developing, motivating, deploying and training the talent needed to steadily improve the organization's software development capability.

Support centre practices (SCP) certification

This certification programme was designed to address issues that affect the rapidly growing technology support industry. SCP certification quantifies the effectiveness of customer support based upon a stringent set of performance standards, and represents the best practices in the industry.

Six Sigma

Six Sigma is a methodology that provides business with the tools to improve the capability of their business processes. This increase in performance and decrease in process variation leads to defect reduction and vast improvement in profits, employee morale and quality of the product. Six Sigma is a rigorous and a systematic mythology that utilizes information (management by facts) and statistical analysis to measure and improve a company's operational performance, practices and systems, by identifying and preventing 'defects' in manufacturing and service-related processes, in order to anticipate and exceed expectations of all stakeholders and thus accomplish effectiveness.

Individual Certifications

CIAC certification

Call Centre Industry Advisory Council (CIAC) certification is the process by which the competence of individuals is assessed, validated, and recognized, in specific areas of expertise based on the requirements of their job role, as determined by leading practitioners in the call centre industry. Achieving CIAC certification indicates that an individual has demonstrated mastery of industry-established knowledge, skill, and behavioural requirements.

Software support professionals association (SSPA)

SSPA offers five different levels of certification for the support professional.

INDIAN BPOs

BPO service providers in India are now vigorously implementing systems and practices that improve the quality of services, in their bid to emulate the success of software firms of the country. Quality of services is a USP for Indian software companies, who have successfully used it to emerge as global players in the software services business.

Currently, India has the largest pool of SEI–CMM Level 5 assessed companies in the world. Today, in India, many BPO companies are implementing COPC (Customer Operations Performance Centre—the equivalent of the CMM-level certification of software firms) as well as Six Sigma simultaneously. To address the quality issues, Indian BPO vendors need to focus on the following:

- BPOs should have a robust process management system that defines processes, identifies process owners, and assigns roles and responsibilities. Process performance is driven by
  - Quality Assurance (QA)
  - Management Information Systems (MIS)
  - Business Analysis team
  - BPO's Six Sigma team of Black Belts which normally focuses on process improvement.
- There should be a proper mechanism to support rapid knowledge acquisition, transition process, performance management and productivity improvement.
- Scalable business process offerings should be there to satisfy the specific customer's requirements.
- BPOs should acquire domain knowledge in order to have a deep understanding of the client and their industry for successful execution of business process outsourcing arrangements.
- Best practices need to be implemented in order to provide value. They should utilize technology and business procedures for information security and compliance.
- BPOs should incorporate process integration and automation for developing sustainable competitive advantage. This involves smart use of technology to automate the entire process and the supply chain.

- Adoption of scientific and engineering tools such as Six Sigma and TQM for significant process improvements is an imperative.
- Transition management in order to make the transition of the client's processes seamless is also necessary.

SUMMARY

In the service sector, quality issues are mainly non-physical. Service quality is measured in the terms of the time taken in the transaction process, its accuracy and completion, and finally customer satisfaction. Service quality requires the entire organization's orientation to quality delivery in order to get overall desirable business performance. The issue of quality is assuming great importance for companies in the BPO domain due to competitive pressure and demanding customers who are outsourcing their business processes to Indian BPOs. Most BPO firms operating in this industry conform to one or more of the leading quality standards in use across the globe. Currently, the quality models that are popular among BPO organizations include the following: ISO 9001: 2000, SW-CMM version 1.1, CMMi version 1.1, P-CMM version 2.0, MBNQA 2002, COPC 2002, and so on. According to a recent industry study (NASSCOM source), existing models of quality often provide limited guidance for ITES–BPO companies due to various reasons. While the ISO 9001 was developed initially for the manufacturing industry and only later interpreted for the service sector and for software development, SW-CMM was created to provide a benchmark for software process improvement. CMMi, on the other hand, was developed to provide guidance for software and systems engineering process improvement, and P-CMM to provide workforce practices for improving the management and development of human assets of an organization.

Review Questions

1. Which practices are followed for managing quality in general?
2. Discuss the major quality issues in the BPO vendor industry in India today.
3. Explain how quality issues are addressed by BPO firms.
4. Which are the prevailing quality standards followed by the BPO outfits in India? Explain their relevance.
5. What is the role of NASSCOM in addressing service quality issues in the BPO sector?

Chapter 17

BPO Analytics

Business process analytics unlocking the power of data and analytics transforming insight into income.[1]

BPO services vendors provide business value to their clients by implementing and running various business processes. They extend this value by mining data from these refined and improved business processes and subsequently partnering and consulting with their client to improve their customer's business performance. Analytics is a value-added service provided by the BPO service as an extension of the BPO services in their service offer package for quite some time. Today, analytics has become very critical and important service offering of BPO as customers started realizing the full potential of these services. A typical BPO analytics function will use the data collected from real-life business.

INTRODUCTION

As against the discrete product offerings in the past, the BPO vendors are currently offering a package covering data analysis, IT infrastructure along with application platform for business solutions. This approach helped them to reduce the operations cost at both (client and vendor) sides. Their approach now provides automation to repetitive processes and build intellectual capital to add value to their offerings to gain competitive edge in market. This is helping BPO clients in their revenue growth and profitability through differentiated services (inputs to clients) of BPO vendors. Analytics, in general, has evolved over the years from batch reporting to data warehousing to dash board visualization to event monitoring to content analysis today. BPO analytics covers analysis of business performance using operational metrics like retention, attendance, customer value, pass rate, resource utilization, revenue generation, etc. The new service is nothing, but to move up in 'Value Chain' in BPO services. The data is collected from operations, HR, Finance, etc., and predictive analytics is done on various parameters.

1. https://www.uk.capgemini.com/insights-data/insights/business-process-analytics.

These parameters are; call quality, customer satisfaction, training performance and revenue generated, etc. Based on analytics, the recommendations are made to help to take business critical decisions quicker and better way in today's competitive environment to gain success in a global market. Today in competitive global economy, the organizations are forced to operate under changing customer demand and regulatory environment. The markets are now mature, with shrinking decision cycles and a short time-to-market. Under such circumstances organizational need to take decisions, which are based on accurate and meaningful data. Analytics, therefore, has become an integral part of the business plan of any organization, helping to assess the business environment accurately and predict future trends.

SCOPE OF ANALYTICS

In today's competitive business scenario business analytics is used by almost all industries. The data analytics is done to get correct analysis of information on customer's behavioural and spent insights, business trends and growth potential, brand value and customer preferences, cash flow analysis, risk assessments and evolving proactive strategies, demand assessment and inventory management all leading to improving the profitability of the business.

The analytics helps management to anticipate and respond quickly to the demanding marketplace and take decisive action to gain leadership by ensuring; increase in sales turnover, campaign response rate and profitability through better retention plans, efficient cash flow management and increased profitability per unit of capital employee, reduction in portfolio risk, early indication of credit defaults, maintenance of optimum inventory levels for store segments to prevent stock-outs. The analytics and solutions, thereof, are in areas such as market positioning, customer lifetime value, price simulation and inventory rationalization help client capture multiple variances and adapt them to business needs. It helps in process transformation from written reporting to predictive analytics and optimization solutions. Analytics platform covers sales, marketing, customer interaction management, human resources, finance, supply chain and procurement. The project governance helps to efficiently track and monitor enterprise performance across all levels in an engagement. Hence, outsourcing vendors and their client's alike need to make use of analytics and find out the ways to increase the value they can achieve and deliver together. The clients expect the cost savings, improved efficiencies and decreased compliance risks from BPO vendor(s). For global competitiveness, organizations today require higher level of insight and performance. The world class BPO vendors uses new generation of IT-based solutions to deploy analytics to extract actionable business insights from huge transactional data. These insights are used by companies to generate positive outcomes. This may include; accelerated speed to market, enhanced innovativeness, stronger customer loyalty and top-line growth. However,

BPO solution based on analytics depends on several factors, including ongoing alignment to business goals, having the right incentives in place and making sure the provider has sufficient visibility across an entire function or process, etc.

VALUE ADDITIONS

Several industry trends are leading to a new generation of BPO solutions. One is that companies are becoming comfortable on outsourcing of critical functions and activities. As companies see BPO vendors can perform multiple business functions better than they can themselves, they are looking for ways to leverage that success across their organizations. Another important trend is the amount of data being generated across the ecosystem. Companies know that this data can be used to improving business operations, developing innovative products and serving customers more effectively. But, few of them have the resources or capabilities to deploy this into insight and finally generate profits. The trend is the increased sophistication and applicability of analytics solutions, and the increased understanding by companies to tap the data and analytics thereof to deploy the same for business success. Many organizations are getting better at generating clean and integrated data to define distinctive customer segments to target. As companies move up the success ladder, they leverage more sophisticated analytics solutions to get greater value. They look for variety of 'analytics' applications that can help to find out different responses for customer segments, predict responses more accurately, and then to actually embed different actions. Finally, companies can use analytics to adapt and optimize processes and respond to real-time needs. At each level of the analytical applications ladder, BPO presents an environment that can lead to distinctive value to its clients based on a foundation of functional industry-specific expertise, along with comprehensive data about a business process and how it is performing. In some functional domains, analytics solutions can result in continuous improvement of business processes, or even embed differentiated actions in the processes themselves. In other areas such as research, analytics is more likely to provide assistance to futuristic decision-making.

ANALYTICAL SOLUTIONS

There are several BPO analytics solutions implemented across the industry segments as per the needs in the analytics ladder. For data quality improvements, BPO vendor may apply analytics to identify errors within the transaction data. They can perform segmented analysis on the transactions and identify key error trends along with the related system components. By addressing the root causes of the errors through system fixes and by making changes to upstream data entry procedures, the organization can eliminate large number of bad transactions at the source itself. This will result in huge cost savings. For attracting customers based on understanding, BPO solution that can take the next step up the analytics ladder and predict a consumer's response, and also realign resources to handle customer interactions more effectively to create a competitive advantage. This type of solution that moves BPO deeper in the value chain focuses on consumer analytics. Predicting and preventing analytics can leverage predictive capabilities to optimize process responses continuously, in real time. In one of such solutions for Insurance Industry, BPO vendor leveraged machine learning to detect patterns in claims data and then take action on segmented queues of claims. The solution also goes a step further and systematically adjusts to trends in the data, predicting sources of errors and directing actions in real time. This will, thus, continuously improve the process and the benefits delivered. In some cases they reduce preventable financial rework for a company from one-third to half of the time. This results into reduced administrative costs associated with rework by preventing over payments, improve BPO vendor and member satisfaction by increasing payment accuracy at the first time. Compliance analytics can help BPO to meet regulatory compliances on price and performance and comply with requirements. BPO clients demand that service providers should deliver value by synthesizing massive amounts of data, analyzing it and then applying industry experience to drive improved outcomes. Organizations that get the most value from BPO, choose providers that bring sophisticated analytics and industry knowledge to enable their clients to go broader and deeper to deliver insights and innovative solutions. This data further can be translated into business metrics, which can be used for strategic decisions.

BENEFITS DERIVED

Analytics helps the businesses to deliver process improvements in the areas of operations, finance and customer services. The internal decision-making process becomes faster on analytics platform. The transactional data on analytics platform becomes single source of accurate information leading to gain in process efficiencies and cost effectiveness. Analytics helps to reduce or eliminate the errors and waste. It further helps to spot the data inconsistency under a broad picture and standardize the process adding distinctive value to the business in data management.

Through Data Analytics it is possible to initiate the innovation process, speed to market and improve customer relationship resulting into revenue growth. In an extremely volatile global environment, organizations are looking for more returns on investments. Therefore, driving profitability cannot be achieved by offering cost savings alone but adding value through analytics. In BPO sector, an intelligent analytics solutions will be the most effective value addition in their offerings. Hence, in the future the following five analytics trends will define the path of success:

- **Customer delight:** The right and timely customer information, can offer accurate customer insights. It may be in the form of customer data, requirements, or feedback. The ability to track and draw intelligence from this information will be major factor in success of BPO (buyer–seller) partnerships. Customer insights, gained from conversations at the contact center, are critical to customer delight.
- **Quality customer data:** Accurate data improves customer satisfaction. It also reduces redundancy and operational costs. Applying analytics to identify error trends in transactional data makes it easier to segregate inaccurate information. This can be done by assigning a task to a teams to fix them.
- **Risk minimization:** Interpretations from customer analytics will be a key factor in minimizing various business risks. Analytical on customer behaviour will significantly reduce the risk organizations need to undertake on new product development or new marketing campaign. This will help organizations to minimize likelihood of losses on inventories.
- **Help in business planning:** A machine learning to detect patterns in consumer behaviour will contribute to predictive analytics. The amount of data that can be gathered allows for analysis that can forecast market conditions and help in business planning. Therefore, in BPO, predictive capabilities can optimize processes and enhance results.
- **Facilitate decision-making:** In today's unpredictable business environment, decision-making cannot be based on human intuition. The data collected and put under statistical analysis will reveal business trends, throwing light on past performance. It will provide much needed clarity of insight and accuracy of prediction of businesses (of partner's).

Hence, analytics will play a major role across planning, operations, and customer service. Analytics will also play a central role in redefining the future of BPO vendors. Customer delight, competitive advantage, risk minimization, business planning, and decision-making will seamlessly flow from efficient analytics management.

PREREQUISITES

To deliver the analytics to clients the BPO needs to have the following in place. The past experience in delivering analytics, scale flexibility and domain expertise of vendor. All these have an impact on the success of its business analytics services practice. The BPO service providers with more and wider experience in specific industries, will have more success in delivering business analytics services. Vendor's capability to match customer requirements cost management, improving operational efficiency, creating a more effective business process, and complying with new or existing regulations are key business priorities for firms that utilize analytics to run their businesses. Hence, BPO vendors in general need to offer a strong and comprehensive suite of business analytics outsourcing offerings to cater to client's needs. BPO vendor has to develop cost-benefit analysis to facilitate an increased adoption of their services portfolio by clients by way of value proposition. In addition, firms in general have to create innovative strategies to improve current management processes and take initiatives to meet the market demand for BA solutions in the future. In competitive analysis customers will prefer consuming the full life cycle of business analytics services, from assessment to process outsourcing, when they partner BPO vendor for their analytics needs. Hence, the vendors that possess the capability to deliver across the value chain of business analytics services will stand to gain a larger market share.

VALUE CHAIN

Basically, business analytics services 'Value chain' is made up of the information management, analysis, and business inference. In addition, the enablers are set of processes and technologies that are delivered across the above three areas. Integration of these processes and technologies with the given three areas makes the complete value chain of business analytics services as shown in the Figure 17.1:

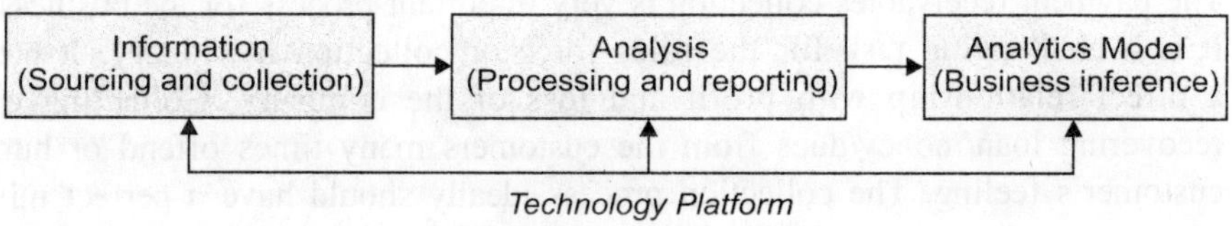

FIGURE 17.1 Business analytics services value chain.

Over the years businesses are using Business Intelligence (BI) Tools to thwart the competition. These tools either installed by clients themselves or BPO vendors. Through BI tools the companies collect data on market trends and industry competition. As the client on his own has limitations to mine data, analyze the same and have insight in his business ecosystem, the help of vendor with domain-specific analytical skills is a must. The vendor can bring in efficiency and cost effectiveness in BI system because of his domain knowledge and the past experience in the industry. Hence, BI outsourcing will help to gain insights in collected data resulting into more accuracy in business inferences.

The following are the major players in BPO Analytics worldwide; Accenture, IBM, Cap Gemini, TCS, HP, Genpact, Infosys, Cognizant, WNS and EXL Services. Today, BPO vendors have established delivery capabilities across cross-industry and industry-specific analytics. They provide finance and revenue analytics, risk analytics, customer insights, and supply chain analytics, but also leverages its strong industry domain expertise to deliver insights in areas such as health-care and pharmaceutical companies, marketing and pricing analytics in retail, and debt management analytics for banking. The analytics capability includes providing predictive and complex quantitative models such as fraud control and anti-money laundering for banks as well as product portfolio mix reports for banking that it provides under its research and transaction processing umbrella. BPOs are consuming business analytics primarily to control cost and operational efficiency. The benefits of business analytics are far beyond just 'finding the business metrics' initiatives. Leading businesses truly understand the importance of analytics to achieve a competitive edge in their markets and utilize business analytics to make their businesses more agile to cater to changing customer needs, to drive innovation in the business processes, and to be an integral part of the growth. Business analytics is not just about getting hold of the right data. It's also about creating the right processes to handle and make use of the valuable enterprise-wide data. To be successful in utilizing the true benefits of a business analytics undertaking, it is important to define and govern all three aspects of business, i.e., information, processes, and people to create a successful culture of analytics.

'ANALYTICS'—IN RECEIVABLES

The payment receivables collection is very important process for the business. It is a challenging task for the sales force or collection machinery. It has a direct relationship with profit and loss of the company. Collecting or recovering loan/money/dues from the customers many times offend or hurt customer's feeling. The collection process ideally should have a perfect mix of efficient operations, man management skills based on intelligent collection strategies. Sometimes, the collection teams have to pay for the misdeeds of sales and marketing team which have used aggressive acquisition policies resulted into accumulation of NPA. This is the reason for data analytics being used in the collection processes. This analytics helps to segregate the customers with different periods for overdue payments receivables. The good and bad ones are separated and more energy and efforts are focused on those receivables, where the chances of collection are more in the given time frame and allocated budget for it. The analytics also gives some insights on the implications on both the cost and customer relationships. This helps in predicting future cash flow using different models. Finally, it also gives some indications on customer's inclination to repay and further to plan differential treatment to some customer accounts. The predictive model that are used in collection processes are; Delinquency Scorecard, Normalization Scorecard, Rollback Scorecard and Recovery Scorecard.

In changing business environment, the data inputs, the BPO vendors get from their clients is changing continuously. Even though vendors are getting data from their clients and that no longer remains with them, they have to dig into industry segment historical data to fine tune the campaign strategies. They have to sometimes use their operational team's expertise to choose the correct data variables. The fine tuning on data analysis helps the BPO vendors to improve upon their client's business strategies and exercise tighter control on their operations leading to reduction in cost, growth in revenue and meet client's business requirements.

BPO vendors use various analytical techniques to gain competitiveness on system efficiency and cost effectiveness fronts. The techniques used are; recency-frequency-monetary analysis, and cluster analysis on attributes. These techniques are used exercise tight segment focus on the campaigns. The other technique like data mining to decide on for strength of resources and predictive analysis for process optimization are often used by BPO vendors to add value to their clients business through strategy implementation process. The base for the predictive models is historical transactional data available with the client. The business solutions also covers the use of regression models to time series forecasts to neural models. As BPO industry operates on very thin margins and, hence, the vendor's efforts are always focused on cost reduction through process and resource optimization. The other important task before BPO vendor is to clean the client's data, which is available with errors and deviations. Here, the BPO vendors expertise to clean data is at test so as to drive performance resulting in gaining distinct positions in the market.

Going by the recent outsourcing trends, the following are areas where analytics outsourcing will have a wide scope—Customer analytics for the energy and utilities sector, Cyber-analytics detect cyber crime, acts of terrorism and IP theft, Analytics to assess students' academic, extra-curricular progress and identify potential issues, Cloud-based business analytics, Fraud analytics in retail banking and analytics from social network data mining.

SUMMARY

The technological advances of the last decades have impacted our world and the business world in particular, in fundamental ways. Massive amounts of data are being gathered and stored, from individual records to every single truck movement via GPS for large logistics providers. Moreover, ever faster computers and optimization methods have become available to transform this data into information for better decision-making. All of this makes it now possible to apply advanced analytical methods to business problems that were not possible 10/15 years ago—ranging from detailed supply chain optimization to manufacturing and service industries. Increasingly sophisticated analytical tools and methods are available to derive business insight from data. However, after getting insight into the processed data the last step in the process decision-making, which is more crucial. Adopting analytics culture brings an organization a step further to connecting analytics insight to high-quality decisions. For the union to be feasible, analytics culture must understand how belief concerning the insight gained from analytics is secured in the organization.

Review Questions

1. What do you mean by 'Business Analytics' and discuss its scope in BPO industry?
2. Discuss the concept of 'Business Analytics Value Chain'.
3. Explain the role of business analytics in enterprise success.
4. Discuss, how analytics is driving new generation BPO solutions.

Chapter 18

Outsourcing in Cloud Environment

There's more than just semantics to the argument over whether cloud is just the latest opportunity to outsource.[1]

Cloud Computing (CC) is new consumption and delivery model for IT services. It is a paradigm shift—or it's outsourcing with a different name. It is a move towards highly standardized racks of servers, with software that manages the racks and allows customers to run applications on them by themselves. It is run on Internet protocols. Cloud computing is a way of using the Internet for client's computing needs, where resources and software are basically provided to client over the Internet and clients are charged for the amount of service they avail of. So, with cloud computing one doesn't have to worry about maintaining the hardware. Client is charged only for the time he is using the applications unlike the traditional services and all the upgrades are automatic. Cloud computing is a service that allows the access of data, software applications or computer processing power from a cloud of on-line resources. It enables access for individual users of data, software applications from any device as well as allowing the big organization to reduce their capital cost when buying software and hardware as a utility service. It lets client access all vendor's applications and documents from anywhere irrespective of physical location in the world and involves provisioning of dynamically scalable and often visualized resources. The cloud computing enables client to drive effectively and respond faster to the market dynamics.

INTRODUCTION

Cloud computing is a new technology used for delivering services of data computation, software, data access and data storage services. The services are delivered at any site irrespective of its physical location and details of the technical system that delivers the services need not be known to the end user or client.

1. http://www.cloudpro.co.uk/cloud-essentials/193/how-outsourcing-different-cloud-computing

In CC, service provider uses Internet as platform for delivering the IT services. The user/client access to the applications from his browser on desktop or mobile device. The service provider stores relevant data and application software on the servers, which are stationed at various remote sites. In some cases, applications are delivered via a screen-sharing technology, while the computing resources are consolidated at a remote data center location. Cloud computing is the concept of converged infrastructure and shared services.

In the cloud computing environment the enterprises have many benefits. They can get their applications platform from the service provider, can run it faster, and manage with low cost, ease and less maintenance problems. It is flexible to volumes (scale) and adjustment to IT resources to meet unpredictable changes in market demand. The cloud computing infrastructure services are data-centers, which are operating on usage sharing basis. However, for customers for their computing needs it appears as a single point of contact.

Cloud computing is broken down into three segments—*storage*. *connectivity* and *computing*. The service offering on these three segments differs with regards to purpose, products for businesses and individuals across the industry. CC is often referred to as a technology leading to significant cost saving. In fact, it is a shift in the business and economic models for exploiting the benefits of Information Technology (IT) without investment on the part of the clients/users. The cost savings is achieved through pooling of the computing resources. According to NIST (National Institute of Standards and Technology), this capability is an essential characteristic of cloud computing. With resource pooling capability CC can serve multiple customers using a multi-tenant model with different physical and virtual resources dynamically assigned and reassigned according to demand. Cloud computing provides strong benefits and economic incentives. Selecting a public, private, and hybrid or community cloud implementation will depend on a customer's specific application, performance, security and compliance requirements. Proper deployment can provide significant savings, better IT services and a higher level of reliability. CC, also known for lower acquisition costs, no capital expenses, free computing scaling as per needed and lower maintenance costs with system flexibility.

OPPORTUNITY TO OUTSOURCE

In general, the client goes for process outsourcing, wherein the service provider performs that process on behalf of the client to get the better process performance. The client does this because he does not have time, expertise or other physical resources to perform that process. Most commonly, the projects are outsourced in the situation, where it is the one, which is odd and it may be required for regular use in future. In general, the non-core functions are outsourced and critical functions are kept for in-house handling and control. Hence, it is not always appropriate for the company to outsource all its functions as some functions are propitiatory (with core competency) in nature and its secrecy needs to be guarded. With CC service the operational cost drops down drastically due to scale economics as CC vendor works with many clients having similar needs. Hence, the fixed cost gets apportioned on volume scale. CC outsourcing differs from other outsourcing contract as once it is locked it is difficult to reverse. As through CC system the clients can get access to data and desired application irrespective of time and the location, the scope for CC is limitless. Moreover, the cost benefits will be enormous coupled will hassle free system maintenance, which will be taken care by service provider. However, the important expectation of clients from CC service providers is faultless IT services with highest standards.

In CC system, hardware costs are down, company-wide access to computer applications possible and no software license fees for every employee are required. As here, option of storing data on someone else's hardware is available, the saving money on IT support for entire network's processing power is possible. In cloud computing collected data is easy to manage, study and use. With services from host providers, a business can be certain that effective messages are delivered to the most appropriate audiences. Cloud computing allows businesses to approach their business endeavours in an inexpensive and efficient manner. In CC the entire infrastructure support is provided by vendor. Thus, it brings hardware costs down. For example, digital learning product in cloud environment—SuccessMaker®—from a Pearson's Digital Learning division of global publishing company offers a digital learning curriculum, which is used by millions of elementary and middle school students throughout the US. This product was originally developed for implementation in school data centers, however, SuccessMaster is now available as a SaaS (Software-as-a-Service) product over the Web managed with the RightScale (www.RightScale.com) cloud platform. It offers a fully automated cloud management platform that enables organizations to easily deploy and manage business critical applications across multiple clouds with complete control and portability. The RightScale Cloud Management Platform is delivered as Software-as-a-Service. On the cloud platform Pearson developers have immediate access to an unlimited number of per-configured test servers, 100 per cent consistency between production and test instances and a self-service approach to create cloud deployments. The Pearson customers now have a much shorter implementation time and easy Web access to SuccessMaker. Pearson looked to the cloud for speedier, more reliable alternatives as against using their own infrastructure. Using RightScale, Pearson developers can create multiple server environments in the cloud from server templates by duplicating production deployments for testing. Hence, this product is quite popular in schools with 30–70 workstations in a lab, where teachers shift students in and out all day long.

CLOUD COMPUTING OFFERINGS

Cloud computing can be classified based on the location where the cloud is hosted. These are, *public clouds*, wherein the vendors install the computing infrastructure at their premises. The cloud computing infrastructures are shared between organizations. The customer has no visibility over the location of the cloud computing infrastructure. In this, not so critical applications are placed in the public cloud. The second one is *private clouds*. These are dedicated infrastructures used for customer and not shared with other organizations. They are expensive and are considered more secure than public clouds. These infrastructures are either externally hosted or in premise hosted clouds. Organizations host some critical, secure applications in private clouds. The last one is *hybrid cloud* which is the combination of private and public cloud. In this organizations use its own infrastructure for normal usage and for peak load they go for public cloud. The other category is *community cloud*, wherein the cloud infrastructure is shared between the organizations of the same community. For example, all the government agencies in a city can share the same cloud, but not the non-government agencies.

SERVICE-BASED CLASSIFICATION

Cloud computing is boon to the organizations today for outsourcing their requirements. There are various forms of CC systems (Figure 18.1) currently available. First one is called *Infrastructure-as-a-Service* (IaaS). It is nothing, but an infrastructure that provides Web hosting and virtual machines such as disk storage and virtual servers. These virtual machines can run on open source, Windows or other operating systems. To name the few companies such as Savvis, GoGrid.com, Rackspace, ATT Cloud Service provide such virtual machines for such services, etc. The second one is Software Application Services, called *Software-as-a-Service* (SaaS). It provide service to specific

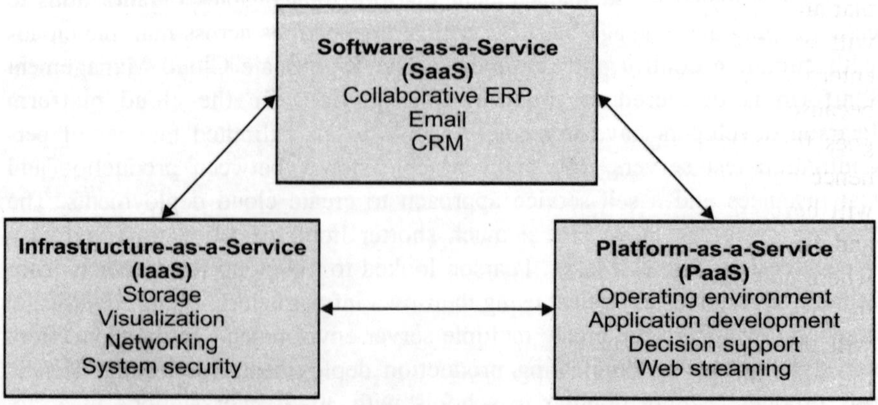

FIGURE 18.1 Cloud computing offerings development platforms.

consumer for desired business application functions. These functions are accessed by the customers on pay per use basis. These services include Hotmail, Flickr, Facebook, etc. Salesforce.com provides such services.

The third one is *Platform-as-a-Service* (PaaS). In this the vendor makes available to the client the computing platform and application design support. With this support the clients do away with owning and managing of IT hardware and software along with running capabilities. This service provides support to all web application development using Internet. The additional services covered are integration of web services, monitoring data base, facilitation of developer community and versioning of applications, etc. The platform may use visualization infrastructure and proprietary software to distribute and manage the computing across wide range of computers and infrastructure. The examples are amazon.com Web Services, Microsoft Windows Azure, Google App Engine, etc.

POTENTIAL PROBLEMS

Being new CC is in process of evolution as the support technologies are yet to attain maturity. Its full integration in the business system with relevant tools is still in the beginning stage. However, CC is being used in the industry as outsourcing option in the following areas by the users as per their needs. The first one is known as Software-as-a-Service or SaaS, known as a means of software delivery and replaces various local IT functions with remote alternatives such as: companies to replace some equipment and staff with SaaS. In fact here, the customer interacts with vendor on applications and not computing infrastructure or development frameworks. SaaS as online Web Services dominate in certain verticals, such as customer relationship management. There are legal issues involved in SaaS for emailing. For example, notification procedures in the event of a data breach or a judicial order, it often don't get clear answers. There are certain types of applications that are relatively standardized across different companies and for which there will be great demand. However, businesses will require offerings that are enterprise process specific. The service providers offer private or hybrid cloud because of the regulatory compliance and reducing the client's risk. The clients goes for private cloud because their own IT infrastructure is not so secured, hence outsourcing. Secondly, their visibility and the control on private cloud will be comparatively tighter. Thirdly, for the expanding business, the large and frequent investments in IT infrastructure are not advisable in situation where customer demand and business environment is changing. Looking into the risk elements the clients invariably want to go in for the cloud, which will use much of their existing IT infrastructure and simultaneously reduce the operational cost. The other concern is future flexibility in the system. The organization appreciates that once the cloud is built it should not lock them into a specific set of products or technology. Today, customers are looking to deal with growing complexities and scale. In addition, compliance and risk management are concerns amongst others. The experts are of the opinion that Cloud Computing should be considered as part of IT governance process. This will help not to allow certain type of data and applications run into the public domain unless certain conditions are met. Today, it is very clear in the industry that when users utilize IT functionality, the software and hardware performing the actual work need not be co-located with them. For example, users of Google Docs can process documents via any computer, merely by knowing a Web address. The physical location of the server and of associated processing platforms need not be known to the user; nor does the storage location of the associated documents. Ancillary client-side software can be automatically downloaded from the Web as needed. In SaaS intensive computing and storage are handled by vendors on a remote just-in-time basis, allocated via available resources. The advantages and disadvantages of SaaS are as presented in Table 18.1.

Table 18.1 SaaS: Advantages and Disadvantages

Advantages	*Disadvantages*
• Ability to easily keep applications up-to-date. • Reliance on third parties for privacy and security. • No particular need to update operating systems. • High computing power. • Automated backups. • Possible improvements in aspects of security.	• Uncertainty as to what occurs when providers undergo changes, especially going out of business. • Reliance on the browser interface. • Limitations on application designer's freedom. • Needs to use a browser interface. • Inhibits the application designer's freedom.

Platform-as-a-Service helps the application developers to develop the applications in the hassle free application support environment, which they may not find in their own organizations. In PaaS, they are not worried about the support infrastructure and its mechanics, which they have otherwise get involved and created. This concept is termed as *DevOps* in the IT outsourcing industry. Here, the role of operator and developer gets merged to large extent. The benefit derived here is that, one PaaS can be used for multiple applications development or one application can be used for developing another one with minimal changes resulting into cost and time saving.

Google's offers CC services. It covers online office productivity tools including e-mail, calendaring, word processing and a simple Web site creation tool and Web Security Services. Google App Engine, works as a PaaS for developers to build applications and host them on Google's infrastructure. Google gone into SaaS for offering packaged software to Web-hosted

Services. The App Engine is alternative to customers in PaaS. However, the concerns are about the security issues in new model. These are; sensitive data access, data segregation, privacy, bug exploitation, recovery, accountability, malicious insiders, management console security, account control, and multi-tenancy issues.

TRADITIONAL OUTSOURCING vs CLOUD COMPUTING

The IT service providers due to varied exposure and their experience with different clients can use their clients IT assets more intelligently and profitably and reap profits. They can even provide the solutions to more complex problems of their clients and manage the resources more efficiently and cost effectively than their customers. However, the vendors providing only IT infrastructure as service in general do not invest in skill development process. They normally focus on automating the process to reduce the human error and cost thereof. As the productivity is enhanced through automation they charge more fees in return from the clients for their services. Private CC providers offers value added services like; hardware isolation against the shared one, services to multiple clients, encryption services using secured line or Virtual Local Area Network (VLAN) and more streamlined and secured procedures for handling the data.

In traditional outsourcing environment scope of infrastructure, application and data processing is limited. However, in CC a service provider decides to offer an IaaS or PaaS on its own standard contract terms. Here, client still manages and maintains, in a self-service fashion, virtual machines running on vendor's infrastructure, program application(s) to be run on vendor's infrastructure. In CC, client is free to install firewalls, anti-malware and anti-spam software, etc. Service provider in CC keeps the client's costs down by passing some of the savings to user by procuring infrastructure for multiple users, using economies of scale as these are not customized for different clients.

With cloud computing, the sequence of events and direction of travel are the opposite. CC service providers offer both customized and standard services which are built on specific or standard terms, respectively. However, the choice of the service package rests with the client depending on processes his needs. In general public CC vendors use standardized services, while private CC vendors allows the greatest degree of customization and control. They do it on the user's own infrastructure and managed by it, and if on third party infrastructure and/or managed by a third party which is closest to traditional outsourcing.

BENEFITS

Over the past 15 years, contract center outsourcing has become a common way for IT organizations to provide consistent quality customer service at a lower cost. Over the past five years, cloud computing has begun to gain entry in the contact center industry with a cloud-based telephony and CRM choices. Today, these two trends are intersecting and, by leveraging both, they can help you drive better customer engagement and loyalty. And this is where cloud computing can help enhance the effectiveness of outsourcing by; improving start-up speed, increasing flexibility to tailor call routing, providing consistency of operational procedures and reporting and lowering the cost of training your outsourcer. Since Cloud solutions do not require onsite hardware or software, vendor can bring up client's contact center in days rather than the months often required to implement a site-based solution. The client's needs are a robust Internet pipe to their facility and a PC with a browser for each agent. If client uses a cloud-based CRM system, then he simply provide the new users and case routing rules. The Cloud components can also interact with and extend client's site-based solutions via APIs. Cloud telephony solutions allow organizations to easily configure and seamlessly route calls between client's in-house center and vendor. Cloud CRM and telephony solutions allow all organization's agents—whether in-house or outsourced—to work from the same system. The benefits are obvious as everyone is recording information in a consistent manner, reporting can be rolled up to show a consolidated view or broken out to show how in-house team is performing compared to vendor's one. Cloud-based telephony and CRM systems are generally designed with a more modern intuitive user interface compared to older legacy systems. Leveraging both outsourcing and cloud computing can deliver a quick, efficient, flexible solution for a cost effective contact center, while maintaining expected quality throughout.

SUMMARY

Cloud computing is a revolutionary concept for many business organizations. Because of the technology's ease of adoption, significantly lower maintenance costs, and greater work flow efficiency, cloud computing is gaining widespread popularity and adoption. For managers dealing with the growing demand for IT in their respective organizations, cloud computing presents itself as an all-in-one solution, being able to satisfy the growing IT needs while, at the same time, reducing energy usage and reducing the cost. In CC, there are two major players, i.e., technology that uses the Internet and central remote servers to maintain data and applications. CC allows customers to use applications with Internet and its efficient computing by centralizing storage, memory, processing and bandwidth. Examples are Yahoo Mail, Gmail, Hotmail, etc.

Cloud computing is relatively new concept referring to businesses sharing, delivering or using services provided remotely by an online host. This host provider maintains these services through an infrastructure, platform or software product that can be used by a number of businesses. Sharing these services between businesses results in a pay-per-use pricing scheme wherein business firms only pay for the services they use. Since the host provides the services online, business firms can access these services from any location without having to install special software or maintain elaborate mainframes. Cloud computing services are broadly divided into three categories—Infrastructure-as-a-Service (IaaS), Platform-as-a-Service (PaaS) and Software-as-a-Service (SaaS). For sales endeavours, there are many automated service tools offered by host providers. The ability to collect, organize and manage leads by simply logging on to the Internet can increase any business' efficiency. Another benefit can be found in the ability to organize and manage accounts, which can strengthen a sales team. In addition, more efficient order processing tools can make a customer happier and can generate more profits for a business. Cloud computing is seen as the consequent evolution of the traditional on-premise computing wider outsourcing stages from total to the selective, and from the multi-vendor outsourcing to an asset-free delivery. While from a technical perspective, cloud computing seems to pose challenges for managing the same. It incorporates a number of challenges on a business level, both from an operational as well as from a strategic point of view.

Review Questions

1. Compare and contrast the traditional outsourcing and cloud computing.
2. Explain 'Cloud Computing' and discuss its various applications.
3. Discuss various offerings in cloud computing services.
4. How CC vendor can odd value to his service offerings?

Chapter 19

BPO Transformation Strategy

Without change there is no innovation, creativity, or incentive for improvement. Those initiate change have better opportunity to manage the change that is inevitable.[1]

In Business Process Outsourcing projects, the client engages a third party to perform certain business functions and processes. The third party is partnered based on its expertise, domain knowledge and past experience in the field. The purpose of outsourcing is to manage and optimize the function/processes by vendor on the mutually agreed performance metrics. To achieve this change, business processes need structural transformation in their functional compositions. The processes need to be aligned to organizational capabilities and business goals to be achieved in future on sustainable basis. Transformation is viewed as an approach to achieve enhanced performance in terms of systems, processes and people. The key to success in understanding of people and the processes therein and the environment (internal and external) they are operating in. Designing a correct metrics for performance evaluation is a must to continuously know the impact of transformation.

INTRODUCTION

Today, any business has the key objectives of increasing shareholder value, quick to market with new products, delivering lower unit cost, scale flexibility, IT solutions that support the business and adding functionality without complexity and growth. This business transformation is all about change within for business improvement. It can be done efficiently and cost effectively if done by somebody who is expert in performing and managing the business processes. The logic is that an expert in performing the process can do the same with less time and cost with no compromise on quality of output. There is always an element of risk in the outsourcing process if not properly addressed. However, outsourcing carries transformational risk in various forms. The critical phase of transformational process is the one at the beginning, wherein costs are not fixed. The both external and internal

1. William Pollard.

environment is changing. In the second phase the client may change his function and locational scope quite frequently. However, at this juncture the service provider should lock in the contract terms and scope. The value delivery of the BPO contract may normally cover; cost reduction, enhancement in service quality and risk mitigation.

The other element to be considered is risk at vendor's end which may be related to his finance, operations, legal compliance and experiential. It will be prudent to address all the risk jointly with rewards and penalty. The lopsided contract may land both BPO vendor and the client in the serious trouble resulting into loss at three counts, i.e., time, revenue and profits. Here, the point to consider is that transformational risks spans across entire life cycle of BPO. In the initial transformational phase the visibility in cost and environment around is very low. In addition, the employees may oppose the change process which makes the change process more complex. Hence, need for conducting change management prior to start of transformation process may sometimes considered as key to achieve success.

Further technology, which is prime mover of transformational process in today's context, can help in integration of different business process within least time frame and with operational ease. The better control on transformational process can be exercised with continuous monitoring of performance metrics and addressing the deviations if any, immediately. The scale factor is crucial in BPO contract as with external changes the scope may assume larger proportion which BPO vendor should build in the project addressing the issue of flexibility at the contract signing stage. Addressing this issue at later stage may be costly proposition as business transformational process calls for investment in both in terms of time and money and is an irreversible process.

TRANSITION

The Transition Phase, while critical to the success of the project, is typically not given importance during the due diligence process, from both the perspective of the client and service provider. The client, having not been through a formal transition process, does not focus on implementation hurdles. On the other hand, vendor assumes that if they can display the ability to meet the client's steady-state requirements, then they stand a fair chance of getting the business. However, they have ignored the fact that transferring in-house process operation to outside service provider can create a volatile atmosphere in a company. In the transition process there are three facets that must be looked into both by client and vendor. These are; people, processes and technology. The technology component is the most widely understood, and involves the migration or replication of the required technical environment. It covers the setting up of all required software, hardware, and network access. The process component is understood by those providers, who are process-oriented, and includes documenting the current processes and transferring this knowledge to the outsourced team members. However, in general, the people component not addressed properly and is allowed to evolve on its own. This is a common wrong step in the transition process. The success or failure of the transition phase will not kill the outsourcing initiative, but it will place the relationship between buyer and vendor on adversarial ground. In the transition, initially, it is difficult to predict costs. In addition, both employees and operations can suffer from the shift. If the transition drags on too long, it can generate resistance to change among employees, make them dissatisfied, and endanger the success of outsourcing project. In such cases a comprehensive and customized enterprise resource planning solution is needed to reduce implementation risk. Enterprises need software that supports best practices. IT should help in seamless integration of client, their customers and service providers and their processes. Before engaging a service provider an enterprise should look into vendor's capabilities to provide solution to its problem and whether the software used fits into the particular outsourcing project. This is the prerequisite of any BPO project for its successful implementation and final results. As transition management is a critical activity in business process outsourcing there should be a robust transition methodology that ensures that all road blocks and potential risks are identified and mitigation plans are put in place during the transition phase are addressed to ensure continuity of services. The stages in this process cover the following:

- **Process documentation:** This enables dedicated vendor's team to become familiar with client's business processes and transition objectives.
- **Leverage experience:** Vendor leverages his experience to incorporate process improvements to meet client's performance requirements.
- **Built-in control:** To monitor and control deviations from norms, built-in control mechanism at various points is created during the transition process.
- **Reviews:** The periodic management reviews with vendor's project team to ensure that the client program is continuously monitored to take care of deviations if any and corrections thereof.

This helps vendor to spot potential risks and work on a corrective action, when and where required. It also keeps vendor updated about the progress and also helps them review the different milestones on continuous basis.

TRANSFORMATION

It is critical to enterprise to know which type of change the organization is undergoing. There are three types of changes and each requires different change strategies, plans and degrees of employee engagement in business process of an enterprise. The changes occurring in organizations today are—developmental, transitional, and transformational. The change management strategies basically support developmental and transitional change. However, these strategies are insufficient for transformational change. Developmental change improves current process, but does not create something new. It focuses on improvements in existing skills sets, processes, methods, performance standards, and conditions such as—quality enhancement enhancing, increasing sales, training in interpersonal communication, work process improvements, team development, and problem-solving efforts. Transitional change requires designing, implementing and bring a new state. This covers reorganizations in post mergers, new products or services development/creation that do not require a significant shift in culture in the organization. The transformational change is far more challenging because the future state is unknown at the start and progress in through trial and error as new information is gathered. This makes it quite harder to manage transformation with pre-determined, time-bound and linear project plans. In transformation process the key change required is in the mindset and the culture of the organization. Here, the viewpoint of the management and the people therein need shift to get into the new future in term of evolving new organizational structure, systems to run the business and training of the people therein to take up the new challenges. The experience in the past shows that implementation of new system fails if required change in organizational culture and the mindset of employees is not happening simultaneously. The suggestion here is to organize for change management workshops so that employees are not dark about the organization's future plans and expectations from the employees. The best way is to go for employee engagement in transformation process. Hence, organizations should engage employees in mindset, behaviour, and change skill development programs to identify enterprise's customers' requirements for transformation. When enterprise engages employees in transformation before implementation, the resistance from employees becomes minimize. The management should use such strategies to support the change efforts, especially if they are transformational. Thus, transformation is more than a new strategy. Its skill development runs deeper into enterprise culture. Transformation includes a new awareness of enterprise's leadership choices, thinking and decisions. It includes altering the culture to sustain the kinds of approaches which are demanded today and which could change tomorrow by developing ability to be agile. In transformation process enterprise has to continually assess requirements and redirect resources as needed. In short transformation, endeavour is an enhanced way of viewing challenges, options and opportunities. It is a commitment to authentic leadership, to being aware of environment and its insight. For transformation to happen organizations need—Leaders, Management skills, Team work, Clear objectives, and Flexibility. Transformation is about change through which the business objectives can be attended. It adds value to the existing business through operational cost reduction and speed to market for products or services irrespective of time and location.

The transformation is done in processes, technology application, people at work and the entire business system. Bringing the change in old approach of the exiting employees of the organization, which is also associated with company's existing infrastructure is more difficult and expensive. But, the change is a must for first survival and then growth. In such cases the focus is more on non-core activities first and then core activities are addressed at the later stage. The success in transformational journey start with basic change in organizational culture. The process is called *unlearning the past and learning the new* for facing the future. If done systematically in organization by taking the help of change management experts the transformational process becomes more easy and hassle free. As the organization dynamics in changing business environment is on shift, traditional leadership is forced to adopt changes such as use of the interactive technology in their business systems and show more transparency in enterprise operations.

For example, Excell Group, a KPO, helped a global, diversified services firm in the Media Industry to transform its finance and accounting (F&A) function into a more efficient and effective operation. In addition to meet the F&A regulatory requirements, the enterprise was realigned from a product-based organizational structure to a geographically aligned organization with standard, global accounting F&A policies, systems, and processes. Vendor provided the program management support to align the country or region F&A operations to the global standard policy and processes. Here, Excell Group not only initiated a required change management program, but also initiated a training program to retained personnel.

In above transformation process, vendor enabled the Media company to achieve its objectives to captured more than 22 per cent cost savings, achieve timeline to implement the global standards in over 75 countries, training of client employees to perform the required F&A activities. The transformation generated cost savings through processes standardization and outsourcing of transaction-based activities, and also supported compliance requirements.

TECHNOLOGY ELEMENT

To lower the transformational risk, the clients should look for the following elements while engaging a vendor for business transformation. This will keep the cost of transformation under control.

- Wider scope of enterprise applications to cover maximum enterprise functions and widespread geographical coverage.
- Proper technology fit by service provider at the optimum cost and less of costly code for its customization.
- Well-defined plan for business processes interfaces and the integration thereof.

- Proper reporting formats and tools in place to boost the comfort level of users.
- Service provider should be well versed with methodology for implementation, without any risk of failure.
- Selection of technology to support wider client base.

To reduce the transformational risk, the support from technology trainers, HR consultants, and experienced project implementers is a must. The scope for software flexibility should be wider to accommodate the future changes and accept higher operational volumes. If done properly, and interactively with in-house processes, the transformation exercise will be risk-free project. It should be kept in mind that transformational risks are not only restricted to transition phase, but covers entire the cycle of outsourcing process. During transition and evolution the organization must achieve short-term successes by reaching desired quality at the earliest. Further, it is necessary to install continuous improvement process to reduce error level in processes control. The predictability of cost items should be built in the system. It should ensure compliance.

TRANSFORMATION APPROACHES

In today's complex multi-locational operational landscape, company's process limitations could make it less agile and result in curtailing its competitive edge. Even retooling the processes in one by one may not produce results. The basic requirement is a right vendor to understand company's processes and catalyzes change by designing a proper model. The Transformation Process helps enterprise make following five essential shifts;

- **Standardization:** Create operation consistency across all locations operation.
- **Mode:** Evolve a model for effective and efficient delivery.
- **Optimization:** Use techniques like 'Six Sigma' and 'Lean Approach' for operations.
- **Technology multiplier:** Use automation or other technologies in process for effectiveness.
- **Decision acceleration:** Use knowledge management techniques, analytics and statistical tools.

In BPO transformational space the vendors in general offers the following modules, transformational support to process engineering through Six Sigma, design and implementation of model for transformation, and managing people risks to gain the success in transformation process.

In general, BPO vendor become a partner in client's transformational journey, offering incremental as well as quantum improvements to client's business. Vendor designs a transformational model both for inshore and offshore application. Their approach is to build a model based on maturity and capability enhancement of client's organization. The model is based on proprietary process framework, the metrics and measurement framework and methodologies for process improvement. The transformational model designed by the vendor is mostly on micro-engineering concept.

The aim of business transformation is to achieve enhancement in profitability in a large quantum. The process of transformation is in fact forced by the enterprise leaders as they foresee the changes in business environment in future and change becomes inevitable. For business transformation which is always done in steps, the enterprise has to create a clear cut road map to tread. Obviously, the first and foremost step is to decide on the objectives and time frame to meet the same. There after map the current processes under existing business environment. Further, do the gap analysis using six sigma tool. The gaps are further identified across the system, covering functions, people and processes. The targets are set for the changes, based on the gaps analysis. The organizational structure is evolved for transformational project implementation to cover all levels of authority and responsibility. The training programs on change management are conducted and required directions for project implementation are given the responsible people at different levels. The entire process is reviewed periodically to track and further to correct its journey. This helps to achieve considerable increase in efficiencies, while moving from a client-based operations model to a process-based delivery model. Vendor provides a re-engineering solution by conducting thorough process assessment and operations modeling using various tools and techniques. The improvements give a significant savings in head counts, reducing error prone activities and drastically improving turn-around. In BTO (Business Transformation Outsourcing) engagement vendor in many cases will create new opportunities for the client to add value and streamline business functions. To transform services successfully, an organization's culture, technology and people all have to support and enable the change. BTO vendor works in partnership with client to transfer the necessary skills, knowledge, technical infrastructure, tools and techniques into the workplace. This helps ensure the transformation runs smoothly, from integrating services to encouraging people to adopt change.

OUTSOURCING BUSINESS TRANSFORMATION

In BTO contract a client's entire business process is outsourced to the BTO vendor. The BTO vendors not only manage the business processes, but also work closely with the company to transform and improve their core business process to add strategic and business value to the entire company. BTO goes beyond the traditional outsourcing model. The vendor will constantly transform and optimize the business process based on the changes in the marketplace. Unlike BPO, BTO vendor will own the entire business process of their client's company and add strategic value by bringing process and business efficiency to the entire company. BTO contracts are fundamentally different and it is complex in nature. As against BPO vendors, BTO vendors possesses deep knowledge/expertise on business processes in businesses. These may be in the domains of accounting, legal, IPR and HR, etc. BTO vendors with his vast experience in various industry segments, in general, will bring in best practices and procedures in their client organizations. BTO vendors will change the landscape of their client business through insights and vision.

In BTO, the vendor and client relationships are for long-term. The partnership is formed to increase shareholder values. Here, for success, the long-term commitment on objectives from both the side is a must. Here, the risks involved in engagement are multiple. Through the managing point of view BOT engagements are complex in nature. The handling requires special expertise on the part of client. BTO vendor needs a full control of the process to adjust and change it as needed. Here, clients interest and policies comes in the way because of internal structure of the company. The greatest risk is to share with IP (Intellectual Property) which gives competitive advantage to client over its competitors. The challenges are changing the policies and pricing models.

BTO reduces the challenges and risks associated with the new technologies. To mitigate risk in BTO contract client can make the BTO vendors accountable to all the technology and business changes. The clients can make the BTO vendor accountable for all the auxiliary, but critical business processes required for the core business processes and they can focus on their primary core competency. Today, Business Transformation Outsourcing (BTO) is not so common. BTO does not have a standard structure evolved yet. Each contract is unique. There are significant risks associated with the BTO contacts. But, leading companies like IBM, Accenture, TCS, Infosys, and Wipro are in the market and offering BTO solutions.

SUMMARY

Transformation is a new wave in the global outsourcing space. It is about eliminating activities which are not adding value to business. In fact, it all about the organizational change to do the things in the right way. It infuses confidence in the organization blood stream to manage the business risk in the changing business environment. With successful transformational process the enterprise can add value to its business through higher performance and economies of scale, sustained savings. For outsourcing vendors to add value is master skill in Business Transformation Outsourcing (BTO). In this BTO vendors has two responsibilities, first one to manage the business processes, the second one is transform and improve their core business process to add strategic and business value to the entire company. BTO partnership involves greater risks which needs to be addressed by client in the BTO contact.

Review Questions

1. What are the drivers of business transformation initiative?
2. How can reliability and predictability of business operations be improved?
3. Discuss various elements of business transformation.
4. Explain the various levels to unlock transformation in business.

Appendix A

Glossary

Application Service Provider (ASP): An ASP is a company that rents applications and related services, such as e-mail, payroll processing and ERP applications, over the Internet.

BOSS: BOSS stands for Burn-Out Stress Syndrome. BOSS is seen very commonly among young call centre executives. The symptoms of this syndrome include chronic fatigue, insomnia and complete alteration of the 24-hour biological rhythm of the body. Gastrointestinal problems are possible for those working at nights, as the body is put under chronic stress.

BOT: BOT is the short term of build, operate and transfer.

BPM: BPM stands for Business Process Management. This involves management of the outsourced business processes.

Business Process Outsourcing (BPO): BPO is the outsourcing of back-office and front-office functions typically performed by white-collar and clerical workers. Examples of such functions include accounting, human resources, and medical coding and transcription. Business process outsourcing means analysing the processes that comprise the business and its functional units, and then working with focused service providers to re-engineer and outsource these simultaneously. BPO involves the full transfer of responsibility for functions to the outsourcing company. The outsourcing service provider then carries out these functions on its own systems to agreed service standards and at a guaranteed cost.

Business Transformation Outsourcing (BTO): Business transformation outsourcing is a natural extension of the more tactical BPO model and involves the transfer of responsibility for all back-office functions, as well as a comprehensive business change management process to an external vendor.

BTO is a strategic relationship between the customer and the outsourcer, having the benefit of sophisticated financing mechanisms. It involves the firm acquiring strategic stakes in the BPO operations that companies have outsourced. BTO involves sharing risks and gains with an outsourcing business partner, and measuring performance improvement in terms of share price, market position, and return on capital.

Captive Centre: A captive centre is a company-owned offshore operation. The activities are performed offshore, but they are not outsourced to another company.

Captive Operation: A BPO captive operation can be set up by a multinational company instead of outsourcing to a third party. For example, GE Capital has its operations in Hyderabad and Gurgaon, while Dell has an operation in Bangalore.

Change Management: Change management involves the structures, procedures, and rules governing the adoption and implementation of changes in the commercial or financial relationship between the customer and the service provider.

Competitive Insourcing: Competitive insourcing is a process whereby company staffers compete with third-party bidders for a defined piece of work.

Contract Manufacturing: Contract manufacturing is the outsourcing of manufacturing jobs to onshore or offshore third-parties which have the necessary infrastructure and knowhow to perform the job.

Copyright: Copyright is a legal right which gives the creators of a wide range of material, such as literature, art, music, sound recordings, films, and broadcasts, the economic rights that enable them to control the use of their material in various ways, such as by making copies, issuing copies to the public, public performances, broadcasting, and online use. Copyright does not protect either ideas or things such as names or titles.

Co-sourcing: Co-sourcing is where a business function is performed by both company staff and external entities such as consultants or outsourcing vendors with specialized knowledge of the business function.

Customer Relationship Management (CRM): CRM is a marketing and order fulfilment system that usually includes a call centre, databases, software, and marketing strategy. CRM initiatives are complex and involve redesign of internal business processes and retraining. Successful contracting for CRM outsourcing involves attention to business as well as technology and legal issues.

Cybersquatting: Cybersquatting refers to a form of unfair competition for websites. A cybersquatter deliberately reserves with a registrar a domain name—consisting of the trademark or name of a company—for the purpose of selling the right to that domain name back to the legitimate owner.

E-sourcing: E-sourcing is a form of Internet-based outsourcing that takes advantage of the application service provider (ASP) delivery model. This approach enables the delivery of business process outsourcing services over the Internet.

Enterprise Resource Planning (ERP): ERP software integrates the various functions of an enterprise on the basis of sharing of data in a common database that, when processed, generates relevant managerial information for purchasing, manufacturing, sales, delivery and other functions.

Facilities Management: Facilities management is an outsourcing solution in which the customer transfers to an external service provider the responsibility for operations and maintenance of one or more facilities.

Glocalization: Glocalization is the condensed form of globalization plus localization. It refers to the ability to take the best from the world's systems, best practices, best ideas, best brands, and weld them with one's own culture in a balanced way, so that one doesn't feel overwhelmed by them.

Gramm–Leach–Bliley Act: The Gramm–Leach–Bliley Act requires financial institutions in the USA to respect the privacy of its customers and to protect the security and confidentiality of the information provided by them.

HIPAA: HIPAA stands for the US Health Insurance Portability and Accountability Act. The US healthcare industry has been involved in the simplification of administrative processes and improvement in efficiency for several decades. The industry leaders concluded that greater standardization of data and transactions was crucial to improve efficiency. This conclusion was subsequently utilized in the development of simple and specific administrative language, included in the healthcare legislation called the HIPAA.

Insourcing: Insourcing involves the transfer of an outsourced function to a department of a company, to be managed entirely by its employees. The term is also used to describe foreign companies locating facilities in the USA and employing US workers.

ITES: ITES is the short form of IT-enabled services. IT-enabled outsourcing involves those outsourcing services that use information technology for processing and delivery. These services are usually delivered through a telecommunications or data network, or other electronic media.

Infringement: Infringement is the invasion of an exclusive right of intellectual property. Infringement of a utility patent involves making, using or selling a patented product or process without permission from the patent holder. Infringement of a registered design involves fabricating a design in a way that makes the fabrication seems almost identical to an existing design, where the resemblance is intended to induce a customer to purchase one thing, supposing it to be another. Infringement of a trademark comprises the unauthorized use or imitation of a mark that is the property of another, in order to deceive, confuse, or mislead customers. Infringement of a copyright involves reproducing, adapting, distributing, performing in public, or displaying in public the copyrighted work of someone else without due permission.

Innovation: An innovation involves the successful exploitation of new ideas in the form of a useful machinery or process, by any person, using his or her own intellect. All inventions are innovations and are patentable, but all innovations are not patentable inventions.

Intellectual Property (IP): Intellectual property is a broad term that includes discoveries, inventions, knowhow, methods, processes, materials, copyrightable works, original data, and other artistic or creative works which may have value. Intellectual property includes material which is protected by statute or legislation such as patents, copyrights, trademarks, service marks, trade secrets, mask works, and plant varieties. It also includes the physical embodiments of intellectual effort, such as models, designs, devices, machines, instrumentation, apparatus, circuits, computer programs and visualizations, biological materials, chemicals, other compositions of matter, and records of research. IP is also a legal concept, inasmuch, like other property, it can be owned, sold, rented, and given away.

Intellectual Property Rights (IPRs): Intellectual Property Rights is a general term covering patents, copyrights, trademarks, industrial designs, geographical indications, layout design of integrated circuits, and protection of undisclosed information (trade secrets). Intellectual Property Rights are statutory rights which, once granted, allow the creator(s) or owner(s) of the intellectual property to exclude others from exploiting the same commercially for a given duration. It allows the creator(s) or owner(s) to have benefits from their work when these are exploited commercially. IPRs are granted to an inventor, creator, or designer, in lieu of the disclosure of his or her knowledge.

Invention: An invention means a new product or process, involving an innovative step and capable of industrial application.

IVR: IVR stands for Integrated Voice Response. IVR systems are automated systems installed in customer contact or service centres, that help in the smooth performance of routine tasks such as accessing account information, product information, and schedules.

Jurisdiction: Jurisdiction means either the administration of justice or extent of authority over a territory, or the territory over which there is such authority.

KPO: KPO stands for Knowledge Process Outsourcing. This involves outsourcing of knowledge-intensive business processes that require specialized domain expertise and deliver high value to organizations.

Licence: A special permission to do something on, or with, somebody else's intellectual property (protected through copyright or patent) which, were it not for the licence, could be legally prevented or could give rise to legal action in tort or trespass. The owner of any intellectual property may grant a third party the use of the property on a non-exclusive or exclusive basis for a period of time in return for payment, usually in the form of royalty.

Local Area Network (LAN): LAN is a group of computers and associated devices that share a common communications line, and typically the resources of a single processor or server, within a small geographic area (for example, an office building). Usually the server contains applications and data storage that are shared in by multiple computer users.

Nearshoring: Nearshore outsourcing or 'nearshoring' involves outsourcing within a territory near that of the client, accessible by short travel or telephone, in the same or neighbouring time-zone.

Offshoring: Offshore outsourcing or 'offshoring' is the outsourcing of business processes overseas or in a separate country.

Patent: Patent means an official document giving the holder of the patent the sole right to make, use or sell an invention, and preventing others from imitating it. A patent is a legal monopoly, which is granted for a limited time by a country to the inventor of a new product or process.

Patent Infringement: Patent infringement involves any unauthorized making, using, offering for sale, or selling of any patented invention.

Procurement BPO: Procurement BPO involves the transfer of management and execution of one or more procurement activities, of the entire procurement sub-segments, or of the entire procurement business function to an external provider.

Request for Information (RFI): RFI is a document that requests prospective service providers to provide general information on their capabilities and overall business.

Request for Proposal (RFP): RFP is a document that requests prospective service providers to propose the terms, conditions, and other elements of an agreement to deliver specified services.

Sarbanes–Oxley Act: Sarbanes–Oxley Act is a legislation that deals with the financial and accounting aspects of a business organization. This act is applicable to public limited companies based in and operating out of the USA. It calls for transparency in financial matters of the company. This act has bearing on those BPO service providers in India who are providing services to US companies.

Service Level Agreement (SLA): The SLA is either a contract or an addendum to a contract that defines the type, value, and conditions of the outsourcing services to be provided. Typically, the SLAs address "quality of service" the issues such as response time, availability and speed.

Strategic Alliance: Strategic alliances are long-term agreements that are generally employed to facilitate significant developments such as the launch of a new manufacturing venture. The agreement lays down the purpose and benefits for the onshore and offshore companies; how they will share risks; and what each will contribute, including capital, process, materials, systems, and management.

Strategic Outsourcing: Strategic outsourcing supports transformation strategies such as restructuring and TQM in order to ensure alignment with overall corporate strategy.

Trademarks: A trademark is any word, name, symbol, or device, or any combination that is used, or intended to be used, in commerce to identify and distinguish the products of one manufacturer or seller from the products manufactured or sold by others, and to indicate the source of the products. A trademark is a type of brand name.

Trade Secrets: Trade secrets refer to any information about the creation of a product or a process that provides its possessor an advantage over the competition and which must therefore be kept secret if it is to be of any use. Such business information is subject to reasonable efforts to preserve confidentiality and has value because it is generally unknown in the trade. Such confidential information is protected from those who seek to gain access to it through improper methods or by a breach of confidence. Infringement of a trade secret is a type of unfair competition.

Zero-based Sourcing: Zero-based sourcing means that the sourcing decision for each and every aspect of a business operation is justified afresh in every planning cycle from an assumed base of zero. This approach ensures that the organization consistently and objectively re-tests its internal operations against the best available external solutions.

Appendix B

Information Resources on BPO

www.bpo.starmatrimonials.com
www.indiawebdevelopers.com/outsourcing/data_privacy.asp
www.kpoexperts.com
www.outsourcing.com
www.outsourcing-law.com
www.24×7bpo.com
www.accenture.com
www.assocham.org/bpo/
www.axiombpm.com
www.banknetindia.com
www.bitscapesolutions.com
www.bixee.com
www.bpoavenues.com
www.bpoindia.org
www.bpomatrix.net
www.bposystems.com
www.bpowatchindia.com
www.cainfotechindia.com
www.capgemini.com/services/outsourcing/bpo
www.cisin.com
www.cogenteservices.com
www.customerfocusservices.com
www.dimensioni.net
www.dqindia.ciol.com/content/industrymarket/bpo/default.asp
www.ebpo.in
www.go4bpo.com
www.hclbpo.com

www.hcltech.com/BPO/
www.icallbiz.com
www.infosearch bpo.com
www.itmatchonline.com
www.itoutsourcingservices.com
www.jvptechnology.com
www.minfosystems.com
www.mphasis.com/offerings/bpo.asp
www.nasscom.in
www.netstarbpo.com
www.nirvanabpo.com
www.nissioutsourcing.com
www.outsourcingking.com
www.pacificbpo.com
www.Qmap.co.uk
www.rayscom.com
www.saibposervices.com
www.services-india.com
www.tamizhan.com
www.telegenisys.com
www.thehindubusinessline.com
www.velai4u.com
www.vservesolution.com
www.webyantram.com
www.wipro.com/bpo/index.htm
www.worldbpoforum.com
www.yantrambpo.com

Appendix C

BPO Organizations

Sr. No.	*BPO Organization*	*Websites*
1	Accenture	www.accenture.com
2	ADP	www.adp.com
3	Affiliated Computer Systems	www.acs-inc.com
4	Atos Origin International B.V.	www.atosorigin.com
5	Ceridian	www.ceridian.com
6	CGI	www.cgi.com
7	Cognizant	www.cognizant.com
8	Convergys	www.convergys.com
9	Covansys	www.covansys.com
10	CSC	www.csc.com
11	IBM Daksh e-Services	www.daksh.com
12	Datametrics	www.datametrics.co.uk
13	Deloitte	www.deloitte.com
14	EDS	www.eds.com
15	eFunds Global Outsourcing	www.efunds.com
16	Ernst & Young/Capgemini	www.capgemini.com
17	Exl Service	www.exlservice.com
18	General Electric	www.ge.com/www.geappliances.com
19	Getronics	www.getronics.com
20	Gevity	www.gevity.com
21	GTL	www.gtllimited.com
22	HCL Technologies	www.hcltech.com
23	Hewitt/Exult	www.hewittassociates.com
24	Hewlett-Packard	www.hp.com

25	HTMT Global Solutions	www.htmtglobal.com
26	Firstsource	www.firstsource.com
27	i-flex	www.iflexsolutions.com
28	i-Gate	www.igate.com
29	Infocrossing	www.infocrossing.com
30	Infosys	www.infosys.com
31	Intelligroup	www.intelligroup.com
32	Keane	www.keane.com
33	MphasiS	www.mphasis.com
34	Northrop Grumman IT	www.it.northropgrumman.com
35	Office Tiger	www.officetiger.com
36	Oracle	www.oracle.com
37	Outsourced Partners International	www.opiglobal.com
38	Patni Computer Systems	www.patni.com
39	Perot Systems	www.perotsystems.com
40	Satyam	www.satyam.com/bpo
41	Siemens Business Services	www.it-solutions.siemens.com www.sbs.siemens.com
42	SourceNet Solutions	www.sourcenetglobal.com
43	Spherion	www.spherion.com
44	Sutherland Global Services	www.suth.com
45	Syntel	www.syntelinc.com
46	Tata Consultancy Services	www.tcs.com
47	TechBooks	www.techbooks.com
48	Unisys	www.unisys.com
49	vCustomer	www.vcustomer.com
50	Wipro Spectramind	www.wipro.com/bpo/index.htm
51	WNS Global	www.wns.com
52	Xansa	www.xansa.com
53	Zenta Technology	www.zentagroup.com
54	24/7 Customer	www.247customer.com

Appendix D

Sample Contract Outsourcing Services

This Agreement is made and entered into as of January 1, 2013 by and between the **Rama Technologies** ("RAMA"), having an office and place of business at 2013 Millennium Park, Vashi, Navi Mumbai, 400703 and **Simon Financial Services** ("SIMON"), having an office and place of 21B, Arpita, D.N. Road, Nariman Point, Mumbai 400001. The agreement will be in force (Effective Date) from January 01, 2013.

WHEREAS, SIMON desires to hire RAMA to perform outsourced management services and RAMA desires to be hired by SIMON to perform such services regarding the operational management (the "Services") for the SIMON customers using a defined set of SIMON Transaction Centers listed on Exhibit A (attached hereto and made a part hereof by reference), collectively known as ("Centers") as an independent contractor according to the terms and conditions set forth herein.

In consideration of the terms and conditions set forth below and other good and valuable consideration, the receipt and sufficiency of which is hereby acknowledged, the parties agrees as follows:

1. WORK DETAILS

1.1 The RAMA and SIMON agree that the general scope and results of the services to be completed by RAMA shall be developed by SIMON and RAMA together. The scope covers the day-to-day management of the Data Processing Centers as described in Exhibit B.

1.2 RAMA shall prepare and deliver to SIMON monthly reports/invoices regarding any services ongoing or performed during each month as per the term of this Agreement.

1.3 SIMON agrees that it will not directly or indirectly, during the term of this agreement, solicit or utilize the services of any other vendor or contractor for the services to be provided by RAMA.

1.4 Both RAMA and SIMON acknowledge and agree that from time to time during the term of this agreement there may be additional services required by the SIMON. The specifications and pricing of these services will be mutually agreed upon and confirmed via written document, which is signed by an authorized representative of each party before such services are delivered. The parties acknowledge and agree that such written document shall be subject to the terms and conditions of this agreement unless specific modifications to this agreement are made to the contrary in such 'statement of work'.

1.5 If a SIMON customer desires to renew its agreement with SIMON without adding new or additional services and/or products towards 'renewal contract', RAMA shall act as the exclusive reseller for SIMON for such renewal of existing SIMON customer contracts. However, this is done beginning 'Effective Date' of this agreement.

1.6 RAMA shall have the exclusive right to sell RAMA applications and other management services to SIMON Transaction Centers customers.

2. FEES

2.1 Towards the consideration of furnishing the services, described herein, SIMON shall pay to RAMA the monthly fee for the 'services' as mentioned in **Exhibit B** ("Monthly Service Fee").

2.2 Monthly service fees shall be payable within thirty (30) days of receipt of invoice. Monthly service fees not paid within thirty (30) days shall be subject to a monthly service charge of 1.75 per cent of the unpaid balance.

2.3 The monthly service fees is based on RAMA's actual costs for providing the services and includes a predetermined margin of twenty-five per cent (25%) which shall be adjusted according to the Margin Plan as indicated. Within sixty (60) days of the Effective Date the parties shall mutually agree on a sliding scale mechanism under which the twenty-five per cent (25%) predetermined margin set forth above shall be adjusted upward or downward based on utilization rates (as well as other factors which may be agreed to by the parties) which actually are occurring in the Transaction Centers. The Margin Plan shall be amended quarterly as necessary and included in the Budget as indicated below. RAMA's actual costs for providing the services shall be calculated monthly and the monthly service fees adjusted up or down accordingly. Adjustments will be reflected in the next monthly invoice for services. RAMA shall prepare a quarterly budget including the resources, costs and other expenses it expects to incur in providing the services for the upcoming quarter. SIMON shall review and promptly approve the budget in the event there are any disputes regarding the budget, the parties shall meet and in good faith negotiate a reconciliation of the budget.

2.4 RAMA and SIMON shall maintain records of all activities subject to revenues, payments, fees, commissions and costs pursuant to this 'agreement'. Each party shall permit a reputable independent certified public accounting firm designated by the other party to have access, at a mutually agreed upon time during normal business hours, to the records and books of account which relate solely to this 'agreement' for the purpose of determining whether the appropriate fees and commissions have been paid. Such audits will be conducted once every year; provided, that either party may audit the other within six (6) months of any internal audit in which a discrepancy of five per cent (5%) or greater is discovered. If a discrepancy is discovered, the party in whose favour the error was made will promptly pay the amount of the error to the other. The party requesting the audit will pay the cost of the audit, provided, that if a discrepancy is discovered of five per cent (5%) or greater in favour of the party requesting the audit, then the audited party will be required to pay the reasonable costs of the audit.

3. LIMITATION OF LIABILITY

3.1 Limitation of Remedies. RAMA's and SIMON's entire liability and exclusive remedy in any cause of action based on contract, tort or otherwise in connection with any Services furnished pursuant to this agreement including its Exhibits shall be limited to the total fees paid by SIMON to RAMA. No action, regardless of form, arising out of this 'agreement' may be brought by either party more than one (1) year after the occurrence of the event giving rise to such cause of action.

3.2 Except with respect to amounts payable arising out of claims based upon willful, malicious or grossly negligent conduct of the liable party, neither RAMA nor anyone else who has been involved in the creation, production, or delivery of the services shall in any event whatsoever be liable for any indirect, consequential, punitive or incidental damages in excess of the total price paid by SIMON to RAMA (including damages for loss of business profits, business interruption, loss of business information, and the like) arising out of the use of or inability to use the services even if SIMON has been advised of the possibility of such damages.

4. INTELLECTUAL PROPERTY

4.1 For purposes of this 'agreement', the term "INTELLECTAUL PROPERTY" shall mean all of the information, data and software furnished by one party to the other, whether in oral, written, graphic or machine-readable form, which may include, but not be limited to, code, software tool specifications, functions and features, integration and shared data block specifications, financial statements, corporate and stock information, file layouts, marketing strategies, business, product or acquisition plans, current business relationships or strategies and customer lists. "Proprietary Information" shall not include information which:

(a) Is or becomes available to the general public through no fault of either party;
(b) Is independently developed by non-disclosing party;
(c) Is rightfully received by the non-disclosing party from a third party without a duty of confidentiality; or
(d) Is required to be disclosed by court order or operation of law.

Before disclosing any 'Intellectual Property' under court order or operation of law, the non-disclosing party shall provide the disclosing party reasonable notice and the opportunity to object to or limit such disclosure.

4.2 Each party acknowledges that, in and as a result of visit(s) to the other party's facilities and/or discussions with a party's officers and employees, a party shall or may be making use of or acquiring Intellectual Property. As a material inducement to disclose such Intellectual Property, each party covenants and agrees that it shall not, except with the prior written consent of the other party, at any time directly by itself or indirectly through any agent or employee—(i) copy, modify, disclose, divulge, reveal, report, publish or transfer to any person or entity, for any purpose whatsoever, any Proprietary Information or (ii) use Intellectual Property for any purpose other than in connection with the consummation of the Proposed Transactions. Failure to mark any of the Intellectual Property as confidential, protected or Intellectual Property shall not affect its status as part of the Intellectual Property under the terms of this 'agreement'.

4.3 Each party covenants and agrees that all right, title and interest in any Intellectual Property shall be and shall remain the exclusive property of the disclosing party.

5. At closing of the activities for SIMON or the termination of this agreement, each party will promptly deliver to the other all copies and embodiments, in whatever form, of Intellectual Property and all other materials containing any Intellectual Property which is in such party's possession or control, no matter where such material is located.

6. For any statement of work, all right, title and interest in and to all products, services and materials provided to SIMON by RAMA under this 'agreement' shall be and remain the property of RAMA exclusively. SIMON shall have no right, title or interest in or to any products, services or materials except as expressly set forth in this 'agreement'. RAMA shall retain all rights and title to any and all capital improvements and Intellectual Property it utilizes or contributes to the Transaction Centers or as part of the services.

7. TERM AND TERMINATION

7.1 This Agreement shall commence on the Effective Date and continue in full force and effect for three (3) years and the term of this Agreement may, upon mutual agreement by the parties, be extended for additional one (1) year period, unless terminated as provided herein.

7.2 If either party (the "Defaulting Party") materially defaults in the performance of its obligations under this Agreement, and if such default is not cured within ninety (90) days after written notice is given to the Defaulting Party specifying the default, then the other party (the "Aggrieved Party") may, by giving written notice to the Defaulting Party, terminate this Agreement as of the date specified in the notice of termination.

7.3 Each party, insofar as it becomes a 'defaulting party', agrees that, upon receipt of any notice of default, it will immediately commence all commercially reasonable efforts to cure the specified default and to commit the resources necessary at the Defaulting Party's expense, to accomplish such cure as promptly as is reasonably possible.

7.4 Upon any termination of this Agreement, RAMA will assist and comply with SIMON's reasonable directions to cause the orderly transition and migration of the Services to SIMON or a third party contractor to whom SIMON chooses to transfer the Services.

8. RAMA may, but shall not be obligated to hire as employees of RAMA the current SIMON employees listed in **Exhibit C**. As part of the 'services', regardless of whether such employees are hired by RAMA, as of the Effective Date, RAMA shall have management control of such employees, but unless hired by RAMA. SIMON shall remain the employee's employer for all purposes, including, but not limited to payroll, taxes, insurance and benefits. SIMON agrees to reasonably assist RAMA in the hiring of any of the employees pursuant to this Section.

9. RAMA shall be paid its compensation without any deductions made whatsoever for state or federal taxes of any kind. RAMA agrees to pay all applicable federal and/or state taxes and all local excise, sales, use, or other taxes which arise as a result of the services performed by RAMA or any employee of RAMA under this Agreement.

10. It is expressly agreed and understood between SIMON and RAMA that RAMA is performing the 'services' as an independent contractor and is neither the employee nor the agent of or on behalf of SIMON.

11. This agreement may not be changed or terminated rally, and no change, termination or attempted waiver or any of the provisions hereof shall be binding unless in writing and signed by both parties.

12. Neither party shall sell, transfer, assign or subcontract any right or obligation hereunder without the prior written consent of the other party. Any act in derogation of the foregoing shall be null and void.

13. Should any provision hereof be deemed, for any reason whatsoever, to be invalid or inoperative, such provision shall be deemed severable and shall not affect the force and validity of other provisions of this Agreement.

14. This Agreement shall be deemed to be made and entered into pursuant to the laws of the Maharashtra State in India and for all purposes this 'agreement' shall be construed and interpreted in accordance with and be governed by the law of the State of Maharashtra in India.

15. Neither RAMA nor SIMON shall be held responsible for any delay or failure in performance under this 'agreement' arising out of causes beyond its control, or without its fault or negligence. Such causes may include, but are not limited to, fires, terrorist acts, strikes, embargoes, shortages or supplies of raw materials, or components or finished goods, acts of God, acts of regulatory agencies or national disasters.

18. RAMA will place SIMON and all affiliates designated by SIMON which are primarily related to the Data Centers under RAMA's umbrella insurance plan.

19. In the event SIMON desires to sell any of the Transaction Centers or its collocation business to a third party, SIMON shall deliver a written notice to RAMA stating the price, terms, and conditions of the proposed sale and the identity of the proposed transferee (a "Sale Notice"). Within a reasonable time period not to exceed fourteen (14) days after receipt of a Sale Notice by RAMA, RAMA shall have the right, but not the obligation to purchase such Transaction Center or its collocation business so offered at the price and on the terms and conditions stated in the Sale Notice.

20. SIMON represents and warrants to RAMA that as of the Effective Date the operations of the Transaction Center and the provision of services to its customers is compliant with:

(a) SIMON service level agreements with its Transaction Centers customers;

(b) Its vendor contracts;

(c) The operating lease and real estate covenants for each Transaction Centers; and

(d) Government laws and regulations requirements related to the Transaction Centers.

21. Neither party may, without the prior written consent of the other party, assign this 'agreement', in whole or in part, either voluntarily or by operation of law, and any attempt to assign this 'agreement' in violation of this Section shall be a default of the Agreement pursuant to Section 7.2 above and such assignment shall be null and void. In the event the majority owner of a party becomes less than a 50 per cent owner and/or the majority owner's equity position drops below 30 per cent of said party, such events shall be deemed assignments for purposes hereof ("Change of Control Events"). An owner of a party which has a Change of Control Event shall have thirty (30) days from the date of the Change of Control Event to declare such event an assignment, or such event is waived as an assignment.

RAMA and SIMON acknowledge that each has fully read and understood this 'agreement', and, intending to be legally bound thereby, executed this Agreement on the date set forth above.

Authorized Signatories:

Simon Financial Services ("SIMON")	Rama Technologies ("RAMA")
Signature:	Signature:
Name:	Name:
Designation:	Designation:

IN WITNESS WHEREOF, the parties acknowledge that each has fully read and understood this 'agreement', and, intending to be legally bound thereby, executed this Agreement on the date first above written.

Witness 1

Simon Financial Services ("SIMON")	Rama Technologies ("RAMA")
Signature:	Signature:
Name:	Name:
Designation:	Designation:

Witness 2

Simon Financial Services ("SIMON")	Rama Technologies ("RAMA")
Signature:	Signature:
Name:	Name:
Designation:	Designation:

EXHIBIT A—SIMON TRANSACTION CENTERS

(Location and Address)

1. ______________________________
2. ______________________________
3. ______________________________
4. ______________________________
5. ______________________________
6. ______________________________

EXHIBIT B—TERMS AND CONDITIONS

1. Responsibilities

1.1 RAMA to provide the operational management services and support for the Data Processing Centers including, but not limited to:

1.1.1 RAMA will support SIMON on customer billing; customer collec-tions; financial reporting and analytical support; certain insurance coverages.

1.1.2 RAMA will assist SIMON in negotiating vendor contracts; making vendor and operating and real estate lease payments; provisioning certain vendor services.

1.1.3 RAMA will provide customer support; executing new sales and renewals or SIMON services; reselling SIMON services bundled with other services and products to New Customers.

1.1.4 RAMA will support SIMON in technical operations—facility management; security services; on-going facilities maintenance and repair.

1.1.5 RAMA will help SIMON in strategic functions such as planning, capital investment advice, business and corporate development advice.

2. Service Levels

RAMA shall perform the Services in a manner that is stipulated in the Service Level Agreements with SIMON Data Center customers. The services will performed within the prevailing government framework and regulations filing requirements as desired.

3. Payment

SIMON shall pay RAMA a Service Fee of ₹15,00,000 per month. The adjustments, if any, will be taken into considerations as per Section 2.3 in the Agreement.

4. Banking

RAMA and SIMON agree for the collection and deposit of money from customers, RAMA shall maintain a separate SIMON bank account and act only as an independent contractor on behalf of SIMON.

EXHIBIT C—LIST OF CURRENT SIMON EMPLOYEES

(Names, Designations and Location Address)

1. ____________
2. ____________
3. ____________
4. ____________
5. ____________

–

–

50. ____________

Appendix E

Draft Service Level Agreement

Between ABF Corporation and Rama Chartered Accountants for Provision of Internal Audit Services

1. PURPOSE

This Service Level Agreement (SLA) document covers the nature and scope as well as the level of the specific services that Rama Chartered Accountants (RCA) will provide to ABF Corporation (ABFC). This SLA defines guaranteed levels of internal audit services and support from RCA for ABFC. The purpose of the SLA serves to regulate the business relationship between RCA and ABFC and therefore covers the following key aspects:

- Principles of RCA
- Rights and obligations of RCA
- Rights and obligations of ABFC
- RCA services and their review
- RCA performance reporting process
- Dispute resolution process
- Communication media
- RCA recovery and contingency
- Continuous improvements
- Amendments and agreements

2. OBJECTIVES OF RCA

RCA is an independent auditing firm to provide financial, performance, operational, and computer audit services. RCA will examine, evaluate and report on the adequacy of internal control as a contribution to the proper, economic, efficient and effective use of financial and other resources.

3. PRINCIPLES OF RCA OPERATION

The following principles should guide the operation of RCA and its relationship with ABFC:

(a) RCA will conduct an internal audit in accordance with the standards set by the Institute of Chartered Accountants of India.

(b) The audit relationship will be guided by detailed operating procedures that take note of ABFC management input.

(c) RCA will report on a quarterly basis to the relevant Audit Committee, detailing RCA's performance compared to the annual audit plan as well as significant findings at ABFC.

(d) Key performance indicators will be benchmarked every year against the local industry and international firms to establish a sound basis for determining RCA performance targets.

(e) The SLA should promote co-operative spirit between RCA and ABFC.

4. RIGHTS AND OBLIGATIONS OF RCA

4.1 Rights

With regard to managing the relationship with ABFC, RCA has the following general rights:

(a) To hire staff and incur expenditure within authority limits designated by RCA management;

(b) To accept with discretion audit assignments, where specialist knowledge and experience falls outside the skills and proficiencies of its staff; these could include legal issues, environmental concerns, technical issues, etc.; to co-source or out-source as and when necessary the skills required to conduct internal audits, e.g. in instances of shortage of staff, large ad hoc projects, etc.; to develop continuous improvement initiatives that have an impact on internal audit services;

(c) To review pricing policies with ABFC as a result of the impact of changes in the prevailing economic climate;

(d) To organize, deploy and re-deploy RCA staff and assets to meet service obligations as it sees fit;

(e) To recover costs from ABFC in a fair manner that reflects ABFC usage of RCA resources, when such a mechanism has been agreed to.

4.2 Obligations

With regard to managing the relationship with ABFC, RCA has the following general obligations:

(a) To consult with the Head of Department (HoD) as well as the Chief Financial Officer (CFO) or Accounts Manager of ABFC to set mutually convenient dates for audit assignments to take place. However, it must be noted that the ultimate timing of audit assignments rests with

ABFC and there may be instances where no notice of the audit is provided;

(b) To determine the scope and objectives of the audit assignment in conjunction with ABFC (normally the HoD and the CFO) to ensure that concerns are identified and that required assurances relating to controls and procedures are addressed. The initial risk assessment conducted with ABFC will also be used in determining the scope and objectives of the audit;

(c) To provide opportunity (with concerned ABFC authorities) to formally respond to the audit reports. The findings and recommendations recorded in the audit reports are open to negotiations, and the submitted management comments will form part of the final audit report;

(d) To agree to recommendations by way of a formal action plan with the Accounts Manager, HoD and CFO. Target dates for the implementation of the agreed-to action plans will also be included in the report;

(e) To issue a report detailing the adequacy of internal controls within two weeks after completion of the audit work regarding individual audited activities;

(f) To issue a final audit report within four weeks after receiving final management comments;

(g) To perform follow-up audit within three months of the issue of the final audit report to ensure that agreed-to recommendations and action plans are indeed practical and have been implemented.

5. RIGHTS AND OBLIGATIONS OF ABFC

5.1 Rights

With regard to managing the relationships with RCA, ABFC has the following general rights:

(a) To request, if required, ad-hoc audit assignments whereby a request to review a particular system is made. This will normally arise as a result of concerns raised, requiring assurance of controls and evaluating procedural efficiency;

(b) To receive the agreed-upon service levels from RCA;

(c) To conduct a regular review of RCA performance;

(d) To bring shortfalls or deficiencies in service to the attention of RCA management;

(e) To be informed and consulted on system and process changes proposed by RCA.

5.2 Obligations

(a) To use RCA services as defined in this SLA;
(b) To make available all information relating to ABFC to RCA;
(c) To raise any underlying concerns, even those that may be insignificant;
(d) To meet appointments, requests for information and deadlines for responses and recommendations;
(e) To implement agreed-to recommendations and action plans;
(f) To perform certain specified activities in order to enable the RCA to deliver the services specified in the SLA (refer to the Annexure).

6. SERVICE LEVEL AGREEMENT REVIEW

RCA is committed to delivering quality internal audit services to ABFC, thereby enabling them to meet its business imperatives. The service levels and their measurements are intended to measure whether or not RCA is meeting the performance levels that are necessary to satisfy ABFC's business requirements. The review of RCA service-level targets and their achievement will be accomplished via bi-annual and annual management review meetings.

6.1 Bi-annual Management Review Meeting

Bi-annual management review meeting will be held by the RCA management team and the ABFC management team to:

(a) Review general performance of RCA;
(b) Monitor the success of meeting the SLA targets to achieve ABFC's business requirements;
(c) Review and accept or deny changes relating to modification of the SLA.

6.2 Annual Management Review Meeting

RCA will review the SLA annually following the finalization of the annual audit plan. ABFC will also review this agreement on an annual basis to ensure that it is in agreement with the expected service levels. In addition, the Audit Committee must comment on the detail of this agreement on an annual basis.

7. DURATION OF THE SERVICE LEVEL AGREEMENT

This SLA includes all of the internal audit services listed and will be effective upon the date of signature by all parties and will continue until terminated. Service scope, charges and performance targets will be renegotiated annually prior to the commencement of the financial year.

8. RCA PERFORMANCE REPORTING PROCESS

To effectively support ABFC's business objectives, it is imperative that consistent and guaranteed service levels are provided by RCA, and RCA's performance will be monitored and reported against a balanced set of business and internal operating performance measures.

Performance against specific business measures, as outlined in the detailed appendices, will be reported quarterly. The targets for these metrics are incorporated into future amendments of this SLA. Service-level targets and their achievement will be documented in trend reports.

RCA performance will be evaluated along set criteria. Any disputes over performance standards will be evaluated on these performance indicators before grievance procedures are instituted. The following list shows specific performance indicators. For details of all the performance indicators, please refer to the Annexure on 'Service Levels'.

(a) The percentage (%) of recommendations that ABFC accepts and turns into action plans will indicate the effectiveness of the service rendered by RCA.
(b) The percentage (%) of actual audit assignments completed against the annual audit plan will indicate the ability of RCA to meet the ABFC's service expectations.
(c) The percentage (%) of audit assignments completed before the planned completion date will indicate efficiency of RCA.

9. SERVICES PROVIDED

This SLA covers services provided by RCA to its clients over and above those covered by operational and financial audits. The services that will be provided are in accordance with the Operational Model Design of RCA. The services are:

(a) Financial record evaluation and authentication;
(b) Evaluation of how effective, efficient and economical strategic objectives are being met;
(c) IT risk-based control assurances and security reviews;
(d) Review of systems accounting procedures;
(e) Fraud risk reviews;
(f) Providing fraud awareness and detection training.

10. DISPUTE RESOLUTION

A standard problem management process will be followed. This process will encompass problem logging, tracking, resolution, escalation, and hands-off processes between ABFC and RCA Client Manager. This process will ensure that the required service levels as per the SLA are established between RCA and ABFC.

11. SERVICE MEDIA OFFERED

RCA will support the following media types for initiating audits and resolving queries:

- Telephone—Contact centre agents
- Mail/facsimile/e-mail
- Internet services—when available
- External messenger.

12. BASIS OF CHARGING

ABFC will pay fees to RCA. These will be reflective of prevailing market charges across the industry.

13. CONTINUOUS IMPROVEMENT

A committee will be established, with both RCA and ABFC representatives, for reviewing service performance and identifying opportunities for process improvement.

14. AMENDMENTS TO THIS AGREEMENT

This agreement is subject to amendment for the addition or deletion of services provided. Any such proposed amendments are to be recorded in an updated version of this document and are subject to the agreement of RCA.

15. APPROVALS

This Service Level Agreement has been reviewed and approved by:

ABFC's Autorized Signatory	RCA's Authorized Signatory
(Date)	(Date)

Annexure

SERVICE LEVELS

RCA process	*Performance indicators*	*Responsible person*	*Service level standard*	*Parameters to measure*
• Draw up the basic scope and objectives with the client	• Approved basic scope and objectives	• RCA Manager	• Documentation of acceptable basic scope and objectives • Reaching of agreement with the client	• Percentage of agreed-to scope and objective sheets
• Determine complexity and scope of client operations	• Preparation of a time budget • Allocation of staff	• RCA Manager	• Accurate time budget	• Percentage of audits completed within planned time budget
• Gather information through enquiry, meetings with the client and his records	• High-level analytical review to gain an overall understanding of the client's operations	• RCA Audit Supervisor	• Understanding of the entity and the underlying risk areas	• Percentage of scope and objective worksheets accepted
• Use chart and document systems	• Documented systems • Obtained understanding of controls	• RCA Audit Supervisor	• Charting and documentation of systems of control that correlate with the actual system of the client	• Percentage of system charts and documents accepted by the client • Percentage of alterations to system charts and documents
• Forward and discuss all queries with the client	• Reported queries to clients and agreement on the most suitable controls	• RCA Audit Supervisor	• Presenting valid, accurate and complete informal control queries	• Percentage of accurate and complete queries presented • Percentage of informal queries accepted
• Indicate to management that the controls need to be tested	• Agreement the scope and objectives concerning the testing of the effectiveness of internal controls	• RCA Audit Senior	• Scope and objective of audit to covers significant risk areas	• Percentage of scope and objective worksheets accepted by client

Continued

SERVICE LEVELS (*Continued*)

RCA process	*Performance indicators*	*Responsible person*	*Service level standard*	*Parameters to measure*
• Discuss the draft audit report and obtain management comments	• Obtaining of management comments from the client and agreeing to action plans	• RCA Manager	• Recommendations and action plans that are practical, value-added and cost-effective	• Percentage of recommendations accepted • Percentage of action plans accepted
• Perform a follow-up audit	• Implementation of recommendations	• RCA Manager	• Practical recommendations and action plans implemented	• Percentage of recommendations implemented • Percentage of action plans implemented
• Approve the basic scope and objective worksheets provided by RCA • Agree to the basic scope and objectives	• Approval of the basic scope and objective worksheet	ABFC • Head of Department (HoD) • Chief Financial Officer (CFO) • Accounts Manager	• Agreement on and approval of basic scope and objectives within 5 working days	• Percentage of basic scope and objectives agreed to and approved by management within 5 working days
• Provide required information for resource planning and budgeting	• Providing requested information to RCA timely	ABFC • HoD • CFO • Accounts Manager	• Providing required information within 5 working days	• Percentage of accurate and complete information provided within 5 working days
• Provide RCA with required information through interviews • Provide system documents	• Providing information required to allow RCA to prepare system charts and documents	ABFC • HoD • CFO • Accounts Manager	• Providing required information within 5 working days	• Percentage of accurate and complete information provided within 5 days
• Meet RCA • Arrive mutually on an opinion of the adequacy of controls	• Agreeing to an opinion on informal control queries	ABFC • HoD • CFO • Line management	• Agreement on meeting within 5 working days • Reaching agreement on informal queries	• Percentage of meetings accepted within 5 working days

Continued

SERVICE LEVELS (*Continued*)

RCA process	*Performance indicators*	*Responsible person*	*Service level standard*	*Parameters to measure*
• Provide all information requested by RCA	• Providing all required information concerning population size	ABFC • HoD • CFO • Accounts Manager	• Providing required information	• Percentage of accurate and complete information requested within 5 working days
• Provide management comments that correlate to acceptable recommendations	• Management comments that correlate with action plans	ABFC • HoD • CFO • Accounts Manager	• Providing management comments and agreeing to practical action plans	• Percentage of management comments provided and practical action plans agreed to within 4 weeks of obtaining the draft report
• Agree on executable action plans				
• Implement practical and feasible RCA recommendations and action plans	• Implementation of recommendations and action plans	ABFC • HOD • CFO • Accounts Manager	• Implementing recommendations and action plans within a reasonable timeframe	• Percentage of recommendations and action plans implemented within 3 months of receipt of the final audit report

Bibliography

"60 anti-BPO laws in US", *Business Standard*, Mumbai, 6 February 2004.

Accenture, "The 7 Things Your Health Insurance Customers Are Not Telling You", 2011 (www.accenture.com/.../Accenture-False-Sense-of-Security-Quality-Measu).

Agrawal, Alok, "Sifting KPO from BPO services", *HindustanTimes.com*, September 29, 2006.

Aissaoui, Najla, Elkafi Hassini and Mohamed Haouari, "Supplier selection and order lot sizing modeling: A review source computer and operation research archive", *Elsevier Science*, Vol. 34, Issue 12, December 2007.

Amritkar, Chandragupta, "Look Who's Talking", *Education Times*, *Times of India*, Mumbai, September 8, 2004.

Babu, Mohan K., *Offshore IT Services: A Framework for Managing Outsources Projects*, McGraw-Hill, Delhi, 2006.

Baburajan, Rajani, "The Rising Cloud Storage Market Opportunity Strengthens Vendors", *infoTECh*, 2011.(Ebizq.net. CNET News. http://news.cnet.com/8301-1009_3-10150569-83.htm l. Retrieved June 04, 2010. http://www.ebizq.net/blogs/saasweek/2008/03/distinguishing_cloud_computing/. Retrieved, January 14, 2010).

Balsubramaniam, N. (Ed.), *Corporate Board and Governance*, Sterling Publishers, New Delhi, 1998.

Bhagwati, J., A. Panagariya and T.N. Srinivasan, "The muddles over outsourcing", *Journal of Economic Perspectives*, **18**, 2004, pp. 93–114.

Boutellier, R., O. Gassmann and M. von Zedtwitz, *Managing Global Innovation: Uncovering the Secrets of Future Competitiveness*, Springer-Verlag, Heidelberg, 2000.

Boyle, Kevin C. and Jeffery A. Tochner, "Customizing SLA in Call Centre Outsourcing Yields Better Results, *Outsourcing Journal*, February 2004.

"BPO and Beyond", *Economic Times* (CD), 3 October 2003.

Braggs, Steven M., *A Guide to Selecting the Contract Business Unit, Negotiating Contract, Maintaining Control of Process*, John Wiley & Sons, 1998, http://ebooks.ebookmall.com/ebooks.

Braggs, Steven M., *Outsourcing: A Guide to Selecting the Correct Business Unit, Negotiating the Contract, Maintaining Control of the Process*, John Wiley & Sons, Chichester, UK, 1998.

Bridges, W., *Managing Transitions*, Nicholas Brealey, London, 1995.

Broadband India: Recommendations on accelerating growth of Internet and broadband penetration, Telecom Regulatory Authority of India, 29 April 2004.

Buyya, Rajkumar, Chee Shin Yeo, and Srikumar Venugopal, "Market-Oriented Cloud Computing: Vision, Hype, and Reality for Delivering IT Services as Computing Utilities",, *Cornel University Library ACM Digital Library*, 2008, p. 9. (http://www.gridBus.org/~raj/papers/hpcc2008_keynote_cloudcomputing.pdf. Retrieved November 02, 2011).

Chesbrough, Henry and Richard S. Rosenbloom, "The role of the business model in capturing value from innovation, evidence from Xerox Corporation's in Technology spin-off companies", *Industrial and Corporate Change*, Vol. II, No. 3, Oxford University Press, 2002.

Click, Rick L., Thomas N. Duening, *Business Process Outsourcing: The Competitive Advantage*, John Wiley & Sons, 2004.

Coscia, Stephen, *Customer Service Over the Phone: Techniques and Technology for Handling Customers Over the Phone*. 5th ed., CMP Press, London, UK, 1999.

Craumer, Martha, "How to think strategically about outsourcing", *Harvard Management Update*, Vol. 7, No. 5, May 2002.

Dai, Williams, "Transitions: Managing personal and organisational change", *ACDM Newsletter*, April, 1999 (http://www.eoslifework.co.uk/transmgt1.htm as on 7 February, 2008).

Danielson, Krissi, Distinguishing Cloud Computing from Utility Computing, *ebiz*, 2008.

Davies, Charles and Hong Per, *Contract Manufacturing: Realising the Potential*, Executive Agenda, A.T. Kerney, Fourth Quarter, 2004.

Davies, Gary, Chun Rosa, Rui V. da Silva and Roper Stuart, *Corporate Reputation and Competitiveness*, Routledge, London, 2003.

Davies, Paul, *Offshoring, Outsourcing and Global Services Revolution*, Nicholas Brealey, London, 2004.

Dawson, Keith, How to Position Your Call Centre for the Business Challenges of the 21st Century, CMP Press, London, UK, 1999.

Desai, Nishit, "Master the art of BPO negotiations: Getting the basics right is paramount while drawing up BPO contracts", NASSCOM ITeS BPO Strategy Summit, June 12, 2003.

Domberger, Simon, *The Contracting Organisation: A Strategic Guide to Outsourcing*, Oxford University Press, Oxford, 1999.

Dubash, Manek, "How is outsourcing different from cloud computing?", *Cloudpro*, March 11, 2011 (http://www.rightscale.com/customers/pearson-manages-digital-learning-rightscale.php).

Duggal Pawan, "Data Security in BPO", *The Economic Times*, Mumbai (http://www.majmudarindia.com/frames/articles/Information_Technology/Outsourcing_Contracts.htm), May 2, 2004.

Duggal, Pawan, "Brief Case", *Economic Times*, Mumbai, 2 May 2004.

Duggal, Pawan, *Laws of Business Process Outsourcing*, Saakshar Law Publications, New Delhi, 2004.

Edward E. Lawer III, Dave Ulrich, Jac Fitz-Enz, and James C. Madden V, "Human Resources Business Process Outsourcing: Transforming How HR Gets its Work Done," *Personnel Psychology*, Vol. 58, 2005.

Ellram, Lisa and Arnold Maltz, "Outsourcing Supply Management", *Journal of Supply Chain Management*, 35(2), 1999, pp. 4–17.

Engardio, Pete, "The future of outsourcing", *Business Week* appeared in (*Economic Times*), under 'World Updates', January 29, 2006.

Eric Siegel and Thomas H. Davenport, *Predictive Analytics: The Power to Predict Who will Click, Buy, Lie, or Die*, Wiley, 2013.

Farber, Dan, "The new geek chic: Data centers", CNET News, 2008. (http://news.cnet.com/830 1-13953_3-9977049-80.htm l. Retrieved July 05, 2011).

Filippo, Edwin B., *Personnel Management*, 5th ed., McGraw-Hill, NY, USA, 1979.

Finch, C., "The Benefits of the Software-as-a-Service Model", *Computerworld Management*, (online), 2006: (http://www.computerworld.com/s/article/107276/The_Benefits_of_the_Software_as_a_ServiceModel).

Ganapati, Priya, "Standardized test for BPO jobs in Bangalore", 12 June 2003, http://www.questresearch.com/news_16june_bbc.html.

Garschhammer M., R. Hauck, H.G. Hegering, B. Kempter, I. Radisic, H. Rolle, H. Schmidt, M. Langer, and M. Nerb, "Towards generic service management concepts: A service model based approach", Integrated Network Management Proceedings, IEEE/IFIP International Symposium, 2001.

Gert, H.N. Laursen and Jesper Thorlund, *Business Analytics for Managers: Taking Business Intelligence beyond Reporting*, Wiley, 2010.

Gopalkrishnan, R., "Education, innovation key to competitiveness", *The Hindu Business Line*, December, 12, 2005.

Greaves, H. and F. Maurice, *Strategic Outsourcing: A Structured Approach to Outsourcing Decisions and Initiatives*, American Management Association, NY, 1999.

Greaves, Maurice F., *Strategic Outsourcing: A Structured Approach to Outsourcing Decisions*, American Management Association, Atlanta, February 1, 1999.

Gurubaxani, Prakash, "Total Outsourcing", *The Economic Times*, Mumbai, March 3, 2004.

Halvey, John K. and Melby Barbara Murphy, *Business Process Outsourcing: Process, Strategies and Contracts*, John Wiley & Sons, Somerset, NJ, USA, 1996.

____, *Business Process Outsourcing,* John Wiley & Sons, 2007.

____, *Business Process Outsourcing: Process, Strategies, and Contracts*, Wiley, NY, 2007.

____, *Information Technology Outsourcing Transactions: Process, Strategies and Contracts*, John Wiley & Sons, Somerset NJ, USA, 1998.

Harmon, Paul, *Business Process Change: A Manager's Guide to Improving, Redesigning and Automating Processes*, Morgan Kaufmann, San Francisco, USA, 2002.

Herriot P., W. Hirsh and P. Reilly, *Trust and Transition*, Wiley, NY, 1998.

Hodge, Mark, "Block and Die: Business Process Outsourcing", *Contract Management*, Vol. I, Issue 1, January 2005, pp. 8–17.

Hogan, Joe, "Strategic Outsourcing: The Importance of Choosing the Right Partner", *Computerworld*, 28 February 2005.

Hope C., *Service Operations Management: Strategy, Design, and Delivery*, Prentice-Hall, NY, 1997.

http://bpmtutorial.com/BPM/WorkFlow.aspx

http://bpo.knowledgehills.com/BPO/Articles/Transition-Management/Transition

http://bponews.blogspot.com/2006_02_01_bponews_archive.html

http://encycogov.com

http://investors.peoplesupport.com/governance/ethics.cfm

http://knowledge.wharton.upenn.edu/092403_ss3.html

http://kpo.evalueserve.com/KPO/BPO-to-KPO-Challenge.aspx

http://outsourcingking.com/BPO/What-Is-BPO.aspx.

http://sourceamerica.net/HIM/WhatBPO.asp

http://www.blogsource.org/bpo/index.htm

http://www.bpoindia.org

http://www.bpoindia.org/research/ethical-hackers.shtml

http://www.business-standard.com

http://www.call-center.net/ccstudy-practices.htm

http://www.cio.com/offshoremap/ A buyer's guide to offshore outsourcing

http://www.csc.com

http://www.ebstrategy.com/bpo/delivery_models/5phases.htm

http://www.entrepreneur.com—contents.

http://www.equaterra.com/summerfestival/support-acts/ERP-executive-summary.html

http://www.estrategy.com.

http://www.go4outsourcing.com/articles/managing_bpo_governance.aspl

Http://www.icsi.edu/DesktopDefault.aspx?tabid=2110

http://www.iflexsolutions.com/iflex/pdf/website/KPO-domainexpertise.pdf.

http://www.infosys.com/investor/corporategovernance.asp

http://www.kminstitute.org

http://www.kpoasia.com/kpo-vs-bpo.htm

http://www.kpoweb.com/kpo_vs_bpo.html

http://www.mpowerasia.com

http://www.naavi.org/cl_editorial_05/cebp.htm

http://www.naavi.org/ponguru/privacy_july1.htm

http://www.nasscom.org

http://www.nasscom.org/bponewsline/jan05/Policy.asp

http://www.nelson-hall.com/bpo-insight/past-issues.html.

http://www.networkmagazineindia.com/200602/analyst'scorner01.shtml.

http://www.nickols.us

http://www.opm.gov/

http://www.outsource2india.com/callcenter/transition-process.asp

http://www.outsourcing.com

http://www.rediff.com /money/2004/dec/31guest2.htm : KPO: The next big opportunity

http://www.russoft.org

http://www.sharedservicesbpo.com

http://www.sla-zone.co.uk.

http://www.sourcemax.com/N010101.html

http://www.sourcingmag.com/content/c060719a.asp

http://www.sourcingmag.com/content/c060802a.asp

http://www.staffware.com/landing/bpo/?link=OvertureBPO

http://www.tutorial-reports.com

http://www.xansa.com

http://www.xicom.biz/bpo_business_models.html

http://www4.gartner.com

http://www-hr.ucsd.edu

Hughes, Kent H., *Building the Next American Century: The Past and Future of Economic Competitiveness*, Woodrow Wilson Center Press (Copublisher: John Hopkins University Press), Washington, D.C., 2005.

Kaka, Noshir F., Shailesh S. Kekre and Saipriya Samrangan, *Benchmarking India's Business Process Outsources*, http://mckinsey.com/clientservice/bto/pointofview/pdf/MoIT8_Nasscom_F.pdf.

Karabinos. David. "May the Source be with you", *Contract Management*, Vol. 43, Issue 9, September 2003.

King Rachael, "Cloud Computing: Small Companies Take Flight", *Businessweek*, 2008. (http://www.businessweek.com/technology/content/aug2008/tc2008083_619516. htm. Retrieved May, 01, 2011)

Knowledge@Wharton, "Reining in Outsourcing Risk," http://www.strategy-business.com/media/file/sb_kw_11-30-05.pd

Kobayashi–Hillary, Mark, *Outsourcing to India*, Springer, Dordrecht, Netherland, 2004.

Kotler, Philip, Kevin Keller, Abraham Koshy, and M. Jha, *Marketing Management*, 13th ed., PHI Learning, New Delhi, 2009.

Kulkarni, Sangeeta, "BPO: It's a different call for IT company", *Economic Times*, June 20, 2004.

Kulkarni, V., "Indian Cos. to Gain from Software Delivery Model", Livemint.com (*The Wall Street Journal*). 2008 (http://www.livemint.com/ 2008/06/01232337/Indian-cos-to-gain-from-softwa.html).

Kumar, Sanjeev and M.S. Krishnan, "Performance Outcomes of onshore and offshore Business Process Outsourcing", Conference on Information System and Technology, 2006.

LaBounty, Char, *How to Establish and Maintain Service Level Agreements*, Help Desk Institute, Colorado Springs, CO, USA, 1994.

Lawler Edward E., III, David Ulrich, Jac Fitz-enz, James Madden, V with Regina Maruca, *Human Resources Business Process Outsourcing: Transforming How HR Gets Its Work Done*, John Wiley & Sons, Inc.

Lovelock, Christopher H., *Services Marketing*, Prentice-Hall, NY, 1996.

Luecke, Richards, *Managing Change and Transition*, Harvard Business Press, Boston, MA, USA, 2003.

Luthans, Fred, *Organisational Behaviour*, 9th ed., Irvin/McGraw-Hill, NY, USA, 2002.

Majumdar, Shyamal, "After BPO & KPO, now comes PPO: The Human Factor", *Business Standard*, Mumbai, 28 June 2007.

Mani, Deepa, Anitesh Barua and Andrew B. Whinston, *Of Process Analysis and Alignment: A Model of Governance in BPO Relationships*, University of Texas at Austin working paper, May 2005.

Mani, Deepa, Anitesh Barua, Andrew B. Whinston, *Successfully Governing Business Process Outsourcing Relationships*, MIS Quarterly, Vol. 5, No. 1, March 2006.

McCormack Kevin P. and William C. Johnson, *Supply Chain Networks and Business Process Orientation: Advanced Strategies and Best Practices*, CRC Press, 2002.

McFetridge, Donald G., *Competitiveness: Concepts and Measures*, Occasional Paper No. 5, Carleton University, Ottawa, April 1995.

Mckee, Sandra L. and Brenda Walters, *Transition Management: A Practical Approach for Personal and Professional Development*, Prentice-Hall, USA, 2002.

Melby, Barbara, "Demistifying Global Multi Tower BPO Transaction: Six Key Issues", *Journal of Sourcing Leadership*, Vol. 2, Issue 4 (http://www.morganlewis.com/pubs/BarbaraMelby_DemystifyingGlobalMulti-TowerBPOTransactions_article_Jan06.pdf), January 2006.

Mensik, Michael and Brian Hengesbaugh, *Outsourcing to India: Key Legal and Tax Considerations for US Financial Institutes*, Baker & McKenzie, Chicago, 2004.

Merchant, Mustafa and Arunachalam Sriniwas, "BPO to KPO: The Indian Journey", IIM Kozhikode, http://mba.iiita.ac.in/jan06/prespective_3.htm.

Meyer, John L. and Carolyn C. Shade, *The Changing Outplacement Process: New Methods and Opportunities for Transition Management,* Quorum Books, Westport, London, 1994.

Michael Miller, *Cloud Computing: Web-Based Applications that Change the Way You Work and Collaborate Online*, Pearson, USA, 2008.

Michael Miller, *Cloud Computing*: *Web-Based Applications that Change the Way You Work and Collaborate Online*, Pearson, Mills, Elinor, USA, 2009.

Mills Elinor, "Cloud Computing Security Forecast: Clear Skies", CNET News, 2009CNlivemint.com (*The Wall Street Journal*); (http://www.livemint.com/2008/06/01232337/Indian-cos-to-gain-from-softwa.html).

Miozzo, Marcela and Vivien Walsh, *International Competitiveness and Technological Change*, Oxford University Press, USA, 2006.

Mujumdar, Anirban and Kamal Poddar, *Managing Attrition in BPO*, Indian Institute of Management Kozhikode, Kerala, 2004.

Nagy Hanna, *Enabling Enterprise Transformation: Business and Grassroots Innovation for the Knowledge Economy Innovation, Technology, and Knowledge Management*, Springer, New York, 2009.

Nakkiran, S. and D. John Franklin, *Business Process Outsourcing (BPO): Concept, Current Trends, Management, Future Challenges*, Deep and Deep Publications, New Delhi, 2004.

NASSCOM ITES–BPO Industry 2005: Background and Reference Resource, 2005.

NASSCOM, *Handbook of ITES Services*, NASSCOM, Bangalore, India, 2002.

NASSCOM, NASSCOM factsheet on ITES–BPO, www.nasscom.org, 2004.

NASSCOM, NASSCOM–McKinsey Report, 2002.

NASSCOM, *Strategic Review*, 2004 and 2005.

Nath, Kamal, India driving competitiveness, *Business Line*, October 7, 2007.

Nelson, R. (Ed.), *National Innovation Systems*, Oxford University Press, Oxford, 1993.

Nickols, Fred, "Transition Management: Tips for managers in times to change", http://home.att.net/~nickols/articles.htm, 2003.

O'Brien, J. and Marakas, G., *Management Information Systems*, McGraw-Hill/Irwin, USA, 2007.

Pantry, Sheila and Peter Griffiths, *The Guide for Preparing and Implementing Service Level Agreements*, Library Association Publishing, London, 2001.

Patrick, Anil R., "Regulations and compliance: BPO.co.in", *Network*, March 2005, http://www.networkmagazineindia.com.

Paul, Davies, *Offshoring, Outsourcing and Global Services Revolution*, Nicholas Brealey Publishing, London, 2004.

Performance Management Practitioner Series, United States Office of Personnel Management.

Poisant J., *Creating and Sustaining a Superior Customer Service Organisation: A Book about Taking Care of People Who Take Care of Customers*, Quorum Books, West Port, CT, http://www.expresscomputeronline.com, 2002.

Porter, M., *On Competitiveness*, Harvard Business Review Press, Boston, MA, USA, 1998.

____, The *Competitive Advantage of Nations*, The Free Press, New York, 1990.

Prasad, R.N. and Seema Acharya, *Fundamentals of Business Analytics*, Wiley, Delhi, 2011.

Raghavendra Rao, N., "BPO: Beyond information technology", *Business Line*, 11 March 2004.

Rajawat, Yash K. "And BPO in Years to Come", *Economic Times*, Mumbai, 19 December 2004.

Richter, Frank–Jurgen and Parthasarathi Banerjee, *The Knowledge Economy in India*, Macmillan, 2003.

Rick L. Click and Thomas N. Duening, *Business Process Outsourcing: The Competitive*, John Wiley & Sons, 2004.

Robinson, Marcia and Kalakota Ravi, *Business Model ROI and Best Practices*, Mivar Press, Alphareffa, GA, USA, 2004.

Robinson, Marcia and Kalakota Ravi, *Offshore Outsourcing: Business Models, ROI and Best Practices*, Mivar Press, 2004.

Ryan, Falvey and Merchant, "Regulation of the Cloud in India", *Journal of Internet Law*, Vol. 15, No. 4, 2011.

Sahay, Sundeep, Brian Nicholas and S. Krishana, *Global IT Outsourcing Software Development Across Borders*, Cambridge University Press, Cambridge, UK, 2003.

Service Level Management using IBM Tivoli Service Level Advisor and Tivoli Business System, www.ibm.com/redbook, December 2004.

Sharma, Samidha and Moumita Bakshi Chartterjee, "BPOs' no-poaching pacts fall apart", *The Economic Times*, 12 December 2006.

Sharma, Sanjeev, "Call Centres in India—Challenges for HR Professionals", http://www.bpoindia.org/research/call-centers-challenges-for-hr.shtml.

Smith, Howard and Peter Finger, *Business Process Management (BPM): The Third Wave*, Meghan–Kiffer Press, Tampa, FL, 2002.

Sosinsky Barrie, *Cloud Computing Bible*, Wiley India, New Delhi, 2011.

Sparrow, Eizabeth, *Successful Outsourcing: From Choosing a Provider to Managing Project*, Springer-Verlag, Telos, 2003.

Sunit, Jilla, "It doesn't do to ignore culture", *Economic Times*, Mumbai, 24 July 2003.

"The Impact of Global Sourcing on the US Economy: 2003–2010", Evalueserve–NASSCOM Report.

Thomas H. Davenport, Jeanne G. Harris and Robert Morison, *Analytics at Work: Smarter Decisions, Better Results*, Harvard Business Review Press, 2010.

Thomas H. Davenport and Jeanne G. Harris, *Competing on Analytics: The New Science of Winning*, Harvard Business Review Press, 2007.

Thomas M. Jorde and David J. Teece (Eds.), *Antitrust, Innovation and Competitiveness*, Oxford University Press, New York, 1992.

Thomas N. Duening and Rick L. Click, *Essentials of Business Process Outsourcing*, Vol. 34 (Essentials Series), John Wiley & Sons, 2005.

Verma, Dinesh, *Supporting Service Level Agreements on IP*, Sams Publishing, London, 1999.

Verma, Shilpa, "Challenges for a HR Professional in BPO", Gleez, http://gleez.com/articles/information/challenges-for-a-hr-professional-in-bpo, 24 July 2007.

Warner Burke, W., *Organisation Change, Theory and Practice*, Sage Publication Inc., London, 2002.

Weber, Matthias and Jens Hemelskamp, *Towards Environmental Innovation System*, Springer, Dordrecht, Netherlands, 2005.

Weerakkody, Vishanth, Wendy L. Currie, and Yamaya Ekanayake, "Re-engineering business processes through application service providers: Challenges, issues and complexities", *Business Process Management Journal*, Vol. 9, Issue 6, 2003, pp. 776–794.

Wever, Kirsten S., *Negotiating Competitiveness*, Harvard Business School Press, January, 1995.

Whitmore, Jim, "BPO Governance—A Strategic Imperative", BPO Insight, May 2006.

Wogart, Jan Peter, Mehta Aasha Kapur, Mehta Arun, *Technology and Competitiveness: The Case of Brazilian and Indian Machine Tools*, Sage Publishing, New Delhi, 1993.

www.ajira.com

www.bpo.nasscom.org

Zacharias, N. and V. Parikh, "Takes Two to Tango", Corporate Counsel, *Economic Times*, July 12, 2003.

Company Index

Subject Index